Eclectica Publishing Intl LLC Titles

2004   *Best Fiction Volume One (7th Anniversary)*

2015   *Tales of Choroni*

2016   *Best Poetry Volume One (20th Anniversary)*

2016   *Best Nonfiction Volume One (20th Anniversary)*

2016   *Best Fiction Volume Two (20th Anniversary)*

2016   *Speculative Edition Volume One (20th Anniversary)*

Eclectica Magazine Speculative

Celebrating 20 Years Online

Eclectica Magazine Speculative

Celebrating 20 Years Online

Selected from *www.eclectica.org*
October 1996 through February 2016
by Tom Dooley

With an Introduction by Tom Dooley
and a Foreword by Jason Sanford

ECLECTICA PUBLISHING INTL LLC
ALBUQUERQUE, NEW MEXICO

In memory of Neil Grimmett, who went on ahead of the rest of us, and dedicated to our four-legged friends, who enrich our lives.

Acknowledgments

Thanks to...

Julie, Lise, and Evans, for enduring a mighty disruption to our family routine so *Eclectica* and this book might exist.

Chris Lott, without whom there would be no *Eclectica*.

Jason Sanford for his generous foreword and multifaceted contributions to the world of online literature, including *storySouth Magazine* and the Million Writers Award.

The 113 contributors to our Kickstarter campaign who footed the bill for this and three other volumes.

NASA, whose public domain photography of the Martian surface not only provided the cover art for this book but encourages the kind of pursuits speculative literature is all about.

Erin Elizabeth Smith, Melvin Sterne, and Charles Yu, who did the dirty but essential job of blurbing.

My mother, who raised me in a log cabin with no electricity, but who gave me *Flash Gordon* comic books to read and later, with the help of a little Honda generator and some bootlegged VHS copies of the original *Star Trek,* cemented my love of possibilities.

Tamara Brenno-Uribarri and Anne Leigh Parrish, who as fiction editors helped select many of these pieces, and Jennifer Finstrom and David Ewald, who selected the poetry and nonfiction included here.

The many editors, authors, and supporters not already mentioned above who have helped keep the boat afloat for two decades.

Contents

Foreword

THE SPECULATIVE STORIES you hold in your hand are not sanctioned nor blessed. They aren't earning million dollar advances or getting optioned for massive box-office grosses while recycling familiar plotlines, characters, and ideas.

No, these stories—along with a sprinkling of poems and essays—in the *Eclectica Magazine* 20th Anniversary Speculative Edition shriek to fantastic delight. They're reminders of when "speculative" was fun and challenging and full of living characters and exciting new worlds for readers to explore. This anthology reaches back to when the heart of speculative fiction beat to the beautiful hellfires of language and ideas and beliefs that could only be created by authors who saw beyond the day-to-day reality of the world around us.

There is history behind this book. A backstory long predating *Eclectica Magazine,* which we know from this volume's title has been around for two decades. A context of science fiction thrills and fantasy dreams, an endless cascade of horror-filled screams and apocalyptic visions, all of which have succeeded in winning the battle but losing the war, or perhaps the other way around.

You see, today the speculative fiction genre is both all-powerful and all-weak. All powerful because the science fiction, fantasy, and horror subgenres making up the speculative genre are beloved by people everywhere. The top films and TV shows and video games are all speculative. The best-selling novels are speculative. If you can't imagine life without *Harry Potter* and *Lord of the Rings* and *Star Trek* and *Star Wars* and *The Walking Dead* and *Twilight*, then you understand the power of speculative fiction in today's world.

But this power has also weakened the genre, with success creating a repeating loop of the same old same old. Why innovate when you can easily make money recycling? The situation has gotten so bad, Hollywood now reboots speculative fiction films after only a few years, assuming no one will care if they're presented with the same story with only minor changes.

This isn't how the genre used to function. For most of the 20th century, speculative fiction was a nonconformist outsider, the kid everyone picked on and hated. "Serious people" (which in this day and age should only be said with very non-serious air quotes) looked down their noses at science fiction, fantasy, and horror. Authors, directors, artists, and others working in these genres struggled to receive even a little recognition and support from the larger cultural institutions and gatekeepers.

Then a funny thing happened: speculative fiction caught hold of the public's imagination. It went from bullied, acne-covered kid to pop superstar. The serious people who had dismissed it began reading and watching the genre. Acclaimed mainstream directors, authors, and artists who only a few years before might have run in fear from speculative fiction began dipping their toes into the genre pool. Speculative fiction works won Pulitzer Prizes and Oscars and became bestsellers and top grossing films and, in short, moneymakers on a scale usually only seen in the wet dreams of venture capitalists.

So all praise the dominating speculative fiction genre! Hail the triumph of imagination over reality!

But what happens when an outsider genre suddenly rules the world? Can speculative fiction still ignite the imagination when the genre's stories are so sliced and diced and homogenized for mainstream appeal, they taste like the expired cans of SPAM you used to find in the back of the cupboard and wouldn't feed to your dog?

Fortunately, the answer is yes, speculative can still ignite the imagination. The contents of this anthology bear witness to that. As said earlier, they are not sanctioned nor approved. They weren't written to cash in on the speculative boomtimes. They aren't retreads of stories you've read a thousand times before. Instead, they are an outsider's outpouring of pure imagination and love.

In keeping with the outsider theme, *Eclectica* is an online magazine—and not just any online magazine, but a *pioneering* one. It was founded in 1996 by Chris Lott and Tom Dooley, who saw the untapped potential of electronic publishing. Unlike other early "ezine" founders, Lott and Dooley didn't focus only on more mainstream literary writing or solely on a particular branch of the speculative genre. Instead, they combined all of the above and more into a totally unique vision of literature, placing science fiction and fantasy and horror stories alongside more realistic stories and poetry and even things too strange to fall under any of those categories, trusting readers to embrace them all.

Basically, *Eclectica* charted an eclectic course through the online literary waters, just as the journal's name promised it would.

Publishing has changed massively in the last 20 years. Today almost every book and magazine and journal is online. E-books can be purchased and read in seconds with the tap of a screen. As I write this, the only practical difference between publishing stories online and in print is that publishing online often results in many more readers.

But that's not how it was in 1996. Back then online magazines and journals were looked down upon, as if publishing online wasn't in any way legitimate. Works in online magazines and journals were overlooked for awards and were rarely reprinted in anthologies and collections of the year's best writings. Tenured academics or ones seeking tenure wouldn't dream of citing an online publishing credit on their curriculum vitaes.

Two decades ago online journals like *Eclectica* were very much outsiders to the literary world, just as speculative fiction was until recently an outsider genre.

I know these things to be true firsthand because in 2001 I founded a literary journal myself called *storySouth*. Despite five years passing between *Eclectica's* founding and my jump into online publishing, the view of the serious people behind most literary magazines and books had not changed. These people still didn't consider online publishing to be as legitimate as words printed on actual paper.

I discovered this truth early on while editing *storySouth*. I had approached the editor of one of the yearly best short story anthologies about considering *storySouth's* fiction for his next edition. The editor's response shocked me. He said *storySouth* looked great and published (in his serious person words) very good fiction, but regardless, he couldn't consider anything in our journal because basically, *storySouth* wasn't a *real* publication.

I founded the Million Writers Award in response, seeking to highlight the year's best online short fiction and refute the idea that a real magazine can't also be virtual. The award has now run for well over a decade, and I believe it has resoundingly made that case.

From the very first year, *Eclectica Magazine* dominated the Million Writers Award, and in fact, it still does, having amassed over a third again as many notable and top ten stories as its nearest competition. And this in spite of another funny thing that happened over the years: all those print magazines and journals who had initially turned up their noses at online publishing? They began publishing online and submitting work for the Million Writers Award! That's when I knew online publishing had become legit in the minds of serious people. And when *Eclectica* continued to not just hold its own, but outperform publications with endowments, paid staffs, university and corporate sponsors, that's when it became clear *Eclectica* was, and is, something special.

And here we are, with *Eclectica Magazine* celebrating its 20th anniversary. An entire generation has passed since *Eclectica* was born, a generation in which both speculative fiction and online publishing have gone from overlooked outsiders to cultural dynamos. I don't worry about the future of either. While both now dominate, there is still room for the outsider voices that made them what they are. There is still space for people who love stories not created to suck up to the current cash cow or publishing trend. There's still room for stories that are more than marketing angles or media spin, stories being crammed down your throat by a multi-million-dollar promotional budget.

As proof, I offer *Eclectica Magazine's* 20th Anniversary Speculative Edition.

Thank you, *Eclectica*, for all you've done to nurture stories like these. And I look forward to reading what you publish in the years to come.

Jason Sanford is an award-winning author of short stories, essays, and articles and an active member of the Science Fiction and Fantasy Writers of America. A finalist for the Nebula Award, Jason has published more than a dozen stories in the British SF magazine *Interzone*, which also devoted a special issue to his fiction. He has also published numerous stories in magazines and anthologies such as *Asimov's Science Fiction, Year's Best SF, Analog, InterGalactic Medicine Show, Beneath Ceaseless Skies*, and other places. In 2001 Jason founded the online magazine *storySouth*, through which he ran the Million Writer Award for many years.

Introduction

A LOT CAN HAPPEN in 20 years. Relationships can run their course. Loved ones and pets can pass away. Cars can be traded in or sold. One might move to a new apartment or a new state, buy and sell a house, change jobs or careers, earn a degree. Kids might arrive in a timespan like that, maybe even grow up and depart. Hairlines recede and waistlines expand, eyesight and hearing weaken, joints stiffen. Entire TV series come and go, as do actors' careers, singers' popularities, cultural trends and artistic movements. Presidential administrations, wars, terrorist attacks and genocides and atrocities, revolutions, disasters, outbreaks... technology changes everyone's lives, and then changes them again.

Reflecting on the intervening years since Chris Lott suggested the two of us start an online literary publication in 1996, I realize all those things not only *can* happen in two decades, but they *have* happened—much of the personal and specific stuff very specifically and personally, to me. Very little remains of the life I led when I was 26 years old, but I have continued to devote whatever spare time I have to putting together a virtual issue of *Eclectica Magazine* every three months.

After the first seven years, we had published so many outstanding pieces of short fiction, I felt compelled to produce a "best of" anthology. Putting together that book was satisfying, but here it is nearly twice again as many years later, and the archives are bursting at the seams. The time has come to shine a light on not just some great stories, but also the nonfiction and poetry that helped make *Eclectica* one of the most respected, longest running electronic lit-mags on the Internet. But even three volumes can't do justice to 20 years, so we added a fourth devoted to speculative literature—the book you're reading now.

The pieces in this volume are meant to be speculative literature, but what does that mean? Ask more than one person, and you'll get more than one answer. In fact, some might take exception to the term itself, since "speculative" is a kind of genre writing, and "literary" is often considered diametric to genre. Drawing the line between speculative and literary writing is no simple matter, and the contents of *Eclectica's* archives make doing so even more difficult. For definitional clarity, I turned to Wikipedia:

> Speculative fiction is a broad category of narrative fiction that includes elements, settings and characters created out of imagination and speculation rather than based on reality and everyday life. It encompasses the genres of science fiction, fantasy, science fantasy, horror, alternative history, and magic realism.

And so we have stories in this volume from the sci-fi, fantasy, horror, alternative history, and magic realism sub-genres, but I would argue every one of them could hold its own as a "literary" piece as well. And then we have speculative poems and essays—and maybe even a piece or two falling altogether outside the aforementioned categories.

If I were to pick an author from our 20 years online who exemplifies what *Eclectica* speculative literature means to me, it would be someone whose work ironically doesn't appear in this volume. You can read Charles Yu's uniquely "complex, brainy, genre-hopping" (says the *New York Times*), often devastating fiction in a lot of other places, though. "Fable," Charles' story in *The New Yorker* this past Spring, is brilliant, profound, and singular, and it demonstrates how a speculative story, meaning one willing to take chances with subject, setting, and structure—in the very way of telling—can rise not just to the level of literature, but blow right on past.

The spirit of Charles Yu's writing—the speculative energy—

exists throughout this book. Whether it's Brigit Kelly Young inhabiting a famous celebrity in the twilight of her fame or An Tran channeling *The Outer Limits*, the pieces collected here are truly varied and inventive. As with any batch of speculative work, there are stories that cast light on political, social, and economic realities. A.S. King's "River 16" has something to say about environmentalism, Lawrence Klavan's "Consensus" has a lot to say about politics, and Dan Malakin's "Stillborn" says as much or more about gender roles and reproduction as the movie *Children of Men*. There is also the sublime and the silly, but don't be fooled. Just because Anthony W. Brown appears to be giving you a user's manual for an aquarium, or Jon Fried's narrator is a baseball glove-shaped phone, or Sean Gill is talking about eating spiders (is that really a thing?), there is heart and intellect and incisive social commentary in all of these pieces. Throughout the collection, there is deep tragedy couched in the lighthearted—Christopher Allen's "Fred's Massive Sorrow" comes to mind—and there is a humor, albeit sometimes dark, in the darkness. I'm looking at you, Niko Vreeland. And because *Eclectica* is a "world wide" publication, there are pieces here like Chikodili Emelumadu's "Jermyn," no less speculative than the rest, and no less unusual for the fact that they're coming from non-Western continents and cultures.

I've referred to a dozen of the authors and pieces contained within, but there are two dozen more equally deserving of mention, each with a story to tell, both literally and figuratively. This volume is dedicated to Neil Grimmett, whose "The Eyes of Dogs to Come" is, were one to plot it on a continuum from literary to speculative, very far to the literary side. Nonetheless, when I contemplated putting together a speculative edition, "Eyes" was the first story I thought to include, and I knew it would function as a kind of entree and cornerstone to the entire volume.

It wasn't until I began reaching out to authors for permissions that I learned the sad news of Neil's recent and unexpected passing. In 20 years or the blink of an eye, it can be all over for any of us. This transience is one of the great mysteries—doubtless the *greatest* mystery—and therefore causes for speculation—in our human experience.

Ultimately, what sets great speculative literature apart from great literature in general is the degree to which it explores and illuminates the mysteries of said human experience. Perhaps, too, the degree of fun involved. These pursuits—seeking understanding and letting loose, being inventive, having *fun*—have been characteristic of speculative endeavors since ancient peoples first looked up at the stars, projected animals and other figures onto them, and invented mythologies. The need to connect dots and make sense of our universe is essential to human intellectuality. It is the essence of imagination, maybe even a key ingredient of whatever it is we call our souls. As such, the pieces in this volume are evidence of the star-stuff Carl Sagan asserted we humans are, and I'm excited to present them in book form.

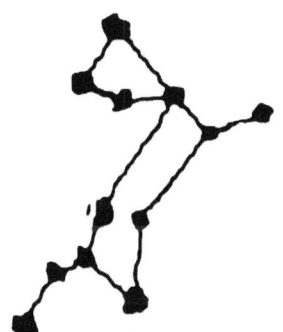

MICHAEL CRANE

A Dog Called Yesterday

From October/November 2010

The man with three heads,
brains, arms, ears, and eyes
is walking his three dogs
past the three factories,
beside the three raging rivers.
He has three choices.
Stop. Set the dogs free.
Or keep them chained
on the leash forever.
The dogs are called
Yesterday, Today
and Tomorrow.
Today is resting
on the grass and sleeping.
Tomorrow is chasing
invisible birds, but Yesterday

is looking up at the man
with three heads, staring
with those sad eyes of the past.
And then Yesterday digs
a deep hole in the ground
and rips the three headed
man's one heart from his chest
and buries it... Yesterday
is a strange beast. One minute
it is barking at the shadows.
The next minute it is holding
out its paws like a beggar.

NEIL GRIMMETT

For the Eyes of Dogs to Come

From July/August 2007

THE MANY OCCASIONS I watched with nothing in mind but eating up some moments of the boredom I suffered to share in my then wife's hobby, I'd thought, *What's all the fuss about? What must be missing in these people's lives to need this as a substitute? Children or some other challenge?* Then I asked myself how these "exhibitors" had the audacity to call it a sport, or to claim it took a lifetime to learn and appreciate its subtleties. I smirked at the displays of despair and elation accompanying their endless reruns of the day's results.

When I looked with a different idea in mind—one born from a madness to prove something or save what was already beyond saving—my stomach turned to jelly and my legs became too weak to walk away. I stood, ringside, with the stench of dog urine throbbing through layers of sawdust, masking the body odors of nervous exhibitors in their finest show outfits, and was close to understanding their emotions for the one and only time. Fleetingly, I'd glimpsed something special, passing along the thin cords of show leads between the dogs and their owners, and I should have crawled away and left them to their dreams. Then the canine eyes turned, alerted to my presence in their dimension by far deeper instincts than anything human. They sensed my future intent and shifted in anticipation and fear as I'd made my decision. I strutted off and would never recognize any of this again until it was far too late.

The rock music drowns out their whimpering, though not the gnawing and clawing from inside the crates, but we are immune to that. Some of the dogs are drugged. It is the only way to get them from one venue to another without them fretting or throwing up so much of their body weight that it's impossible to get them back in condition for the show. Just crumble a couple of ACPs, a dab of a moistened finger passed between the little pile of gold dust and the dog's kissing tongue, and it's more than enough for most British journeys. The trouble is some cannot shake off the drug, and they betray us with their leaden movements. They have to be starved well before the show and often force-fed back into shape after arriving.

Tonight, there are about 15 dogs in the back of the van, bolted in wooden travelling boxes, piled on top of each other nearly to the roof with no chance of getting out for a stretch until we reach the showground. Some are champions, some just starting out. Some will never amount to anything, but their owners go on paying and paying again to prove that's a lie. They believe every negative decision against their dog is a slur on their lives, another rung deliberately kept out of reach. The world has been shrunken to the stage that is the show ring, with the masked players in this drama fooling no one with their disguises.

Mostly, people just get used to being beaten and carry on, turning up with the family pet, watching the big names getting bigger, and becoming more bitter and disappointed with each exit. Sometimes, though, one of these also-rans happens to breed a good one. One that attracts the wrong sort of attention. Then the ever-present whisperers start offering their placings, confirming an unprovable truth, and exposing the injustice of it all. The owner begins to crave a fair decision. A first place to start with, then surely that so-desired Challenge Certificate—the ultimate bit of green paper, stating in print and forever that the animal is good enough in the judge's opinion to become a champion. Only three of those "tickets," and you've done it. Then, as they try to come to terms with another unjust defeat, someone spills our trade into their chaliced ears: "What about a professional handler? They can win with anything."

And of course, we can.

The music closes, and my colleague Gabby lights another cigarette off the butt of his last. He is one of the great handlers of all time, and though he cares to state that I'm an upstart and only winning through luck, we've become something of a team. Gabby likes to tell stories between CDs. To let me into a few more secrets of our brotherhood, and to reveal the truth hidden behind each lie we must promote and pretend to believe.

"The Pawnbroker," he says, "is judging the group next month. One of us better stand him a bottle or two, just to steady his nerves, you know. Did I ever tell you how he got to be called 'The Pawnbroker?'"

He has, but I'm just glad to be a part of all this and will listen and listen, for now. More people show dogs than go to football matches, and in this country there are only about ten full-time professional handlers. Always the center of attention, charging from ring to ring, class to class, piling up the rosettes and prize cards until at the end of the day we usually arrive in the Big Ring for the group (Terrier, Working, Toy, Utility, Hound or Gundog) judging. Every exhibitor's dream: the Best-of-Breed animal on the end of their lead, groomed and perfect, the exemplar of its race with the owner's name attached for all to see. "Read 'em and die," we tell the ringside experts with their veiled accusations.

The Pawnbroker had bred this puppy, Gabby tells me again, a real one with everything going for it except for the fact it had decided not to let its balls appear. Some rich American heiress had spotted it a few days after it was born and just had to own it, no matter what the cost. He did everything conceivable to get the testicles to descend into the scrotum sac, but they refused to oblige. So he came up with a cunning plan: he slit the pooch's flaccid pouch open and sewed in a couple of squash balls. The dog went over the pond and everyone was happy. Then one day it was in the ring and the judge—with an unusually impressive display of understanding the breed standard—managed to count three testicles. A normal one had dropped to join the rubber imposters. All hell broke loose, and the Pawnbroker got his sobriquet along with a five-year ban.

I laugh at the story again, while from the darkness of the van, a dog whimpers as if in sympathy. Maybe it even knows about blades and cuts. We have to alter some, those unfortunates with minor faults that might get in the way. Say, like a tail. Such a little thing to get in the way of all that potential winning. If the tail goes over too far, we call that "gay," or if it is hooked in a loop, a "toby jug." Whatever, it spoils the picture and is so easy to spot. And so easy to correct, for the right price, of course. Just take a blade—home-made in the coldest silences, thin, with two flat cutting edges. Let the dog race about with another animal, close enough to get it excited, but always tantalizingly out of reach. Watch the tail to determine its fault as the dog becomes more and more wound up, as it should always be in the show ring. Then pounce with the old and new images locked in your mind. You usually need at least two or three strong men to help hold the creature because anaesthetic is out of the question. It's not that anyone wants to be cruel, but a numb tail won't respond before or after, and you must, like any true artist, see the reality behind your creation. The blade probes its way between the bones, then turns so the edges can sever the ligaments and tendons—you can hear them ping like elastic even above all the other noise. A couple here, a couple there, until everything is as nature surely intended.

Ears are a lot harder and messier. They take longer to heal, the aftercare is more complex, and they often need more than one go at correcting. "Top and tail," we say when both ends have been fixed. Like, "That Best in Show winner at Crufts was top and tailed, twice!" Could you imagine all that glory being taken away from someone for the sake of a little blood and pain? Besides, we are not like some countries where major surgery is carried out—grafts and tucks, false teeth, contact lenses. No wonder they can't breed anything when no one knows what is for real. We would never let things get that bad. We just want to be your patron saints, not God.

Gabby lights another cigarette, and I quickly stuff a CD in the player and turn it up. He is starting on about his wife, and I know where that sad, old song will end. She left him a couple of years back with a message pinned to the kennel wall waiting for his return from a show—drained and beat and just wanting to get the dogs unloaded and make bed. She said she just couldn't take the smell anymore.

"What smell?" he's always asking anyone who will listen. "Can you smell anything?"

The first time I met Gabby, he was setting fire to a dog. In the middle of a busy showground with all the public and officials just a wall of canvas away. I was mooching around one of the grooming tents, hoping to pick up a tip or two from the professional handlers, and there was Gabby with a dog on the stripping table. A Welsh terrier if I remember correctly. Another of the professionals was standing in front of the table blocking off the view from anyone passing the entrance.

"Come here," Gabby said to me, "and you might get to learn something." I stood shoulder to shoulder with the other handler to help hide what was going down. Gabby lit a length of thick cord and used it to paint the dog in flames, singeing its fur, inch by inch, slapping out the sudden flare-ups without any sign of panic. When the dog's coat had been transformed to a tight, hard covering, he plastered it in a mixture of chalk and dye and left it standing to dry. "It can't grow a hard coat," he told me, "no matter what you do. This is the only way." I was impressed, not only by his skill and knowledge, but by the fact the dog had actually gone to sleep while it was happening. At least that is what I'd thought at the time.

I watched him in the ring later as he went on and won the ticket with that dog and all the other exhibitors stood there with their efforts at grooming and breeding left in his wake. I learned plenty that day. "You never stop learning in this game," the old breeders love to intone. And they know. They are more than just custodians. Theirs was the vision of type and ideal that shaped the world of pedigree dogs. The perfect animal, always just one more litter or cull away.

When I say "breeders," I am talking about the proper ones, a dying breed themselves these days, who actually love their dogs and want to promote them through the show ring. Not the new sort who find the animals incidental to their goals. They are just in it for the power and kudos with the ultimate aim of qualifying to judge. It has very little to do with money and everything to do with the ultimate accolade of becoming a championship judge. To be able to travel around the country, then the world, with their opinion unchallengeable and sending its ripples backwards and forwards forever. To have bred a champion is the first step, to keep winning helps the momentum until each new appointment is assured, and the fact most of them couldn't tell a three-legged rocking horse from a dog is lost behind their unimpeachable reputations. We just help get them there. They, in return, make certain we keep going.

I've got one of them today—two, if you count the judge as well as the client. The client is desperate for her first British champion and starting to become impatient. She and her hubby are from one of those wealthy Scandinavian countries. They have been involved in showing dogs over here for about 18 months and already feel things are dragging. Their bitch has won two tickets, and luckily I'm on for the third today. It is a crappy little creature with close, tied movement and a spooky temperament. But that doesn't matter. What matters is today's judge. He is giving tickets for the first time and will be shit-scared of making a fool of himself or offending the wrong people. He will be glad of any help received—and will already have been got at. Not with money. Remember, money means nothing. Pressure and promises.

"Give my bitch the ticket," my owner will have said to him, "and you'll be making up a champion on your first appointment. Two other judges can't have got it wrong. Why risk anything controversial? And, of course, you know that when I am made a judge, I have always truly been a fan of your dogs."

On and on it will have gone, until, so long as I give him the nod it is the right animal in front of him, my winning is guaranteed.

One time, when I was new to all of this and just starting to become established, through what I then believed was my own hard work and efforts and nothing to do with other people's schemes, I had a client's bitch on two tickets and took her to show under a lady judge doing her first number. She was well out of touch with the scene but had fucked her way to this position in an earlier time and was still out to collect any dues owing. "Tell her," the owner instructed me, "when no one can hear you, that the dog has two tickets." I loved that dog. She had the most stunning head and expression I had ever seen. It dominated the whole ring and drew attention from everyone, friend or foe. So I kept my mouth shut. I wanted to win on merit alone. To prove that all the susurrations blowing around the huge tented village were just sighs of disappointment. I was showing in "open" bitch. The open class is considered the toughest as all dogs are eligible, including those that are already champions. Usually, the winner of open is a certainty for the ticket. I won open against tough competition. I stood in line for the Challenge Certificate knowing I was about to make up my first champion. The judge, clinging to some vestige of the looks that had got her there, strutted up and down the line making a fine show of assessment. She handed the ticket to the winner of the limit class and the reserve ticket to the junior winner.

She spoke to me outside the ring and said she liked my bitch but felt the animal wasn't quite ready for her first ticket! She told the owner on the phone that night she had been scared to give what she thought was a first CC to a handler she hadn't recognized, and so she went down the line to more familiar faces.

"Why," the owner said, she kept on asking him, "didn't a 'professional' tell me?" The breeder took that bitch off me and gave it to another handler who made her up at the next championship show. It broke my heart.

Now I know. And though it is strictly against the rules to speak to a judge in the ring during judging, I will chant it out like a mantra: "It's on two, make it up. It's on two, glory for you."

The owners of the bitch will turn up today dressed for the occasion. They will have hampers of food and crates of champagne at the ready. As soon as I win, they'll throw a party. All the other exhibitors and the judge will turn up—and everyone will act surprised and delighted. I am required to put in an appearance and accept my praise. It will be minimal and given reluctantly. Professional handlers are not liked. We are mercenaries, tolerated for the duration of each battle. We don't care. The war goes on and on.

Bruce Springsteen is screaming "Born in the USA" as we descend the final hill to the showground. The massive car parks are already starting to fill with early arrivals. Some people have been here all night, sleeping in vehicles, their hopes and pets steaming up the windscreens as they dream and wait. We are allowed to drive straight into the show. The guard at the gates recognizes us from a long way off and is joking as we drive in. "Now there is going to be trouble," he tells his young assistant. "Now the show really gets underway." We speed by with the music drowning out our replies.

Everything is off-loaded. The dogs that needed force-feeding—including nearly all of the would-be sick travellers and too-closely bred anorexics—have been stuffed. Most of the coloring and other illegal activities have been done before the public was allowed in. We have changed into our suits and ties and are standing around trying to look mean and unapproachable. And if you could call the endless barking and yelping of thousands of dogs and the excited babbling of their owners calm, then this is the calm before the storm. Soon the loudspeakers will give out their little welcome speech and wish everyone luck and fair play. Then we'll be on a rush with everything moving so slow it hurts.

I've seen a few of my clients getting into position, including the two who are expecting a win. They nearly managed a smile before darting into one of the V.I.P. tents to await their moment of glory.

Gabby comes over and says the usual: "I have the feeling this is going to be our day." Then he adds something another famous handler is credited with quoting after a day's monumental winning: "Leave them just their eyes that they may stand and weep."

For some reason, as he walks away, I look into the travel box where the future champion waits. It is black inside, and yet I feel I can see her eyes staring out through the mesh front of her prison at everything happening. It makes me remember something my father once said. We were talking about art and how it could say things about great issues and injustices by using an image that could be endlessly enlarged and reinterpreted. He said that he liked the cartoonists and one piece, in particular. It had been on the occasion of some Russian space flight, when they had blasted this dog named Laika into the firmament and left her up there drifting about, waiting to die. This cartoon had shown the huge void that is space, silent and infinite, with the little capsule in the middle of it. Inside was Laikas, nicknamed Mutnic, staring out wide-eyed, trustingly, into our lives. The caption read, "A giant step for man."

Through another space the PA system barks out its order, and I slip a lead around the dog. It is time for the judging to commence.

CHIKODILI EMELUMADU

Jermyn

From January/February 2014

OUR DOG JERMYN ate everything. So at my brother's naming ceremony, it did not seem unusual to see him attacking a gift-wrapped box so vigorously. It was easily the best-wrapped present, all pink and green and shiny.

"Jermyn!" I took it from him. He leapt to snatch it back. Standing on his hind legs, he's almost taller than I am.

"What's wrong with that fool dog?" My mother asked. Her lips thinned.

"Dunno." I was enjoying having Jermyn leap for it. Even if he was almost pushing me to the ground.

"Well you better lock him up before he ruins things for us today." She gave him an evil look.

Jermyn was my step-father's dog. He had a taste for my mother's lace skirts. He waited until they were washed and hung out to dry, flapping in the breeze. And not any old ones. The ones with sequins or diamante. Expensive lace. He liked to shit sequins. Afterwards he'd sit and lick his bloody bum dry. Right now, he looked at her like she was lunch and all she had on were oversized earrings and a silk robe.

"He likes you, you know."

Her response was a harrumph. Then she sashayed upstairs.

"She likes you, Jermyn. And so do I." I swatted him on the rump.

Everyone said my mother would marry again. But when she did, it was with a lightning speed that surprised a lot of people.

"What kind of woman does not wait the full mourning year before marrying again?"

"She carries the stench of her dead husband."

"She is lucky a man wanted to take her on with two children."

"Can't blame him. The woman is as fine as Mami Wata."

Indeed. If anyone could be compared to the water goddess, it was my mother. She was stunning. And charming. And graceful. Everything I was not. You should have seen the way she used her hands. Even moving them in silent commands to the servants, they whispered through the air as if motion could bruise them. I admired my mother.

I liked my step-father well enough. He was crazy about my mother. Not crazy enough to give up the dog, though.

"I'll buy you new ones," he said to my mother when confronted with evidence of Jermyn's misdeeds.

"That's not the point!"

Jermyn stole meat from the pot while it was still cooking on the fire. He crept in through the back doors, nosed the lid off and snapped up as much as he could. It was his howls of pain that brought us running.

My step-father gave him the whole pot of meat when it was done.

"I'll buy you another pot," he said to my mother.

He wanted us to call him "Dad" straightaway, and I did. It helped our image. I am pragmatic about such things. My sister is not.

"He disgusts me," she said. I knew she didn't mean it. She was a daddy's girl who missed her dead dad.

"His beard is too weird. He looks like Pharaoh." That was true. Our new dad had a beard, heavy, black, shaped so it curved away from his face like a banana.

"What kind of man does not wait for a woman to take off mourning clothes anyway?" Now she was just listening to gossip. Nwala did not know anything about funeral rites before our father died. We had never been exposed to death.

"I bet he cannot have children." She was wrong. My mother was pregnant within the year. She gave birth to my sister Ugo, and now three years later, our baby brother was finally born.

Our step-father had taken him in his arms after he was born and performed the full Lion King. He raised him up high. "All of this belongs to you!" he exclaimed. "I will give you the world." Nwala hissed and left the room.

"Darling, mind the fan," said my mother, filing her nails.

"Yes, yes." He handed my brother over and went out to give cash gifts to all of the hospital staff and anyone who so much as looked at him.

I stroked the tight O curls on my brother's head. His eyes were open. I lowered my face to his. "Hello, baby. I am your sister. Edwina."

When I looked up, tears were pouring down my mother's face.

"Are you in pain? Should I call a nurse?"

But she merely laughed, the sound of gears grinding. "I wish your father's brothers could see me now."

Throughout my brother's ceremony, my mum shuddered each time Jermyn barked, fingering her newest frothy attire: creamy yellow lace, fine as cobwebs. It looked fit to collapse like a Victorian maiden if you looked at it sternly. I should have put that in quotes since I borrowed it. My new grandmother said it first.

Finally, my father could take the staccato barks no more.

"Somebody release that mutt," he said. "I'll give him some palm wine. He'll soon join in the swing of things."

My grandmother tutted. She said in Igbo, "When you treat a dog like a son, why be surprised when it acts like one?" In English she added: "He's just jealous you finally have a boy. He's going to be replaced."

"No, never." My father sipped his tankard of palm wine. Foam clung to his moustache. He did not wipe it off.

My grandmother looked at him as he said that. I could tell she wanted to ask him if he was "having brain waves," her code for crazy. But she didn't want to insult her son in front of all the guests milling about. She circled her head with her fingers and clicked them to nullify his words.

"Where is your sister? Go and get her to help." My mother looked with alarm as a servant girl laden with plates of oily *onugbu* soup came her way. She side-stepped quickly. Her fish-tail skirt made it seem as if she was gliding. Her earrings threw patterned sunlight all over her bare shoulders.

"That girl is always dodging. Why do you let her spend so much time by herself? It's not healthy, always going into that bush behind the house." Grandma's legs were almost useless, which is probably why she could only carry my sister Ugo for as long as she did. Ugo was the size of an adult pig.

My mother bristled. "You know how she is, Nne," she said. "Can anyone stop her?" She said this in the syrupy tones which meant she was really, really annoyed.

"Don't look to that one for bride price," said grandmother. "But my darling Ugo will fetch more than twice whatever your other two do. Won't you?" She tickled my sister under her dimpled chin. Ugo squealed. My mother pretended not to hear her.

My sister Nwala stood by our fish pond, squeezing *udala* fruits. She twirled her favorite short twig in her hand. It was a knobby bit of bark she'd picked up from god-knows-where, which she used as a soother. It stained her hand dusty green.

"Mum's calling you."

She said nothing.

"What are you doing?"

"Feeding the fish udala seeds. What does it look like?"

"Do they like it?"

She shrugged.

"Mum says you're to come and help.

"Why? It's not my baby."

Nwala had not even held our brother since he had been born. She despised Ugo, called her "half-breed" because she "looks like a pig and has ears like a teddy bear." Don't ask me.

On my way back from the backyard, I saw Jermyn sniffing about in the pile of presents, whimpering. I watched him for a while, nosing packages aside. He saw me and barked, two short high ones. He didn't wag his tail.

"What is it, boy?" I asked like they did in films. "Did Nwala fall in the fish pond? Did dad choke on a fish bone? Is baby on the balcony?" I looked up. "No. So stop that racket."

Jermyn ignored me. He went back to his search.

"You can stop looking. I hid it upstairs. Honestly, you and shiny things."

Jermyn's ears pricked up.

"Don't even think about it," I said.

But he ignored me and rushed to the backyard, making an even bigger racket than before. Many of the serving girls from the local caterer shrank back from his slavering form. He pawed the mosquito netted patio doors.

"Oh, no you don't!" I took him away and locked him up in his kennel again.

A long howl split the air. Even the live band stopped playing. Their lead singer, resplendent in sunglasses and trendy dreadlocks, crossed himself.

"Jesu Kristi. That dog is behaving like somebody's died," he said.

"Why has the music stopped?" My step-father yelled. They started up again. I noticed the lead singer turning a ring rosary around his fingers.

When I went upstairs to keep the rest of the gifts in the cupboard in the baby's room, the first one was gone.

"Hey, where...?"

There was a piece of the pink and green wrapping paper on the floor. I picked it up and put it in my pocket. I would look for the present later.

My brother was named Emmanuel Kaosisochukwu Dimazoro Ogugua Achufusi. Everyone agreed his names were fitting.

Jermyn's howling woke me in the middle of the night. I heard a rustling in my room. I thought, "Cockroach!" My skin responded with gooseflesh. I listened. Silence. I was dropping off to sleep when it came again. I sat up.

"Hello?" I definitely watch too many films. I reached beside my bedside table and picked up the metal torch. I clicked it on and aimed the beam at the sound. Again. Rustle, rustle.

It came from my dirty linen basket. My mind swarmed with images. Had a rat managed to get in there? Was it a cockroach? If yes, was it not better being trapped under the lid of my basket until one of the girls could get it out? But no, cockroaches could gnaw through clothes like moths. I had a few clothes I really liked in there.

It was the last thought that sent me almost flying across the cool tiles in desperate bravado. I took the lid off and shone the beam in the basket. The sound stopped. I poked the clothes with the torch.

Nothing.

I bent down to pick up the lid. Something flew straight out and into my face. I dropped the lid. The torch clattered to the floor and went out. I slapped my face several times, my hair a few hundred, my body a thousand. I stomped on the ground, picked up the torch and shone it around.

The piece of wrapping paper from earlier in the day lay on the floor.

As I stared at it, it moved. Slowly at first, as if it didn't want to startle me. Then it scuttled across the floor to slip under my bedroom door.

I stood there holding the torch in both my hands, fogging up the glass with my breath.

"The hell...?" I decided it was probably the wind.

I told you I was pragmatic.

It wasn't the wind. The heat in my room made it impossible to go back to sleep. The windows were closed, and there was no breeze. I timed myself on my mobile phone, trying to talk myself into getting up. Nine minutes. Nine minutes before the rustle started up again. It sounded bigger this time. Like a... what is the collective noun for bits of wrapping paper? A swarm? It was a swarm of wrapping paper. I shone the torch before I stepped out of my room. I caught the tail of it, tapering off in twos and threes.

I stepped on a piece. It wiggled underneath my feet.

"Ouch!" It cut the skin between my big toe as it fled to join the others. I followed it, hopping on one foot. It was going upstairs. My parents slept upstairs. And so did my baby brother.

My sister's door opened on my right.

"Yaaaa!" She ploughed into me. I fell, scraping an elbow on the pebbledash walls. The torch slid away, spun and caught us in its beam. Nwala looked as if she hadn't been sleeping, either. More than that, she was awake. Too awake. As if she hadn't slept for days. How had I not noticed?

"Nwala, get off me. There is something...!"

"Leave it Edwina. It only wants a little blood. Then it'll go away."

I wanted to ask her what the hell she was talking about, but some part of me must have known not to. In films, this is where people get killed. Asking stupid questions instead of fleeing.

"Get off me, Nwala!"

I struggled, but Nwala was strong. Bony, but strong. She pinned my arms to the floor with her knees.

"Don't you understand? It was hungry. It's been hungry all this while."

"Get off! It could hurt the baby!"

"Good! I'm so sick of that stupid baby!

I pushed her off. She hit her head on the wall. I ran.

"Edwina!" she called after me. Her voice bounced all over place. I could hear her coming as I ran upstairs. Her feet slapped flipper-like against the tiles.

"What's all this racket?" My mother appeared at the top of the stairs. She seemed soft-lit, all rose gold and pinks, her silk nightgown creaseless.

"Nwala is trying to kill the baby!"

"I am not!"

"What?" My mother's hand whispered through the air around her head. Any other person might have scratched their head. I rushed past her into the baby's room.

All was calm. Too calm. The baby breathed softly. I turned to flick on the light and saw it. It swirled in the air behind the door, in the shape of a person. Not a real person. A logo person, the kind cooked up by smart ad men. Pointed arms and feet like the Tour de France cyclist.

It came towards me, swirling, swirling like dust motes. I picked the baby up and held him to my chest.

"Edwina! All it needs is a little blood!" Nwala burst in. "I promised!"

"Then give him yours!" The thing stretched out a swirling, shimmering arm. "What the hell is this thing?"

"Edwina, I promised him the baby. Don't you see? This could solve all our problems. Mum could love us again!"

"Huh?" The nearer the thing moved, the more I could feel the breeze it generated. It tickled the hairs on my face.

"Ugo is a girl, she's no real threat, but a boy, a boy changes everything!"

"I love you," said mum, gliding in. She glanced at the creature. Her lips pursed. "I don't know what she's told you, but if you think I am giving up my son, you have another thing coming."

The paper man looked from one to the other of us. It hovered uncertainly.

"Where did you find this thing?" asked mum. "Is this what you've been doing all this while in the bushes? Good lord."

"It's not my fault. I'm starved for attention. And I want my daddy," said Nwala. She wiped her eyes with the sleeves of her pajamas. "It found me. It said we could be a family again."

"Your father is not coming back, Nwala, you know that." Mum touched her face. "He left us, and that is that. This is our family now."

The creature shimmered into the rocking chair. It held its head in its hands. We could hear Jermyn going crazy, scampering about the compound, looking for a way into the house from the kennels.

"And you," she turned to the creature. "Why don't you get off your lazy behind? Stop looking for small girls to do your dirty work. If it's blood you're after, why don't you pay a visit to my greedy ex-brothers-in-law? They threw me out of my house just because I didn't have a son to carry on the family name."

The thing looked up. I could see its face, swirling like a school of fish. It paused for a moment, then stood to its full height. It almost touched the ceiling. The baby began to wail. Jermyn howled louder.

"Mum, it can't fly that far without a body. It needs..." Nwala began.

"Yes, yes. We know. It needs blood." I rolled my eyes and handed the baby over to mum. She pulled down the neck of her nightgown and attached him to her breast. "How did it get here anyway?"

Nwala brought out the gnarled twig.

"Why don't you take Jermyn's body? He won't mind. He's a loyal dog." Mum sat in the chair the thing had just vacated. She re-latched the baby and rearranged the kimono sleeves to spread out like butterflies' wings. "And he's always eating my clothes."

"Mum, you can't do that!" I stopped. It would be just like the revenge-dog film, *Teri Meharbaniyan.* My dad loved old Bollywood films. The uncles had taken those DVDs as well. I had begged and begged. I knew the uncles would not watch them. They just had to have all his stuff. It was tradition, they said.

"Actually, that is a good idea," I amended.

"Yes?" She looked to Nwala for confirmation.

"Yes." Nwala's smile was shaky. She stared at the thing as if wishing to communicate something.

"What going on?" Our step-father yawned. His stale palm-wine breath filled the room. He rubbed his chin. "Why is everyone up?" he picked at his eye crust. He clocked the creature near the window.

"Argh!" He turned to run. He slipped on the rug. He fell. He was out like a light. Blood seeped from a cut to his head. The creature stared at it.

"Why isn't it taking that blood?" I asked.

"It didn't earn that. That's just taking the piss," said Nwala.

"I told your father not to put that rug there." Mum burped the baby and put him back in his cot. "Let's go."

We trooped downstairs.

Jermyn barked and barked and barked. The thing just stood there shimmering. Jermyn tried to bite it. It disintegrated and reformed. It made Jermyn chase his tail.

My mother cleared her throat. "This is all well and good, but are you going to take the dog or not?"

The swarm whipped round and round until it was a mini cyclone. In it went arrow-straight into Jermyn's barking mouth. Jermyn howled one more time and then stopped. His eyes flickered, now green, now pink.

"All right, Jermyn," said mum. "Kill!" She pointed in the direction of my father's village.

We gaped at her.

"What?" she shrugged. "I've always wanted to say that."

Jermyn barked. No sound came out. A single piece of paper like the one I stepped on escaped his mouth and flittered over the gate. He gathered himself and leapt after it.

"Sorry mum," said Nwala as we went back to the nursery.

"You should apologize to your father. I'm not the one who's going to wake up with a headache," she looked at herself in the full length mirror in the baby's room. I'd always wondered what it was for. Now I knew.

I yawned. I needed my bed.

"I do hope Jermyn eats your Uncle Christian's wife first. The thought of her fat ass forced into my jacquard wrappers gives me the creeps." She patted her hair in its fat, long plaits. "It's such a shame isn't it? The things we women have to do to earn society's protection?"

She lifted my step-father in her arms. Her footfalls were still light, her hips still swung from side to side as she went down the hall to their bedroom.

"Edwina? I think mum's crazy," Nwala whispered.

I sat in the rocking chair and fell asleep.

The next morning at breakfast, Nwala shoveled cornflakes and *akara* balls into her mouth. Her three-year semi-fast had come to an end.

"Morning, darling," said mum as our step-father came down for breakfast.

I handed him a glass of orange juice, freshly squeezed from one of the trees at the back.

"I must have had too much to drink last night," he winced.

"You fell out of bed." Mum kissed him. So did Nwala. He looked up in surprise. His face melted in pleasure. He wasn't so bad after all.

"So, where is Jermyn today? He hasn't come to greet me."

"I sent him on a little errand," said mum. "He really is a good dog."

ALICE WHITTENBURG

A New Definition of Treason

From April/May 2011

(PASQUELINA)
1. Defense Prop 2020

"Of course it makes sense," my dad said. We were getting ready to go
to dinner, just the two of us, because Mendel, Gabriella, and Curtis
were obviously not going to show. "We live in a democracy, and we
should vote before going to war."

It was Saturday. It was Dad's first time home from the capital in
over a year, a surprise visit. On Friday night I invited Mendel,
Gabriella, and Curtis to come see him. Each gave a different reason
why that wasn't possible. Dad and I played chess before we went to
bed, and in the morning we watched the news. There was a report on
the war referendum, Defense Prop 2020. Dad and I had been arguing
about it ever since.

"I don't want any part of it," I said.

"Then just vote no," he answered.

"It's a scam," I said. "If the government really wants to go to war, will they let the voters stop them?"

"You're very cynical," Dad said, and we went outside and got into separate cars and drove to a restaurant he and Mom used to like.

"War has always been with us," Dad said as soon as we got a table. "At least now we can vote on it."

"But who in their right minds," I said quietly, "would ever vote to go to war?"

"People who think our enemies deserve to be punished, people who want to see justice served, or who just want some excitement." He shrugged.

"Crazy people," I said.

"Our enemies will vote for their wars, and if we don't vote for ours, they'll have the advantage over us. Sensible people know that."

"That's not my definition of sensible," I said. The waiter came just then, and we ordered wine and pasta.

After the waiter had gone, Dad said, "Don't you want to see those bastards get what's coming to them?"

"What about diplomacy?" I said. "What about forgiveness?"

"What about it?" he said.

"If I hadn't been willing to forgive, we wouldn't be here now."

"Don't start on that," he said. The wine came, and he drank his first glass quickly.

"So how could we stop them if the voters said no but the government wanted war?"

"Vote out the warmongers, too," Dad said, smiling. He poured another glass of wine.

"What if we had voted? What if Mendel, Gabriella, Curtis and me had voted that you and Mom shouldn't fight any more? What would you have done?"

Dad said, "Don't start on that," and he drank down his wine.

"We could never stop you," I said. "Kids should have more power."

2. Replacing Giselle Trieste

Dad and I were sitting in my living room after our dinner out, and I asked him again to tell me where Mom was.

"About a year ago Agency was investigating a cell, and your mother was supposed to infiltrate it. She made contact and arranged to meet them, but when she arrived, there was just one woman: Giselle Trieste. Your mother asked, 'Where are the others?' Giselle Trieste said, 'This is how we operate; a cell of one can't betray itself.'"

I was going to say, "You expect me to believe that?" but instead I asked, "How could Mom replace another woman?"

"Your mother asked Giselle Trieste, 'How do your people communicate?' And the Trieste woman said, 'Like the cells and tissues and organs of the body, we use a biologic code.' So your mother entered that cell the way a virus invades its host, and she replaced Giselle Trieste."

"How can you know all this if you weren't there?"

"I have my ways. She reported back for a while. Odd intelligence. Non-specific information. She gave Agency a key to that biologic code, but they haven't quite cracked it yet."

"That's not what you told me on the phone. When I asked about Mom."

"Isn't it?"

"I want you to tell me what happened to her. A true story about where she is and where I can find her."

"I'm sorry," he said. "I can't do that."

"So why tell me fictions?"

"To reassure you. To comfort myself."

Angry, I went off to bed. He sat and drank whiskey in the dark, making up new stories he didn't expect me to believe.

3. My Mother's Smile

After Dad was gone, I called Mendel, Gabriella, and Curtis so we could video-conference. I said I understood why they hadn't come to see Dad, and I told them about the visit.

"Obviously, he's a liar," Mendel said. Mendel is my older brother. "Dad's not big enough in government to know about Agency."

"He drives a black Jag with digital plates," I said. "He has some pretty sophisticated mobile security."

"That doesn't mean shit," Mendel said.

Gabriella is a middle child like me; in fact, we're twins. "Next time Dad visits, I'll come over," she broke in.

"I think you should stay away from him," Curtis said. He's the youngest. "Dad can twist your words and steal your secrets. You don't even have to say nothing."

"Anything," Gabriella corrected. "So what exactly did he say about Mom?"

I hesitated for a few seconds. "This time he said Mom replaced a woman named Giselle Trieste."

Mendel laughed an ugly laugh. "Giselle Trieste is probably the bitch Dad was with when Mom decided she'd had enough."

"But why did he tell me Mom turned into another person? Like a woman in a science fiction movie?"

"There are viruses that can reprogram DNA, that can change living things," Curtis said.

"You've been reading too many comic books," Mendel said.

"You don't know ten percent of what you think you know," Curtis said.

"Stop it," Gabriella said.

I wanted to change the subject. "Dad thinks we should all vote on Defense Prop 2020."

They didn't pay any attention to me and continued to bicker.

So I said, "I asked Dad what would've happened if we would've voted. Us kids."

"Voted on what?" Mendel asked sharply.

"On them fighting like they did."

"They would've just done what they wanted. Like they always did," Mendel shouted. His video-conference window disappeared from my screen.

"Listen, guys, I gotta go, too," Gabriella said, and her window blanked out.

It was just Curtis and me. "Stay away from it," he said. "Agency and government and that. Of course they'll win the vote, and of course there'll be a war if that's what they want."

"I'm going to try to find Giselle Trieste," I said. "In case she is. Mom, I mean."

"You're so sweet," he said. "You're such a forgiving nature." He waved, and then his window blanked out.

I kept thinking about the virus idea—the possibility of invading cells and rewriting DNA and becoming someone else. Or they might become you. And what would that mean during wartime? Would we replace our enemies? Would our enemies replace us? Maybe they already had.

I began a search and found somebody named Giselle Trieste in a group photo at a barracks somewhere in Nevada. Her smile was something like Mom's. Her smile was something like the enemy's.

(CURTIS)
4. Pod/God

I was laying on the floor with the dog. The dog's name is God—for obvious reasons. I was using God as my personal therapist.

I said, "Pasquelina asked Dad where Mom is. Dad said Mom became somebody else. Like a pod person from *Invasion of the Body Snatchers*. Why did he tell her that?"

God didn't answer.

It was getting dark. My apartment was cold, but there was a warm spot where God huddled up to me. I was just almost asleep. Then my phone rang.

"What?" I said into my phone.

"It's your father," Dad's voice said. It was his sad-drunk voice.

"I don't believe in my father," I said. I hung up and turned off the phone. Five seconds later it started ringing again.

"What?" I said again.

"Why didn't you come to Pasquelina's house?" my father asked. "We had fun. Like old times."

"I don't believe in old times," I said.

There was silence. God started running in his sleep.

"I'll come back soon," Dad said. "I really want to see you."

"How'd you get my number?"

"From Pasquelina."

"I know that's a lie."

"You shouldn't accuse your own father of lying."

"My own father shouldn't lie. About Mom and all. We need to know what happened to her."

"There's a special program at Agency. She volunteered. Do you remember that magician at your party? Tricks with coins and cards? Your mother is a kind of magician. She'll help us win the war."

"You told Pasquelina she became someone else. Giselle Trieste. But Mendel says Giselle Trieste was your girlfriend."

"Giselle Trieste doesn't exist."

"She doesn't exist? She does exist, and she's Mom? Make up your mind."

"My mind is made up. What about yours? Have you signed up yet?"

"I'm never going to fight."

"You will if they pass Defense Prop 2020. You'll have to go. The girls, too, maybe. Mendel's got a wonky head. They won't want him."

"I'll leave the country."

"What's wrong with you? Are you as bad as I always said you were?"

Dad was using his mean-drunk voice. He was trying to get me worked up. God could feel my tension, and he sat up and barked.

"What was that?"

"My dog."

"I like dogs. Mom had one at the base. It was trained to sniff out rare elements they needed for miniaturization."

"So you're going to tell me Mom is miniaturized?"

"I'm not going to tell you anything. Except that you should sign up."

"You sound like some pod man who replaced my dad."

"I'm better than that. I'm in charge of the pod squad. I'm the pod god." Now he was using his crazy-drunk voice.

I hung up and turned off the phone. I put the phone under a pile of clothes. Then I huddled up to God. The phone kept on ringing and ringing, but my father couldn't make me answer.

5. AKA Orion

After I hung up on my dad, after he stopped trying to call me back, I couldn't sleep. So I went out on the balcony and looked into the night sky to see what I could see above the glare of lights. Orion was there, and while I looked at the line of stars making up his belt, I planned how to free some information about Giselle Trieste. Pasquelina is smart, and she's good at infometrics, but if I'm trying to find Giselle Trieste and Pasquelina's trying to find Giselle Trieste, nine times out of ten I will find Giselle Trieste first. Or whomever I'm looking for.

I went back into the apartment and called Chloe. "Meet me at Squid's," I said, and she said OK. God looked sleepy, but I brought him along anyway.

"No dogs allowed in here," Squid said, and then I sat at a table, and God laid underneath it, and I drank Mexican beer until Chloe got there.

"Problems with my dad," I said. "I have to go out of town for a couple days." She knows enough about my dad not to ask questions.

"It's getting cold," she said. "Wear that coat I got you."

"Tonight I looked at Orion for a long time," I said. "He's been in a constellation, hunting, for like thousands of years."

"I don't know about hunting," she said. "I'm a vegan."

"Could you take God while I'm gone?" I asked. She said she would and we kissed and I had another Mexican beer.

When I went back to my place it seemed lonely without God. I slept for a few hours, and got up while it was still dark. I put some clothes in a gym bag along with my hardware, and I went to the bullet train station. I bought a ticket to the capital. By morning the train was full of government commuters coming in from the ring cities, giving me the bad eye for the way they thought I smelled.

I worked my hardware all day, and I learned three things: There is something called genetic transformation, and cells can be reprogrammed. Dad does have top portfolio clearance. And Mom hasn't been at Agency for over a year. But I couldn't find anything about Giselle Trieste, so I decided to try again tomorrow.

After dark I went to a Draft Resisters meeting. I got as far as the door. I thought I recognized a few people, but then I saw a guy I knew was a narc and somebody from Agency. I turned away, and a big guy yelled, "Hey! Aren't you coming in? The meeting's starting."

"No," I said, walking fast.

"Hey! What's your name?" he shouted.

"Orion," I said and kept on walking.

(GABRIELLA)
6. Killing Lambs and Sending Kids to War

Mom hasn't seen Krista for two years, and Krista has no memory of her grandmother. Now I'm having trouble remembering Mom, though to be honest she started fading away right after Mendel fell.

Krista cries when I fight with Anderson, just like Pasquelina and I did when Mom and Dad fought. Mendel used to try to stop them, until he fell down the attic stairs. He got a concussion and stayed in a coma for a while. He was bruised from head to toe.

"What were you doing in the attic?" I asked him in the hospital when he could finally talk.

"Spying on Mom and Dad," he said. He sounded like his mouth was full of wet cotton. His eyes were dark and hollow-looking.

I knew he used to do surveillance on all of us, put cameras and mics in unexpected places, make recordings. "Why?" I asked. "When they fight we can hear them down the block. Why do you need to spy?"

"I don't remember," he said in a spooky, dead voice. "I really don't remember what it was about."

When Mendel finally got out of the hospital, Grandma Steenie came to live with us, and Mom and Dad mostly lived in the capital. "Help your grandmother," Mom said to Pasquelina and me. Pasquelina immediately started studying all the time so she could get all A's. That left me to do the hard work.

I guess that's what made me a practical person. When I got pregnant, I married Anderson even though I knew he drank too much. When I turned 18, I joined the Guard. I took an oath. And when Dad asked me about Curtis and Mendel and Pasquelina, I told him what I knew. I'd do the same with Anderson. I'd even do it with Krista.

"Are your brothers or sister disloyal in some way?" Dad asked.

I said Mendel had changed since he fell, and he was just a guy with a damaged brain. But I gave away a few secrets about Curtis and

Pasquelina. I felt like I was the disloyal one, but Dad always says, "The right thing to do is a hard thing to do." Don't people kill lambs to eat them? Don't parents send their kids to war?

Next week's the election for Defense Prop 2020, and I plan to vote for war. Even though it means I might get called up. Even though that means being separated from Krista. It's so cold over there, I can imagine crying and having the tears freeze on my cheeks.

The last time I saw Curtis, I tried to get him to do the right thing and sign up for the Guard. He pouted and turned his back on me like Krista does when I tell her to put her toys away and she's not done playing. I wanted to smack him. He was 12 when Mom and Dad went away, and he's like a clay boy who wasn't ever really properly formed. War, I think, will finally form him.

7. Not Identical Twins

I decided I needed to talk to Dad and it couldn't wait until his next visit. I searched and searched for the number he once gave me, but I finally had to call Pasquelina and ask her how to reach him. She's so smart, she might as well be good for something.

"So, why are you calling Dad?" she asked.

"I couldn't make it to your house, but I did want to see him."

"You used to say you were glad he was gone. Because of Krista," she said.

"I just want to ask him something. About the war."

"He thinks it's a good idea."

"So do I." There was a shocked little silence. "We're not identical twins, Patsy. We don't see things the same way." She gave me Dad's number, and we mumbled our goodbyes.

I left a message, and it was about four hours before Dad called me back. "Gabbie!" he said when I answered my phone. "How's my granddaughter?"

"Great," I said. "I wanted to tell you I'm sorry I couldn't come to Patsy's house to see you."

"All's well that ends well," he said. He sounded far away, and his voice was drug-cheerful instead of drunk-cheerful.

"Can we go on video?" I asked. I was surprised to see how different he looked—his hair and face were the same shade of grey. "I'll be there next time you come," I promised, smiling into the camera.

"You might be overseas by then, sweetie-pie." He said it with a certain ruthlessness, as though he almost enjoyed the thought.

"I need to ask you something," I said. "If Defense Prop 2020 passes, will Anderson and I both have to go?"

He thought for a few seconds and said, "Not my bailiwick, honey. I don't know. Is Anderson in the Guard?"

I nodded.

"You'll have to talk to somebody locally, kiddo. I couldn't really tell you."

"It'll be short though, won't it?" I asked.

"Short and sweet!" he said. "We have tricks up our collective sleeve you can't even imagine. Stealth technology upgrades. Big news in camouflage and encryption. Personnel enhancements galore."

"Personnel enhancements?" I asked.

"Just wait till you get there, doll babe."

That was when Krista stumbled into the room, fresh from her nap. "Say hi to Grandpa," I said, but I could see she didn't know who he was and didn't care.

"Hey, my big girl!" Dad yelled, and Krista cringed away from the phone like she was scared. "She's grown so much, it's amazing."

"She has," I said. "I wish Mom could see her."

"Your mother," Dad said, "is on a very special mission."

"Why did you tell Patsy she became Giselle Trieste?"

"You know how your sister is. She needs a lot of reassurance."

I said I understood, and for a few minutes I felt glad Dad saw me as stronger and braver than Patsy. Which is true. But after we hung up, I held Krista for a while, and I wondered what kind of reassurance the Giselle Trieste story was supposed to bring, and I wondered why he didn't know I need reassurance, too.

(MENDEL)
8. Head Case

I'm proud of myself. Pasquelina and Curtis both tried and failed, but I'm the one who found Giselle Trieste.

Tonight after work I called Patsy. "Can you come over here right now?"

She started whining about being tired and having an exam to study for. "You think you're tired?" I yelled. "I worked all day at a mind-numbingly boring government job, so quite bitching and get over here."

Patsy came through my door about 20 minutes later. She looked at the mess and made disgusted noises. "I'm a head case, remember?" I said. Then I put a strange vocal thing by Glee Monkeys on one player. I put a screechy dissonant thing by Jazzing for Power on another player. I turned on the water in the sink full blast, and I stood really close to Patsy.

"What the hell is going on?" she hissed.

"It takes one to know one," I said, "and I know surveillance guys. I don't want us to be overheard."

"Can we sit down?" she whisper-shrieked, making her eyes big and kind of crazy. We pushed a bunch of wires and plastic covers off the couch and sat as close together as we could.

"You know the only reason I have this job in government is because Dad felt guilty," I said.

"I know that's what you think," she said in that university-rationalistic way she has. All-"A" math student. Big-time programmer.

That old and unreasonable rage started bubbling up inside me. "And I know what you think! Everything that's wrong with me is because I fell and cracked my skull!"

I was whisper-shrieking, too, and gesturing wildly. Patsy had that scared-little-sister look, so I made myself stop. "I was a spy in a house of spies," I said quietly, right into her ear. "That's why it happened. Afterwards I shut the hell up because I wanted to survive. I shut the hell up because I didn't want you or Curtis or Gabbie to get hurt. But I was a pretty good spy, and over time I've remembered my secrets and kept them."

"So why are you telling me this now?"

"Because I found out who Giselle Trieste is."

She looked wild, and tears came to her eyes. "But how?"

"At work."

"Oh, Mendel..."

"I've never done a single thing like this before. As far as anyone knows over all these years, I'm a head case who doesn't remember anything. I'll tell you about Giselle Trieste, but first I'll tell you why Dad beat me up. Did you know that Mom studied genetics? That she dropped out of a Ph.D. program before she went to Agency? That she was on the Crop Resource Board that forced other countries to use patented seeds? Mom started to have second thoughts. Dad was a play-it-by-the-rules guy. So they fought, and I listened in."

I could tell Pasquelina didn't know what to think, so I said, "Now I have some real information. Help me go through this stuff, and we can find out where Mom is." She looked scared, but she nodded once, and I got out my most secure machine. We started to look at files.

9. Code is Poetry

By the time Patsy and I had convinced ourselves we knew what there was to know, it was the middle of the night. I decided to call Curtis anyway.

"Hey, I need to borrow some money," I said when he shouted "What?" into his phone. "Meet me at Tacos y Mas and bring some cash." This was code; neither of us could imagine a universe where I would borrow money from him.

Tacos y Mas is open all night, and it's what they used to call a greasy spoon. By the time Patsy and I got there, Curtis was sitting in a booth sucking beer from a fingerprint-covered glass. There was loud Banda music playing, and the waitress was at the other end of the room. I sat next to Curtis and said into his ear, "I just found Giselle Trieste."

He rocked back and forth with silent laughter. "I was in the capital looking for her," he said in a normal voice, "but I couldn't find anybody besides narcs and agents."

"Shhhh!" Patsy said. She was sitting on the other side of the booth. Her face looked blue, but maybe that was just from the fluorescent lights.

"You're gonna draw attention to us," Curtis said. "So just act normal and talk in code. Code is poetry, remember?"

The waitress came, and Patsy ordered coffee. I realized how hungry I was and ordered chimichangas. "How can you eat at a time like this?" Patsy asked.

"Easy," I said. "I feel very proud of myself."

"You should," Curtis said, but he seemed a little reserved. Jealous, maybe?

For a while we all fiddled with our phones. Then I said, "Basically there are three reasons why I need to borrow money off you."

Curtis said, "Yeah, well they better be good because I'm getting tired of bailing you out."

My chimichangas came, and I smothered them with salsa and ate two big forkfuls. "I'm waiting," Curtis said, and he did look eager.

"First," I said, "that bitch Giselle is seriously fucked up. Which is why I'm out of options."

"But where is she? I thought you were trying to find her."

"We have to distinguish between Giselle and the woman I love. That woman is in prison. And the reason she's in prison is because of her husband. We really, really do need to stay out of his way!"

By which Curtis understood that Mom is in prison. And she's there because of Dad. Which are two of the things Patsy and I learned. What I couldn't easily tell him is Giselle Trieste means Genetic Transformation, the weaponized version, a process allowing a modified virus to enter seeds and rewrite DNA to make them toxic. Mom wanted to blow the whistle, and Dad stopped her. He got a big promotion for his troubles.

I told Curtis whatever else I could. Then Patsy asked, "Should we tell Gabbie?" Curtis voted no, but Patsy and I outvoted him.

"She needs to know," Patsy said, and I nodded while Curtis nursed his beer and scowled. Then he slid a couple of bills across the table, just to cover our story about borrowing money. He paid for his beer and left. I figured I'd probably never see him again.

(DAD)
10. A New Definition of Treason

After the arrest I called Gabbie, and I said, "Sweetie-pie, I'm proud of you. You did the right thing."

She was very quiet, and her little girl, my only grandchild, was crying in the background.

"What about Patsy and Curtis?"

"Curtis, that good-for-not-much little bastard, is nowhere to be found. So we'll see where and when he surfaces. Patsy is on probation, but she can still go to school. Mendel's the problem and always has been."

"Where is he?"

"I'm not entirely sure, doll. That boy has had some serious head trauma in his life, so he needs medical facilities. I don't really know where all those facilities are, but some of them, as I understand it, aren't even in this country."

"Oh, Dad, they told me..."

"Honey, we're all just doing what we have to do. And we're all just fighting the bad guys. I know you are. I know I am. And we have to take treason seriously."

"So was it? Treason, I mean?"

"I don't think there's any doubt about that."

"And what about Mom? Can you tell me where she is?"

"You shouldn't ask me, angel-cake. Asking is a kind of treason, too, you know."

She was very quiet again. She's my girl, and she's a lot like me. But she is a woman, and I don't expect her to understand everything.

"That must be some new definition of treason," she said, sounding like she was fighting tears.

"Definitions of treason come and go. They can be re-written, when necessary, to help you do what you need to do. Didn't I always tell you that the right thing to do is a hard thing to do?"

"I keep telling myself that."

"Good girl. Because Defense Prop 2020 passed, just like we thought it would, and we're going to war."

"Was it a landslide?"

"I think it got 42 percent of the vote."

"You mean 52 percent, don't you, Dad?" she said, but I just said, "Bye, sweetie," and hung up the phone. Because I know what I mean, God damn it.

D. HARLAN WILSON

My Barbarian

From October/November 2001

THE BARBARIAN WASN'T working out. It kept defecating all over the upholstery, and whenever the wife and I had company over, it insisted on tackling and molesting every last cleavage-toter it could get its bony, gritty fingers on. I decided to return it.

"You sure you wanna take that route?" said Harry Arboreal, the manager of The Barbarian Boutique. We were standing in the middle of the store. Surrounding us was an ersatz jungle laden with barbarians like mine. Most of the barbarians were swinging on vines or whaling on each other with femurs or logs. A few were masturbating. One was banging its face against a tree trunk. "I mean, I'd be happy to take your barbarian back, but maybe you're being a little bit hasty here," Harry added. "Maybe you should give your barbarian another chance. After all, he's your barbarian."

He had a point. I thanked him and greased his cold calloused palm with a fifty for the advice, then grabbed the barbarian by its leash and clicked my tongue.

On the way home, the barbarian gnawed through its leash and attacked a street mime. The street mime saw it coming, and thinking it was a dirty crazy person instead of a barbarian, tried to reason with it by gesturing at it in a certain way with his face and body parts. The barbarian paid no attention to the gestures; it leapt on and began strangling the mime. The mime didn't have a voice box—it was stolen and sold on the black market by his stepfather when he was a child, an awful thing in that he lacked the capacity to express himself by means of speech acts, but a good thing in that, had his voice box never been stolen and sold, he never would have become a mime, a profession he thoroughly enjoyed—so all he could do was mouth, "Help! Help! Help!" in silence.

I felt sorry for the mime and said, "Leave that thing alone!" The barbarian didn't listen to me. I took what was left of the leash and gave the barbarian two quick, bloody lashes across the back. It squealed like a piglet and jumped off the mime. Urinating uncontrollably, it gamboled into traffic. Horns blasted, tires shrieked, cars crashed and exploded. I waited patiently for the smoke to clear, but when it did, the barbarian was gone.

I spent the rest of the day looking all over the city. I looked in dumpsters, manholes, every house of ill-repute. No luck. So I started knocking on people's doors and asking if they had seen it. Nobody had. Then, as I was leaning up against a lamppost catching my breath, I saw the barbarian running down the middle of the street. It ran right by me, saluting me with a curt fart as it passed.

I pushed myself off the lamppost, flagged down and leapt into a taxi. "Follow that barbarian!" I pointed. The taxi driver refused. "It's against my religion to acknowledge the existence of barbarians," he said, "and if I follow that barbarian, well, that's precisely what I'll be doing, isn't it?"

"Not if you pretend that barbarian is a haberdasher," I said. The taxi driver grabbed his chin with the tips of his fingers and began fondling it. I waited patiently for the fondling to come to an end... but it never did. And by the time I leapt out of his taxi and flagged down and leapt into another one, the barbarian was long gone. After having a little fit, I told this taxi driver to take me to police headquarters. I wanted to look around for the barbarian some more. I wanted to tell it that, even though it had been misbehaving, I was sorry for abusing it. But I was too tired and depressed. I filed a missing barbarian's report and went home, wondering how I was going to explain everything to the wife.

As it turned out, I didn't have to explain anything. I walked into my house and there was the barbarian, *my* barbarian, micturating on the couch. It was squatting on an armrest, and the wife was yelling at it, trying to convince it to go use the toilet. But the barbarian wouldn't budge. And when I nodded at it, it nodded back at me.

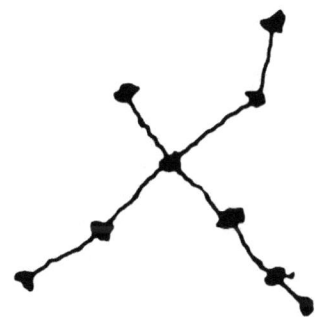

DAVID MATHEWS

Butter Fairies

From July/August 2015

For Meredith Boe

Look.
Like tiny thin
idle old men
they lurk in
your azaleas,
almost
too weak to lift
their little lanterns,
or raise their petite
grappling hooks
above their hoods
with hollow hopes:
today is their kind's
resurrection.
No one knows

how many
they are who crave
fresh creamy dairy
daily, no one
fears them climbing
in and swiping
anything.
Each time their
appetites labor,
it makes them more
humble creatures.
They all feel
it's quite queer
more people
should mean
butter's loss.
Some have asked,
"Do birds have
trouble finding worms?
Can mice find meals?"
Few remember
the long ago days
when what they wished
was placed at the doorstep
to snatch
without question.
They just keep
lingering in
your azaleas,
wondering
if they'll ever be
believed in again.

A.S. KING

River 16

From July/August 2007

H-125 HAS ONE river. One polluted river. It's like wading through chest-high, metal-flecked molasses loaded with floating industrial waste and dead people. On Earth, the closest comparison would be the Ganges, the Lot, and the New River all rolled into one. When I work on the river, they pay me $700 (Earth dollars) per hour.

Other than the river, H-125 doesn't offer much by way of familiar scenery. The surface is potholed like the moon, but uglier. Half of it is covered in mines, so we can take every last ounce of aluminum ore and ship it home to Earth for just one more year of them living like a planet full of deluded assholes. The few monochromatic canyons and peaks are interesting enough, unless you've seen the Grand Canyon or The Rockies, like I have. Of course, I never will again. Even if I do make the lottery, I'll be too old to go. And I should have never been sent here in the first place because none of it was my fault.

I'm getting ahead of myself.

Let me start this another way.

I was shipped here 14 years ago as punishment for a crime I did not commit. I worked in the mines at first—back-breaking prison labor—and then graduated slowly to my freedom and this job sifting through the polluted River 16 to weed out bodies, refrigerators, televisions, transports or any other things the population here tosses in that might clog the hydro-generator. Of course, if a dead body gets to me, then Frank in sector 2-H isn't doing his job. And if a small household appliance floats this far, that means Denny in sector 2-D isn't doing his job either. I can't say I blame them, though. I used to work in sector 2, and the smell of the crematorium is enough to make you pass out sometimes. Plus, Denny and Frank, like most of us, are crippled after working so long and hard in the mines.

The planet's population is divided now, after 40 years, between prisoners who work off their crimes and don't get paid, and ex-prisoners like us, who work with industrial independent contractors for more money than we'd ever see on Earth.

The only problem with making $700 an hour is there's nothing on H-125 to buy. Nothing. It's a 100% free society. We're the ultimate combination of socialism and communism and anarchy. Everything is free. But they pay us, anyway. So life is a constant state of financial impotence. It's like living inside of an eyeball but not being able to see out.

Here's how the math works. Seven hundred an hour is $7,000 a day. That's $42,000 a week, which is $2,100,000 a year. And I get to look at it (glare at it) every month on payday: my balance. The balance of my life. Ten digital numbers on a screen. My $24,864,990.11. Say it with me. Twenty-four million, eight hundred and sixty-four thousand, nine hundred and ninety dollars and eleven cents. I can't send it home, and I can't buy anything with it. Unless I win the lottery in the next seven months, my time is up. My luck runs out. I'm done for, and my imaginary money comes with me down River 16, the waterway of the euthanized, to be plucked out by Frank or whoever replaces me in section 3-C, and reduced to ash the color of an H-125 sunrise. The few who make the lottery before they reach age 50 are allowed to transfer their credits earned here to a bank on Earth and return home, but unless you get lucky, all you have is a number to look at until they retire you.

Back home, I used to fish on the Niagara River when I was a boy. The Earth Corps had restored it in the 23rd century after centuries of abuse and neglect. They paid for projects like river restoration and oceanic filters and arctic ice cleanings by discovering and mining distant planets filled with what Earth consumers were still buying. Like some bum at the turn of the millennium, they were trading soda cans for nickels and using the nickels to pay for more soda cans.

I had a beautiful family. Two boys, a baby girl, and Jean, my supportive and loving wife. We lived in a small, solar-heated home on the east side of Rochester, in a community known for its low population, which, when I was sent away, was around two million people. The rest of New York State wasn't so lucky. When Manhattan sank, the 30 million survivors scattered to the most nearby places. And the lust for higher ground crowded the Catskill, the Pocono, and the Adirondack Mountains. Rochester, being lakeside, was spared too much of an influx.

I was never any good at history, but from what I remember, recycling laws came into effect in the USA sometime in the 21st century. After the second revolution in 2234, when Earth became a global entity, the laws went lax for a while, but by the time my eldest boy Ginero was born 100 years later, the squads were out in full force every waste collection day, with their detectors and their electronic citation devices. Until Ginero became a teenager, we never got a fine.

Two soda cans in the regular paper/composting trash cost me four thousand five hundred dollars. Five weeks later, my dear wife Jean mustn't have been paying attention one day and threw a Ragu glass jar in the wrong bin and that cost me a second fine, which was double the first, and a strict warning that the limit was five. Five fines, and then prison for the homeowner. This was the 24th century. Mistakes of this sort would not be tolerated.

I held a family meeting explaining that if we weren't careful, they could put me in jail, and so, we would no longer be buying anything in glass jars or bottles, and every bag of trash that went from the kitchen to the garage would be inspected by me. At that, Ginero tried every single day to slip something in past my eyes. It was his teenaged way of pressing authority, I suppose, but he didn't understand the consequences. It's one thing to stay out later than curfew or start drinking alcohol, but this would damage our entire family. I would lose my job at the advertising firm. Our upper-middle class existence would drain so quickly that soon we would be no different from the riffraff that settled in the mountaintop cities of New Harlem or New Brooklyn or New Bronx. Ginero was 13 and a smart-ass. Nothing we said made him understand that this was not a game.

The third fine, $12,000, was for a crushed soda can he'd stuffed in the bag after I'd inspected it and put it at the end of our driveway.

The fourth was for a glass bottle he must have pinched from a neighbor's bin and tossed into the trash on his way to school.

Another family meeting. This time, just me, Ginero, and Jean.

"Son, do you realize what my being put in prison will do to your mother?"

He shrugged.

Jean slapped his arm. "God damn it, Ginero! What the hell has got into you? Don't you understand you are about to send this entire family into poverty?"

"So?"

"So?" Jean repeated. "So? Is that how you want to live? Like those children who have no shoes? Like the Manhattan refugees? Are you so spoiled, you can't see how good you have it?"

He sneered at us and yelled, "You call this good? I get everything I want! The kids at school make fun of me for being a spoiled rich kid. They call me 'Ginero Dinero'! I never have to struggle for anything! I hate it! I'd rather be poor like everyone else!"

I received the fifth fine in the mailbox, for two more crushed soda cans. Along with the bill for $20,000, which was three months' salary, was a letter from the Rochester sheriff explaining the procedure for taking me to prison or one of the mining colonies, which would happen the next time we failed to recycle.

Jean hugged me in bed that night and swore up and down that she'd testify it was Ginero's fault. That Ginero should be sent away, not me. But he was thirteen. And he was our son. She couldn't send him to prison any more than I could.

For three weeks, Jean and I would sift through every little bit of garbage in the garage on Tuesday nights. We'd re-bag it, put it in the bins, and I'd lock the new padlock we put on the garage door to keep Ginero out.

On Wednesday mornings, I'd stand with the cans until the trucks and inspectors came, making sure Ginero didn't drop anything in on his way to school. It was at those times, while guarding my waste bins from my own son, I got angry about the whole mess. Part of me wanted to stand back behind the oak tree in the lawn and catch Ginero in the act, and then beat him senseless, like my father had done to me on a few occasions to teach me how the real world worked. Another part of me asked if his behavior was in some way my fault.

It was a ball of tinfoil that sent me to H-125. He'd wrapped a paper towel around it, and when Jean and I went through the trash that fourth Tuesday night, we just didn't think to unwrap the thing.

Not a day goes by up here when I don't think of Jean and the kids. Even Ginero, the little bastard. He'd be 27 now. I wonder how they made it, if they stayed together, or if my arrest ripped the family apart. I wonder if Jean is still as beautiful as she was when I first met her at the little diner two miles from the Niagara River. I wonder can she still afford to fill the hummingbird feeders and sit and wait for them to come and stick their long tongues in and drink the sugary water. I hope she never had to be hungry.

My walk home from River 16 takes me through Hermes Sector, where I can see the docking station for the biannual round trip to Earth. Today, the ship has come with 300 new prisoners, each dressed in a color-coded thermal jumpsuit to designate his crime. Red are the white-collar polluters, CEOs of dirty corporations, who get sent to the depths of the mineshafts to do the most dangerous work. Green are the litterbugs, whether a gum wrapper from a car window or a transport trailer full of scrap or garbage, who go to work in the civil service. Yellow are for personal-use criminals like FR (Failure to Recycle), water wasting, sewer violations, or OEL (Over Energy Limits) who get sent to the mines to become human trains, like I did, to move the tons of slag with their bare backs.

The arrival of the ship means in two weeks, there will be a departing flight, with 300 lucky lottery winners on it, which means a week from today will be my last lottery.

At an intersection, a transport bus stops to let opposing traffic through, and I look at the men, who gaze, in shades of awe, out at their first dead planet. Are they disappointed by the endless gray? The lack of clouds and wildlife? The dim light from a too-distant sun?

Suddenly I am looking at Ginero, who is looking back at me. We lock eyes for two seconds before the transport jerks him toward whatever quadrant his mine will be in. He raises a red-suited arm to acknowledge me, and I say, "Wait," but the bus is gone, turned round a corner and out of sight. My son is on H-125. A slave. Like he made me 14 years ago. I run after the bus, hoping it might stop, hoping I was wrong, that it wasn't him, hoping I can rescue him, but it accelerates and I stop, wheezing, and realize I do not want to save Ginero. I realize I want Ginero to save me.

A week later, on payday, they announce 300 lottery winners. I'm not on the list, and I ask my payment officer if transfers of Earth credits are allowed to H-125 prisoners. He tells me it's possible, if I pay the right people the right amount of credits.

"So, would five million be enough? Do you think? To get the job done?" I ask.

He grins. "I think that ought to do it, yeah."

"So what if an old man wanted to find someone here? Would an extra two million buy him a quadrant location?"

"That sounds reasonable," he says, looking over my shoulder at the line of men to be paid, "but the old man had better hurry up."

I hand him a slip of paper with Ginero's name on it, and after a quick tussle with the computer, he hands it back, with the address. I scribble it onto my palm, and slide the paper back to him, because he knows what to do next. Can I trust him to only take seven for himself? No more than I can trust Ginero, if he ever gets off H-125, to take the money home and help our family. No matter. At least when my body is hooked and dragged from the river, I'll have lived for something up here in this wasteland. For now, I stare at the numbers on my palm and wonder what kind of man I will meet when I visit, and whether I will like him.

Ginero stares at me through the thick glass, and the lines on his forehead stretch wide with worry. I want to put him at ease and smile, but I admit part of me wants to break through and strangle the 13-

year-old boy he once was. I notice his manicured hands and compare them to my splitting thumbs and septic calluses, and for a second, I feel happy he is here. Happy he is about to experience real work for the first time in his life. Until I remember he will be worked to death like the rest of us, and no matter what a boy does to his father, it is never a good thing to contemplate the death of your child.

We stare like this for a while, eyes darting from the floor to each other, to the other prisoners, until it is our turn to meet at one of the four visitor booths for our ten-minute conversation. When we are face to face, no glass between us, I see he looks like Jean. Her chin, her eyes.

"Dad."

"Son."

He purses his lips, and frowns. "I'm so sorry."

I nod and squeeze my brow into the same frown. "How's your mother?"

"She's fine. Still lives in Rochester with Annie. Annie'll graduate school this year."

I feel hot tears run down my face. "Graduate? Annie?" I sigh. "How did Jean afford to stay in the house?"

"I don't know how she did it for the first years, but I got a job at the plant as soon as I turned 16, and so did Darren."

"Darren. How is he?" The last time I saw Darren, he was ten, and playing with plastic toy soldiers in the flowerbeds Jean had just mulched. I can smell the spring air and the tree bark.

"He works in advertising. I stayed in the plant and worked my way up to the office jobs. Soon, I was bringing home as much money as you were before you got... sent... here."

"So you lived with Mom? Took my place?"

He nods. "Until I met Stephanie, yes. Then we moved into a place on Harvest Street. You know, near the park?"

God. The Harvest Street Park. The days I used to spend pushing Ginero's little denim covered butt on those swings. The fun we had in the snow on the sliding boards. The time Darren slipped on the steps and split his lip.

"Stephanie? Is that your girlfriend?"

"My wife. We had a little girl three years ago."

I think about Annie when I left her. She was three as well. "I'm a grandfather?"

"Yes." Ginero is crying now, too. He wipes his eyes with his red sleeve. "We named her Jeanie, after Mom. She looks like her, too."

"Jeanie," I say. I can't hold back the sob. I am a grandfather. I pinch the bridge of my nose with my finger and thumb and then look at the timer. I have two more minutes.

"I miss them so much," he says.

"I know, son. I know you do. I guess you know by now that up here, they put out your candle once you hit 50, right?"

Ginero suddenly looks at me, concerned.

"Well, if they haven't told you that, then I'm glad I'm the one who broke it to you. Up here, you aren't much use as an old man, and the fumes in the mines age you double, anyway. But that's not why I'm telling you."

"Go on."

"Once you get free of the system, you'll get work, like I did, doing something else. And you stand to make a fortune doing it, too. I made a fortune, but I'm never going to make it home."

"Oh, Dad."

"It's okay," I say, glancing at the timer. Sixty-two seconds left. "Look, Ginero. I transferred all of my money into your prisoner account. You won't be able to access it or spend it up here, and you can't tell anyone about it, but if you're luckier than me, and you make it back to Earth, you can take it with you and assure our family never worries again."

He looks guilty. This secures my trust, and I smile and touch his hands. "You must tell your mother I love her, and your sister and brother, too."

"Will I see you again? Can't you come back and see me again?"

"Only once every six months, son. And in six months, I'll be floating down River 16, another lump for Frank to drag out and put on the conveyor."

"But," he begins to sob and grips my hand like he used to when he was a frightened boy.

"You'll make it, Gino. I know you will. Remember I love you. Think of your wife and daughter often, and you will serve your years here with purpose."

The buzzer sounds, and we hug over the wide table. He is crying, and I see his mother again, crying, having lost her husband and her son to this environmental tyranny. What sort of pitiless world divides a man from his young family for the sake of mere litter?

Walking through Hermes Sector on my way home, I see the launch pad and imagine Ginero flying home to his family. I see him at the bank on the corner of Elm and Green streets with Jean, transferring $15 million into her account. I see Annie going to college and becoming a doctor, like she wanted when I last saw her as a three-year-old, grasping her play stethoscope and laminated eye chart. I see Jean smiling a little, knowing I thought of them every last year of my life, knowing I loved them through all of my suffering.

I hug myself away from H-125's dismal horizon and imagine I am holding my granddaughter, my Jeanie. These are the things that give life meaning. Not numbers on a screen, or job security with hospital benefits. As I squeeze myself, I feel her squirm and nuzzle me with her soft, little-girl skin. I hear her giggle and squeal with ticklish laughter. I see her growing tall and broad-shouldered on the sweat money from my toiling, and I am happier than a man has ever been on this awful, dusty rock.

I near G sector and begin to smell the river. I am happy to go to work today, to keep my mind from melancholy, to remind myself of the realities. But still, I have a granddaughter. This, somehow, makes the scent sweeter than it's ever been, and though I know it must be my brain playing tricks, I remember the smell of a freshly washed child and baby powder. As I suit up, I breathe in baby oil and diaper cream. As I walk to my chest-deep platform in sector 3-C of River 16, I hear soft lullabies. As I hook a rusty old filing cabinet and motion to the crane man to pull it out, I feel, for the first time in 14 years, like a proud father again.

CHRISTOPHER ALLEN

Fred's Massive Sorrow

From October/November 2015

Flat 61c—Tanna Kolvea

THE STEPS LEADING up to Tanna's sixth-story flat hawed and hemmed. Six flights, 12 steps each. When the other tenants were about, the house was a Babel of 12-tone rows, but today Tanna's footfalls sawed and moaned an ascending series alone. Alone. Finally. She enjoyed her own company, which she had so much more of now that she'd finally got rid of Fred.

Needy Fred: the lumbering, hairy galoot who loved Tanna with every bit of his lumbering, hairy heart. To say Fred had fawned on Tanna would be mildly underestimating the stretch of his devotion. He'd lavished Tanna with all manner of gift, from the daily necessities of, well, food, to life's little luxuries: prettily scented soaps, pralines, and poems. Oral epic poetry he performed for hours until Tanna—and sometimes Fred himself—fell asleep. This situation had gone on for so long that Tanna wondered, as she squeaked and squawked up these infernal stairs, if it hadn't always been this way, if it really was over, if anything epic once begun ever ended.

At the sixth floor, she gripped the banister, pulled herself up to the landing, and ran headlong into it: an enormous potted tree, head bent like a giant in a pillbox. Or, with its broad red ribbon round its belly, a deciduous genie. Or was it an evergreen? Some sort of pine? Maybe a banyan?

There was a note. And it had her name on it—Miss Tanna Kolvea—in large loopy letters. Inside it read, "My hard-bitten Miss Tanna Kolvea. Our parting has germinated and sprouted within me like a seed into a sapling, and here is the sorrow it has become. Remember me, Miss Tanna Kolvea, and my massive sorrow." Tanna rolled her eyes. Fred had such a wordy way with words.

"Goodness," she said and smiled at Fred's massive sorrow. Sorrow was almost always ironic in its grandeur and spleen: it was so green; it blossomed and thrived. "So vital," Tanna said. "And kind of sexy." But where was she going to put it? Not in the flat. Fred's sorrow needed more headroom than she'd ever be able to provide.

The roof terrace would be an excellent place. It wasn't far, and Fred's massive sorrow could grow up to the stars if it had a mind. Tanna turned her attention to the last flight of 12 steps up to the roof terrace. She'd need help. Fred's sorrow looked as if it weighed a ton. There were the two sweet, burly men who lived together on the first floor and did odd jobs around the building. They'd help if she made a rhubarb pie. She'd made one once, and Bernie, the smaller burly man, said he'd have climbed mountains for a fork of it. "Well, let's just see about that," Tanna said, moaning and creaking back down six flights of stairs.

Later that afternoon, Fred's massive sorrow sat comfortably on the roof terrace while two sweet, burly men feasted on a pie so tart yet so sweet Bernie would have carried Fred's sorrow to the moon if that's what Tanna had required—which, in hindsight, would have been a much better place for it.

In a rusting lawn chair, Tanna sat next to the tree and watched it grow. Alone in the last few hours, it had produced cones and dropped them, buds and dropped them, blossoms and dropped them. It was already a foot taller, and the pot had begun to bulge as if the roots were seeking sustenance.

"I'm not going to water you, if that's what you're thinking," Tanna said to the tree. "That's not how break-ups work, you know. One doesn't cultivate the other's sorrow. I mean, really," she said and left the tree to sort out its mess of grief, which was deepening by the second.

The Roof Terrace

One could hardly say that Fred's massive sorrow was happy on the roof terrace, but it did thrive. It went through the four seasons—football, rabbit hunting, beach, and opera—in one day, every day. Its cones, catkins, and seeds sprung out and tumbled over the edge of the grand six-story building and onto the ground below. Each day at noon it blew billows and billows of jaundiced pollen, then at four its opera-season coat of brittle brown needles. At six o'clock every evening, the songbirds who had nested in its boughs in the a.m. dropped dead, rolled off the roof and dappled the ground below with cheery pinks, greens, and blues. A spectacle. A show. A miracle—albeit a rather morose one.

"Pretty!" the tenants agreed.

The tree at first peeked demurely from the roof's edge. Passersby would remark upon the novelty of a tree—was it an oak, a spruce, a banyan?—perched up there all alone. But as the years ticked off, Fred's massive sorrow became true to its name: a shadow over the building, purging all manner of mess around it, infusing the neighborhood with the sweet smell of decay.

"Like presents, the birds," some tenants remarked. "Like when a cat brings you a mouse."

"Hogwash," said others.

"We should get rid of the tree," one of the tenants suggested.

"Who'll pay for the removal?" another asked, and before anyone could answer, "Not I."

"The tree will be the end of us. We'll be buried alive in rot and dead robins."

"The end," someone said, "will be the end of us. And the end will surely come. As it always has."

"Hogwash."

"Fine points."

"Hear, hear!"

So that was that. It was decided the end would be the end of them, and there was nothing they could do about that, so why waste money on tree removal when they could spend it on, say, the opera? Or food?

It was not long until the first floor became known as the cellar. The tenants still lived there; they simply weren't at street level any longer. They were anxious and scuttling creatures, like moles or badgers or—

"It's cozy down here," someone of indiscernible gender said, leaning briefly out of its dank recess.

But up on the roof terrace, it was not so *gemütlich*. Exposed to the elements, Fred's massive sorrow grew stern. Defiant, proud, erect—all the qualities, in fact, of a tall and somber thing. Like a tree. Which it was.

Yet as it grew toward the stars, its roots were starting to press against the terracotta pot like eager children, fingers and noses squashed against car windows, leaving home for the last time. Hairline cracks spread across its bottom until a tiny capillary poked through and plunged through the pitch toward flat 61c. Sorrow knew its way.

Flat 52a—The Jollys

The Jollys first noticed the damage when they arrived home, sunburnt and two kilos heavier, from their three-week all-inclusive holiday in Barbados. A corner near the ceiling in the living room was plumper, as if an arm were pressing against the drywall. Or something like a pipe or—

"A root?" Mrs Jolly ventured, gawping up at the corner. She was still holding her suitcase in one hand, her three-year-old's arm and a sombrero in the other.

She called Bernie, the sweet and burly superintendent, who also gawped up at the corner awhile before deciding it had always been there.

"Always been there," he said.

Mr Jolly, gawping now, too, started to disagree but got a swift elbow from his wife. "Ah, yes," he said. "Always been there—long before we moved in, I'm sure. It's a pipe."

His wife smiled, nodded. "Yessiree. A pipe."

The pipe grew and eventually branched out into smaller, hairy pipes, which grew and branched out into yet smaller, hairier pipes— which was all quite unpipelike. Though the walls were beginning to crumble in places, there was no way in hell the Jollys were going to pay for repairs. They kept referring to the roots as pipes for years after it was obvious the roots were roots.

"They're harmless, the pipes," Mrs Jolly said, because no one had suggested to her the roots might curl around her or her son Zak in the night as they slept. No one had mentioned the whispering, so wordy and love starved, coming from the walls. No one had conjectured there might be a sinister life force in these hairy, supernal fingers springing up here and there—and then suddenly *here*. But then, the family hadn't been strangled in their beds, had they? Well, not yet.

Years passed as years always have, and the Jollys forgot they'd ever had anything but rustic, hirsute panelling. The flat was dark but cozy. They hooked crystal Christmas ornaments on the curtains of aerial roots hanging down from the ceiling in the living room and sang "Deck the Pipes" as they decked them. If they'd ever known anything different, they certainly didn't know they knew.

Zak, the then three-year-old, was now 13 and a dark little creature of indiscernible gender. It listened to contemporary German opera, John Cage, and Pink and rarely left its room. It talked—but of course mostly listened—to the wordy walls in its sleep and scraped faces into its skin with the jagged tip of a perfectly straightened paperclip. Of bats. Of skulls. And of the bugs who tunnelled through the walls.

Flat 26c—Justice and His Grandmother

When Justice brought home finger-painted art of his family, there were only two figures squidged in bright green and pink: a small boy and a bug. A soldier termite.

Sadly, Justice didn't have the talent to draw an anatomically correct soldier termite or the English language skills to describe her, so his teacher assumed the child's grandmother was merely—albeit monstrously—bottom-heavy with an odd hair-do. And Justice wasn't actually aware his grandmother was a soldier termite. But she was.

She hadn't always been a bug. When she was a little girl in Dortmund, she was a little girl. But then the vagaries of age and worry—and Justice—shrank her. By the age of 40, she'd become pretty much the soldier termite she was now.

Justice was supposed to have been called Justin, but in the hours following Justice's violent birth, his mother had lacked the energy to spell neatly. Then shortly thereafter she'd lacked the energy to live— and that's why Justice lived in the tiny guest bedroom with his German grandmother, the soldier termite. At first she spoke German to Justice, but as she shrunk she also began to click, more and more, until all that was left of her German was a guttural rasp and a bit of a rolled *R*.

The grandmother catered to her grandson's every need with super-soldier termite strength and a mandible-to-the-wheel sort of determination. Her whole life was Justice. She stood guard over him when he slept, nibbled dead skin cells from his nose, and six-leg tickled him under his knees in the evenings. She gave him a mud mask on Sundays and made him a tasty mush each morning from the roots growing down through the walls; it was of course regurgitated, but what he didn't know wouldn't hurt him. Her bedtime stories, clicked with waving, flailing, and pumping legs, were epic. They transported Justice to a world where boys were encouraged to nestle down deep into themselves, to a world rising or sinking depending on how one looked at it—to a world, in fact, very much, if not exactly, like his own.

His window was boarded up, had been for decades, maybe forever. The first and second floors used to be above ground. At least that was the legend. Justice lived in a magical place. A changing place. A massively sad place. Which he found fascinating.

"*Sinken wir, oder werden wir begrabben?*" he asked his grandmother, who clicked that it didn't much matter if they were sinking or being buried, did it? The effect was the same.

"*Na ja,*" he said. "*Wäre aber schön zu wissen.*"

Click, click.

"*Schon gut,*" Justice said, brought his bowl to the sink, and rinsed the woody residue of root mush from its rim. He faked the ambivalent deadpan he knew his grandmother so needed to see, but inside he boiled with wonder and empathy for the sinister viral spirit spidering through the house.

Flat 61c—Alacia and Stephin Dornstown, 1901

Alacia and Stephin considered themselves lucky beyond words. The building on the corner was the newest, the swankest place to live in town, and they'd gotten a flat. South-facing. Never mind that they'd borrowed the first year's rent from Stephin's parents and lied about their jobs—Stephin was not a lawyer and, despite her odd name, Alacia was not a famous actress from Portugal—they were in! In! In! In! In the first high-rise building to be built in Dornstown in this new, grand century.

But as it turned out, they weren't the first, and Alacia despised not being first. She would have loved to enjoy the supremacy of firstness; she always had. She could have welcomed subsequent tenants into her home—her building—but now she was forced to grin and accept welcomes from speedier tenants with their supreme smiles and firstly bunt cakes, the traditional confection of welcome. Alacia despised bunt cake. The name didn't really say what was in the cake, like a chocolate, coconut, or caramel cake would. What is *bunt*?

"Thanks!" She grinned down at the bunt—whatever—cake. Really, there could be anything in that cake. Gravel. Kangaroos. Sorrow. Nuts. She despised nuts.

"Vee are having a séance today evening on ze rrrroof!" Wren from 44b was still holding out the bunt cake. She was a stout, German woman who wore large floral patterns because she thought they made her look happier.

"A séance?" Alacia said.

"Ze most famous mentalist of our time vill be zere." Wren sounded like a brochure with a strong Teutonic accent. "She has promised to schpeak to ze departed."

"Goodness."

"You vill come." This was not a question.

In the end, Alacia and Stephin went because neither one had ever been to a séance. They took their seats at the large, round table set up for the performance and introduced themselves. They were Alacia and Stephin, obviously, and the other tenants at the table had names as well.

"The table is round!" the mentalist began. She was an elderly, black-turbaned woman who swooned a lot and whose chin was stuck at a 100-degree angle as if to embody her levitating force. "And therefore it has no corners." She panned the tenants as if to invite praise for this revelation.

"Even I knew that," whispered Alacia. She despised the obvious.

"Silence!" The mentalist swooned, stretched her arms across the table, and spread her palms toward the darkening sky. "I will now summon the departed."

"Aren't we meant to join hands or something?" Stephin asked.

"And close our eyes," Alacia added, "so you can pull some rabbit or thingy out of your what's-it?"

"Hogwash."

"Silence!"

"Not very séancelike," Stephin whispered—Stephin who'd never been to a séance before.

"I am beginning to feel an energy. A presence. A massive one. Some massive sorrow," said the mentalist. "Somebody's very, very put out."

Stephin and Alacia looked around. They didn't really care much for the word sad. They were keener on swank, lucky, supreme, supernal—all that stuff. They were in the newest building in town in a new century. Sorrow belonged blocks and blocks away.

"It's emanating from that corner." The mentalist rose slowly—Alacia gasped, thinking at first the mentalist was levitating—and crept over to the edge of the roof. "Here. Here! A massive sorrow. Clearly massive."

"But there's nothing there," Alacia whispered.

"Well, of course there's nothing here," the mentalist said, a wee bit out of character. "That's why we call them the departed, you mule."

"Goodness," said Alacia.

Stephin sniggered. He hadn't married Alacia for her smarts.

"Its name is Fred." The mentalist swooned back into character. "Fred!" she called out. "Speak to me! Speak." She threw back her head and screeched. "Speak!"

"Goodness." Alacia despised this woman and this Fred, who was obviously not very swank.

"Fred is sad," said the mentalist. "Wait. Fred... is what? You're not the departed, but the not-yet-arrived? Ladies and gents, Fred is from the future. What? He's come to warn us, well, you, that is. I live in Leicester. *Shhh!*"

"We didn't say anything," said Stephin.

"Fred says your great grandchildren will be buried in his sorrow. Buried alive!"

"Well, that doesn't sound too bad," said Alacia. "We might not even have children, and even if we did, they'd probably be living in America by then. Or Portugal. What year is this boring Fred person from?" Alacia asked.

But no one was listening. The other tenants, who were not so ambivalent, worldly, or child-averse, were leaving. There was pandemonium, or at least as much pandemonium as could be wreaked by six upper-middle-class tenants on a roof terrace. No one jumped over the edge. No one cursed. No one forgot his coat.

But the middle-aged couple from 31d vacated their flat before the week was out, forfeiting almost a month's rent. The remaining tenants agreed to never speak of the séance again, to never, ever speak of Fred's (potentially) massive sorrow.

Flat 61c—Tanna Kolvea

The building survived the world's wars; but in the years that followed, mounds of debris—rubble, appliances, and the corpses of those who hadn't fared so well in the wars—lingered, mostly in black and white documentaries shown in America and Portugal.

"A true survivor," noted a passerby.

"A gem," one of the tenants remarked when it became apparent the owner of the building had died in the bombings, leaving the building—the only one left standing in Dornstown—to the tenants in his will. Life, although surrounded by heaps and heaps of debris and dead people, was good.

Until one day, rather suddenly or gradually, depending on how one looked at it, the town was bright and pretty again in pastel greens and pinks. Dornstown was so bright and pretty, in fact, that hardly anyone—if anyone at all—noticed it had ever been anything but. The children, never having known the pangs of war, thought the town had always been a quaint hamlet graced with 20-year-old three-story villas and the occasional bungalow (since these were the *dernier cri* in California, and the people of Dornstown were enamoured of California's pink-and-greenness from San Diego to Yosemite).

On the square, statues—of men on horses, of men wielding guns, of men waving flags, of men on horses waving guns, flags in teeth—were fables and myth, frozen in time. Life was simply too still and manly to be anything else than what it was: stunned, like a photograph, for decades.

On the stateliest corner in Dornstown, the building sat and sat in this glass-calm sea of oblivion until one day a little girl was born into the inherited stately squalor of her great grandmother's home, flat 61c—a girl named Tanna Kolvea with a face and heart of granite. Her violent birth split her poor mother right down the middle but woke the world from its post-war depression. She was so pretty, the tenants agreed. She'd break hearts. Well, at least one.

Flat 52a—The Jollys

Elmar Jolly was born into the world a tiny gem who could see angels, yet by the age of six, his disposition had darkened. He still saw angels, but now they agitated him. They kept him awake, orating epic poetry.

At night the needy walls wrapped around him and tried to cuddle. They whispered they empathized with Elmar's sensitive nature, that they wished him serenity, that they wished him success, that they wished his named weren't Elmar. "Such an ugly name," the walls whispered. Elmar's parents had given their only child the name Elmar, never thinking for a moment they'd actually use it. No sooner had Elmar popped out than they started calling him Zak.

"Also ugly. So ugly."

The walls called ElmarZak Angel, a logical choice. They talked to him about the woman known as Tanna, how she'd crushed the heart of a man named Fred, how Fred's sorrow had grown from a seed into a tree, probably a banyan. The walls taught the little boy about sorrow and the pandemonium it causes, an enervating, spreading, sprouting pandemonium.

But as he grew, he began to listen more closely, to understand. Sorrow was no light fare. Sorrow turned one inwards, deep down into the depths of oneself, where confusion is cozy, freeing, and Germanic.

At 13, Angel spent most of its time listening to atonal symphonies and drawing pictures of hairy, oblong creatures it called Freds, which it showed to no one, especially not its parents.

The Jollys were the type of people—the type of tenants—who cheerfully refused to do anything about anything. Everything, from the stove to the toilet seat, was broken in the flat, but Mr and Mrs Jolly would do nothing about it.

"It's always been that way," Mrs Jolly would say.

"Yep," Mr Jolly would confirm. "Always been that way."

But Angel knew better. Angel knew things were changing all around. In spring, the walls sprouted little blue flowers, and regardless of what the rest of the tenants said, the ground outside this building was heaping up around it. It was easy for Angel's parents to deny this: they lived on the fifth floor. When Mrs Jolly's bridge club would ask why the fourth floor was on street level, she'd simply smile and say, "It's always been that way."

But it hadn't. Angel remembered distinctly leaving the building once on the second floor. Or was it the fourth? Angel hadn't left its room in so long, and for good reason: Angel's parents, with their cloying smiles and doe eyes, were out there on the other side of its door. They were always there. Smiling.

"One day," the walls whispered to Angel, "you'll have to leave. You know that, right?"

"I know."

"You're different," the walls said. "You understand sorrow."

Angel knew this but didn't answer. Different could be good or bad, and Angel never knew the difference. Angel was confused: the sudden seemed so gradual, change so permanent, and depth was hardly distinguishable from height. Nothing meant anything one wanted it to mean.

"You're special," said the walls, "You see how intricate and enervating the effluents of sorrow are."

Angel nodded but also thought the walls were a bit verbose. If a word wasn't used in a contemporary German opera, Angel probably didn't know it. It knew it'd have to leave the building, though. Often, it dreamt of living in a flat alone, or maybe with a man or a woman.

Of living somewhere else, like America or Portugal. Of living, generally.

"Zak?" Angel's mother was at the door.

Angel rubbed a finger over the rough, hairy door frame, stood there in silence. If it didn't answer, its mother would think it was asleep or dead or had never lived, which it hadn't really.

Flat 12b—Tanna Kolvea

Tanna had to get out. Everyone said her imagination was running away with her. Roots didn't curl around sleeping tenants and cradle them, someone said, although Tanna had never used the words *curl* and *cradle*. "Ridiculous, you stupid cow!" they said in a curiously affectionate tone. "Roots don't possess telic sensibilities to seek out—"

"Yes they do!" Tanna would cry. "That's exactly what roots do. They press through mountains to find sustenance! Through bedrock!" Tanna was quite hysterical, hadn't slept in months.

"You could have the tree removed," someone suggested, which at first seemed an excellent idea.

"You could apologize to poor Fred," someone else said, which was way down low on Tanna's list of ways to solve this problem.

So she made rhubarb pie and invited the assistance of Carl and Bernie, the sweet, burly superintendents from 12a. Yet, after surveying the scene—the root system was so intricate and remarkably strong (in a word, massive) that chopping down the tree at the base of its trunk would hardly guarantee success—Carl and Bernie, both vegetarians and members of several tree-hugging associations, decided against any chopping.

"It's too massive," Bernie said, cheeks bulging with pie. "It'd crush the building when it fell."

"True," said Carl, cheeks equally bulging. "And this building is all we've ever had."

Tanna told the other tenants she was living in 12b only temporarily until she found a flat in another country. She'd done the maths. Wellington, New Zealand, was the furthest city from Fred's massive sorrow. The only thing keeping her from realizing this plan was abject poverty. Tanna was penniless. She'd inherited the right to live in the building rent-free in any space that came available from her great grandfather Stephin Kolvea, the divorcée who'd reportedly been married to a very ill-tempered Portuguese actress.

Living next door to Carl and Bernie relieved some of her fears. They assured her Fred's massive sorrow would take years to burrow through the house. The roots were still knocking about the third floor.

"*Hmmm,*" said Bernie.

"What? What?" Tanna was hysterical.

"26-C has reported protruding pipes," he said, "but I think they said they'd always been there."

"And they're Irish," added Carl.

Tanna caulked every corner and seam of her flat, every crack and cranny, every thing. She'd read about the impenetrability of silicone and hoped it was at least less susceptible to sorrow than bedrock.

Flat 16c—Justice and His Grandmother

Justice's grandmother used to talk about the old country; now she only clicked about it. The old country was a place called Germany where they spoke the language she used to speak. The old country was full of beerhalls with wooden tables reeking of stale beer and blood sausage: "A homey, quiet place," she'd click in German with a swoon of nostalgia for an era when she wasn't 4,000 times too small to wear a *dirndl.* Even without the *dirndl,* she'd return in a second if she hadn't inherited this flat from her Auntie Wren, legendarily a large woman who'd thrown wobbly fits about some impending sorrow whenever she was lent an ear.

Auntie Wren had been the family nutter, the huge, exotic aunt who lived in the foreign country. Then the bombs fell. When the dust settled on the detritus of war, she became the quite attractive nutter with the free flat in the only building still standing in the foreign country. So one thing led to another, as things have always done since things began leading to other things—in this case Justice, who was having trouble at school.

Justice didn't speak English. He clicked. And when that went un-understood (which was pretty much always), he spoke German (which was not much better). This went on for several more years than it should have, until on the first day of sixth form, Justice was sent home with a note neither he nor his grandmother could read, but which, his grandmother clicked, tasted very nice. Recycled paper was so tender, blue ink so sweet.

The next day Justice was sent home again with a similar note, and the next and the next, until Justice's grandmother, feeling a bit bloated and dizzy from all the ink, finally got the message. She could teach her grandson better than anyone anyway. She was excited by the new project. First subject: mud shelter tubes!

Flat 12a—Carl and Bernie

Bernie lit another candle. Cozy cost a lot in wax and matches. He sat in his den—at four floors underground, he had nothing but dens—and read Proust by candlelight. In French. He didn't understand French, so it didn't much matter that the light was too dim and Bernie's eyes too weak. At 96 he only pretended to read anyway.

Carl, Bernie's partner of way too many decades, was in the kitchen-den cooking a root vegetable soup (unrelated but possibly subliminally suggested by the roots peeking through their ceiling). Carl was adding garlic and paprika to the pot because he knew they gave Bernie indigestion.

"It won't be long now," said Bernie.

"Oh, no, the soup'll need another 30 minutes at least," Carl shouted, squashing another garlic clove and scraping it into the soup.

"Confound it. I mean till the roots reach soil. Real soil! Confound it! And that'll be the end of it. Of her."

"Fred's sorrow ain't dumb," said Carl, standing at the door to the dining-den.

"Wonder why she didn't just say she was sorry," said Bernie. "Could've saved everyone a lot of grief. Get it?"

"Ha. Good one."

"It'll all be over soon," said Bernie. Although too deaf to hear the roar of termites in the wall, he was nonetheless more than correct in his prediction.

"It'll find her, and when it does..." Carl rubbed his hands together and grinned.

"I suppose you're right. May she rest in peace—until then of course."

They laughed heartily. They both thought Tanna had been a pain. Her last wish had been that Bernie and Carl bury her beneath silicone-slathered bedrock in New Zealand, and she'd stockpiled enough rhubarb pie in the freezer to pay for the trouble. But when she died her unremarkable death, Bernie and Carl schlepped her body to the third cellar—the farthest from the building as they, at 96, were prepared to drag a corpse—and bricked Tanna's rigid corpus into the crawlspace. There was something literary about this, but since neither Carl nor Bernie enjoyed literature, they were oblivious to any allusion it might call to mind. They simply wanted to be done with the woman. It was her fault, after all, that the building was sinking, becoming a six-story, termite-infested hill with a single, massive tree at its top. If she hadn't handled poor Fred so shamelessly, Bernie and Carl wouldn't have had so many dens. It was that simple. Still, they enjoyed the pies.

"And when it finds her?" asked Bernie.

"Dear Old Fred's massive sorrow?" Carl shook a big, red cloud of paprika into the soup. "It won't be pretty. It'll scratch and bore into her with its jagged, woody fingers and lick up her cells, it will. It'll lap all the juicy bits and gnaw on the hard ones—and you know there were many hard ones—till its sorrow is plump and sated. Soup's ready!"

Flat 16c—Justice and His Grandmother

Justice hadn't meant to kill his soldier termite grandmother. In hindsight, it probably had not been the best habit for her to sleep nestled in her grandson's left armpit. Cozy, but rather unsafe. In hindsight.

Justice had crushed her. And now he was faced with the task of burying her, if one buried termites. Burying a subterranean termite seemed a tad redundant. He didn't know, but it didn't matter, because before he could finish Googling the topic, he lost her.

Reality hit him that evening as a stabbing pain in his stomach. Without his grandmother to regurgitate mush from the wood of the old house and the roots networking through it, what would he eat? And how would he rear himself? Being only forty?

He nibbled on one of the smaller roots protruding from the walls in the kitchen, but it just wasn't the same. Not like grandmother's mush.

He'd heard once from the walls that there was another boy living on the fifth floor. His name was Zak or Elmar or some other ugly name. If anyone knew what boys ate, ZakElmar would. It was worth a shot.

Four 12-step flights of stairs was a bit much for a boy who hadn't been out of his flat in 20 years. Justice was still catching his breath when Mr Jolly came to the door.

"My, my," Mr Jolly said. "You're a hairy one."

Justice had not seen himself in a mirror since he was a young boy, but he assumed this was a compliment. "Thank you, kind sir," he clicked.

"Excuse me?" Mr Jolly smiled.

"I've heard there's a boy here named ZakElmar or something ugly like that," Justice clicked, trying to click politely like his grandmother had taught him.

"Huh? Boy, you're clicking like a bug. Can't you speak English?" Though this sounded impolite, the stupid grin on Mr Jolly's face said otherwise.

Justice stared at the man and cocked his head to one side. Of course he was clicking. Didn't this creature understand clicking? Maybe German?

"*Ist ElmarZak zuhause? Ich suche einen Freund,*" Justice said. "*Ich hab Hunger.*"

"That's not much better." Mr Jolly's grin grew and grew.

"Who's at the door?" Mrs Jolly's grin appeared behind Mr Jolly's.

But then another creature, naked and slight, appeared behind Mr and Mrs Jolly. Like an angel, his hairless body was scrawled in myth.

"*Ich bin da,*" Angel clicked.

"*Ich freue mich,*" Justice clicked back. He was so hungry.

The Crawlspace

The space Bernie and Carl had provided Tanna was not much larger than a coffin. So little air was let in—so skilful was their masonry— the degeneration of Tanna's body was achingly slow, as if it were delaying its inevitable end—something which can hardly be substantiated or refuted. After all, she was well holed up: anything could be true behind all that brick and silicone.

So perhaps the truth is this: that Miss Tanna Kolvea had never been anything more than the sum of her bits and cells and bacteria—

in their zillions, each a loveless and thankless little creature of indiscernible gender. All they needed to thrive was a bit of oxygen, yet thriving was not happiness. Tanna had never needed happiness. And now oxygen was the last thing she needed.

The crumbling began in a corner and progressed downward until a root not larger than a galoot's hair poked its way through into Tanna's chamber. This happened slowly or quickly depending on how one looked at it, but it happened as all things do. The hair drooped more than dropped toward the corpse—so sad was the little fellow. Perhaps a tear or two fell. Then with the force of the world's mightiest, meanest armies, the root charged—rabid, ardent, vicious, starved, all that stuff—into the corpse. Into its heartless chest cavity.

A moment passed, something pregnant like a sigh. Then the walls burst. Brittle mortar fell all around Tanna, while roots—hairy and haggard, driven by insane thirst—wound themselves round and round until nothing of the woman, not her bits nor her cells nor her zillions of bacteria, was left. Until, in fact, Miss Tanna Kolvea had never been.

Sorough's Hill

The tenants were vague, nameless shadows of indiscernible gender. Myths and legends. But genuine people? Made of flesh? The building had always been vacant as far as anyone knew, so they filled it with legends of sad creatures oblivious to the crumbling walls around them.

But there were the two persons thought to live in a cave on the outskirts of Dornstown, the persons referred to as Angel and Justice, which were of course not their real names, who were thought to have once lived in the house, if there'd ever been one. Except for the occasional less than human clicking sounds coming from the deep recesses of the cave, there was no hard evidence of their existence. Children wrote stories about them, which proved they weren't real.

But fact was, the tree's intricate root system had reordered the architectonics of the building. Rooms were halved and quartered by aerating roots; entire floors had collapsed under the massive weight of the lateral meristems with a bit of help from a massive termite infestation. Then suddenly—or gradually, but the two are barely distinguishable—there was no building at all. And of course there never had been.

What there had always been was a hill. And depending on who wrote its name, it was Sars Hill, Sorrow's Hill, Sorough's Hill, or simply Fred's Hill as some of the locals liked to call it—but always a hill, proving to everyone who came to see it that it had always been a hill.

A perfectly massive, bell-shaped hill—verdant and stately—with a singular, magnificent tree atop it. A banyan, some people said. Some sort of pine, said others.

"So ironic," said a tourist.

"How so?" another asked.

"Sorrow's Hill," she replied. "Get it?"

"Ah, yes. Anything but sad, eh?"

"It's absolutely charming."

"And calming."

"And green."

"Yes, quite green."

"And kind of sexy."

LAURENCE KLAVAN

Consensus

From January/February 2014

WHEN THE RESULTS came in from their Informers, Tab proposed a toast and Abner lifted his glass, as did everyone else. All offered and accepted congratulations, even though, of course, none had done anything except support the winning candidate. But Abner could not help feeling wistful or worse, and it showed on his face. It would have been better if Belle had been there, he thought, and he felt acknowledgment of this in the hard, slightly painful grasp Tab took of his shoulder. His former brother-in-law had already seemed tight, as if he'd been bothered all evening by his sister's absence; it wasn't just that he was so happy their guy had won, the presidential candidate who'd promised peace.

"She would have been glad, too," Tab said about Belle.

"Yes, she would," Abner nodded, even though he wasn't sure. Belle had never cared much for politics—or parties, for that matter, two more things he and his wife had had in common and which had made her death from cancer a year ago that much harder to bear. Still, agreeing was one way to wiggle out of Tab's embrace. His host's thick fingers were now digging into Abner's arm, as if he meant to attach himself to Abner, since he could no longer touch, address, or see his sister. "I better be going," Abner said, swiveling enough so Tab's fingers snapped free, the way a frozen fly does from a window sill when you finally dust it clean.

Tab placed a big wet kiss on Abner's cheek, one smelling of Scotch and shrimp hors d'oeuvres, again as if saying goodbye to his sister and not him. Then he staggered away, chanting, "We won, we won," words which seemed to have many meanings, though Abner was unsure what the others might be.

Approaching the front door, Abner reflexively checked his device to see what else their Informers had to say about the election. So many at the party were doing it that the little lights looked like candles in a funeral ritual held in the dimly lit living room.

"Would you mind giving me a lift?" someone asked as he put on his coat. "I could use a ride."

Abner turned. He saw a woman he didn't recognize: small, boyishly built, younger than he (early 30s, maybe) with dark hair frosted in places by blonde as if there were little poppies planted in it.

"Oh," he said, surprised both because he usually knew everyone at Tab's parties and that the woman's request was so helpless. "Uh, okay, sure. Why not?"

"I'm Signe."

"Abner."

He drove them in the near-dark with only a few lights left on in the suburban streets. Signe sat in silence, which perturbed Abner and made him speak up (Belle had once told him people could be defined by how they responded to silence, and, as usual, she had been right). "Are you a friend of Tab's? I don't remember seeing you around."

"A friend of a friend. But my friend left early without telling me. Some friend."

"Sorry."

"It's all right. I have a thing about being left early, I guess."

Signe explained her husband had recently died—also of cancer—and this had made her feel trapped between flights in an unfamiliar airport, as if her connection had been canceled and would never be rescheduled.

"Or something," she said. "I'm not being clear."

"No, no," Abner said. "I know just what you mean."

And he did. Not only had Signe gone through the same trauma he had, but her analogy about the experience was the exact one that had occurred to him. It was uncanny, one of those things that suddenly make you feel close to a total stranger. Abner could see more lights going on in houses as he drove, as if in happy acknowledgment of what had occurred.

They spoke more as they went, and Abner found himself reducing his speed to make the trip last longer. Both were the youngest in their families, had been stammerers as children and bedwetters long after they should have stopped. Each had two older and bullying siblings of the same sex. His mother had ended up an alcoholic; her father had been one all along.

"Here," Signe said, suddenly and with regret, as if snapping out of a reverie they both were in. "Please, take a left. This is me."

Abner blinked, as if he, too, had just awakened. He was shocked to see where they were.

It was the other side of town, a neighborhood he had never entered, not intentionally, anyway, had used only to turn around or take as a shortcut back to what he knew. He looked down to the passenger seat and saw with a start that Signe's device was on and sitting in her lap, its light like a small round X-ray of herself. On it, her Informers were celebrating the election of the other presidential candidate, the one who was warlike.

Now Abner was additionally stunned Signe had been at the party. There was rarely if ever any fraternizing between those who believed one thing and another.

"It's peculiar, isn't it?" she said, as if he had spoken this aloud. "My friend said it was like entering enemy territory for me and thought it would be funny, a prank. She didn't know I'm not obsessed with current events. And look who I met."

She meant him. He pulled up outside her house.

"Would you care to come in?" she asked, obviously overcoming shyness, something that had also plagued him his entire life.

"I'd like to," he blurted out. "But maybe next time."

And his even saying that was a sign of something big between them; both knew it would have to stay their secret.

A few weeks later, Abner was set up on a lunch date by his ex-brother-in-law. At first, he thought it was strange, if not unseemly, as if Tab were encouraging a posthumous infidelity. But maybe, he thought, Tab was being positive, compassionate, and forward-looking. Or else Tab was being controlling, allowing Abner to move ahead only if he, Tab, could be in charge of it. Abner didn't know. In any case, the image of a quizzical Belle seemed to appear in the air above the deli table as he ate with Edna, a woman Tab knew from work.

She was pretty, pleasant, and bright, divorced with two young children. She alluded to her ex-husband being depressed or at least moody and withdrawn, something which bothered Edna and about which she seemed judgmental. Abner began to suspect she had been the one to initiate the break-up, in order to free herself from a husband she felt dragging her down. This disquieted Abner, since he tended to be downbeat himself and had emotional "issues" of his own.

Edna was active politically—kept on top of things all day, in other words—and spent much of the lunch on her device, excitedly discussing the peace talks of the new president (the one they believed had won), which were already in the works. The light from the object held in her hands reflected up onto her face, giving her a scary Jack-O-Lantern look. He wondered if she was so animated because she was nervous or because she was heavily invested in the information and just assumed he would be, too. He wasn't sure.

Abner had not turned on his own device, had not done so for days, had no idea what his Informers were saying was happening.

"This is on me," he said at the end, placing down his card. Edna fought him perfunctorily, then gave in with a smile. Paying made Abner feel less guilty, because he knew they had no future and she had seemed interested.

Afterward, right before dark, Abner found his way back to the other neighborhood, as if led by an invisible convoy in a dream. When he entered, a cop drove by, checking out his car, deciding if he belonged. Abner did not stop or even turn his head to see the remaining lawn signs for the other winning candidate. He acted as if he were right at home, for this was how he felt. The cop moved on.

Signe had left her living room curtain half-closed, as they had arranged, so he would know she was home. Her door had been kept unlocked, and he went through it, as he had almost every night for the past few weeks.

Abner had learned Signe hated the heat and liked air conditioning, was not vegetarian but took it easy on the meat, had a little wine every evening but had not smoked dope for years. There were many other things they shared, and he hoped he would find out more tonight, as he had all the other times.

Signe was standing in the vestibule and moved toward him as he entered. She wrapped her arms around him, then closed the curtain all the way.

Signe enjoyed a fair amount of biting and spanking in bed, as he did, but liked to start soft with nibbling kisses and tender stroking, so this was what they did once more as she drew him to the floor.

Tab had another party a month later. It was to celebrate the signing of their president's peace pact, which their Informers had announced. (Signe said hers was planning a ramp-up to war when she went on, just to check the weather.) It was the familiar crowd, and this time Signe wasn't invited by her friend. Abner saw his former brother-in-law had again started drinking early and, barely an hour in, was already red-faced and weaving.

"So," Tab said, cornering Abner in a hallway and leaning his big body in to bar his escape, "Edna has been asking after you."

"Who? Oh." Abner nodded, self-consciously. He had never followed up with Tab after the lunch. "Is that right?"

"Yes. Weren't you going to call her? Didn't you hit it off? That's what she thought."

"It was fine," he said, evasively. "Maybe I'm not—maybe I'm just not ready yet."

It was a silly lie, but Abner felt uneasy telling Tab anything now. He had not mentioned who he was seeing and where. And, here, in a gathering of like-minded people—one which suddenly seemed loud and crowded, as if at that second it had shifted into a higher gear—it seemed unsafe. Abner had never felt that way in Tab's house before.

"You were seen," the other man said, his boozy breath brushing Abner's lips. "Coming from that street. I want you to know that."

Abner felt chilled hearing this, imprisoned in the space between the kitchen and the living room, Tab's wife Lee only steps away, cracking ice into a bowl and possibly about to turn their way.

"What would Belle say?" Tab whispered, his voice growing lower as his words became more accusatory, like a flame getting hotter the tinier it sank.

"I—I don't know," Abner answered, feeling his stammer threaten to return after, what, 25 years?

"Well, I do. I do know. She wouldn't like it. She wouldn't like what you're subscribing to now. And I meant that punt intentionally. That *pun*."

"I'm not subscribing to anything," Abner said, sincerely, for he had not switched any beliefs. "I think she would have given me her blessing." And this was something after much back-and-forth he had decided for himself.

Now he saw his ex-brother-in-law was on the verge of tears, and not just from a sense of being betrayed, of Abner's taking on different ideas of the world. He was afraid of losing Abner, which would mean Belle would go with him for good, the way something swirls down a drain—an old wedding ring or something else invaluable—and can never be retrieved.

The feeling made Tab strike out at him, ram a fist into Abner's side, striking him like a knife thrust from someone's sleeve in a secret agent film. He said, right into Abner's ear, "Go on, then. Go to those horrible people on the other side, if that's what you want. Just don't come back."

But when Abner peeled away, squinting in pain, his right rib sore from where Tab had punched him, he saw the other man's face said the opposite: Don't go or, if you must, come back, I'll be here, where I always will be, waiting.

Abner drove without feeling it, oblivious to his feet touching pedals, his hands on the wheel. He drifted as if floating to the now-familiar street, the turn that would take him to where she was.

There was a new booth set up at the entrance to the area, as if a toll were being enacted. Seated at a table inside its glass like someone presiding over everyone (or being punished?) was the cop Abner had often seen making his rounds. An automatic weapon leaned against the wall behind him. His device was unusually large and propped up on the table; it showed his president standing beside an electronic map of military movements.

The cop nodded at Abner and waved him ahead, urged him to hurry, as if he were the last one he could allow. Abner drove in, and two soldiers placed construction barriers at the mouth of the lane to prevent anyone from following.

Every house light he passed was on, as if all the streets were screaming. Other soldiers put sandbags where front lawns met sidewalks. Gas masks covered their faces. As Abner pulled into Signe's driveway, he knew there was no going back, and it felt good.

The living room curtain was again half-closed. Abner walked toward the open door. Before he knocked, he glanced up. He saw fighter planes of a hostile force hovering in the sky, bent on bombing them all into oblivion. Abner smiled, for now it looked like love.

BRIGIT KELLY YOUNG

Pretty, Pretty Britney

From July/August 2013

6:00 pm

WHAT IF HE thinks I'm stupid? Britney thought as she put on her eyelashes.

She knew she would say "cool" too much. Back before, she had thought she sounded cool when she said cool, and now she realized that cool was a stupid word all along.

This one time, back then, when Britney was crying really, really hard, her assistant had told her, "Honey, older people say they wish they were young, but if we had the chance none of us would go back to being 19 again. It's all insecurity and stupid men." But Britney was older now. And being older sucked, too. Really, nothing ever changes.

Britney lifted up her blue sequined shirt and stared at her stomach in the mirror. *That* stomach, over there, not *hers*. It couldn't be hers. She couldn't see her abs anymore. But the new part, the puff in the tummy where the babies once were, each little cutie-pie-poo-poo-poopsie baby, it still seemed kinda beautiful to her. Like a perfectly toasted marshmallow above her pelvis. Like the belly of a pin-up model in the 1950s or Marilyn Monroe or Elizabeth Taylor, whom Britney adored and had since she was a little girl. God, the women were so beautiful back then. No one would put Marilyn in a magazine today. Well, maybe a plus-size catalogue or something, but not real magazines. Poor fucking Marilyn. Touched and fucked and made fun of. Marilyn could be kind of a bitch, though, and that made it less sad. Britney had read most of her biography on the bus but never finished it.

Britney lifted her shirt higher still and took in the hollow dents of where her ribs met below her breasts. Once they were half-tunnels in between the bones of her body, and now the rib-dents were barely perceptible. There was skin like a badly planted tent between them.

Britney always knew she would never be as sexy as someone like Marilyn Monroe, and sometimes she got depressed when she saw Marilyn's pictures. How can someone be *that* beautiful? It hurt to even look at her. That's what Britney wanted. She wanted to have a face that hurt. Being pretty didn't count if you weren't the most pretty.

Britney unbuttoned her jeans and pulled town the top of her thong to gaze at her C-section scar and bikini line. Sometimes Britney checked to see if her scar was still there, and she moved her fingers up and down it. When the boys weren't with her, the scar was, and she needed to finger it, to tickle it like it was her babies' feet. A smile, a frown, a curse, lit up underneath that scar. It was getting whiter, pink no longer, and it looked stark against the creamy caramel of the rest of her. She pulled her jeans down farther. Her pelvis was too prickly. She'd shaved two days ago, and if she shaved it again today, the new stubble would bleed. She should have brought the waxer lady over, but she couldn't seem to remember to do anything these days. Anything, anything, anything.

"I can't do anything," Britney whispered to the reflection of her groin.

Moving her eyes up from the body, Britney looked into her own face.

There it was.

She felt the tears come, then saw them, rising into the bottoms of her eyes like a calm ocean's wave on the shore, and then going back to where they came from.

She was ugly, she saw. And beautiful. She saw that, too.

Britney did her habitual mirror-face. She looked down demurely, then up sexily, down, then up, down, then up, until she got dizzy. She saw in her reflection how he would see her eyes later. Later, that night, she imagined, when she was half-undressed, moving from kisses between his legs back to his chest, gazing up at him the whole time while she did it, as he looked at her, feeling like a god for getting to see her climb out of the fantasy of the TV and onto his lucky body, while she felt nothing except a tired libido that had given up and an ego needing to see that awed look on a guy's face as he came, came wildly, moaning with the moan only she could give him... *that's* when she would make the mirror-face. Guys loved her, even in person. They went crazy for the way she looked at them, they said. And it was true that sometimes when she watched old videos and saw her up-down looky thing, she even wanted to fuck herself. One time J.M. had said her dad was really unlucky, because he was the only guy in the world who couldn't whack off to her. "What about my brother?" she'd asked, concerned, not exactly getting the joke, and John had just laughed at her. She'd done her up-down looky-thing with him, and he hadn't even noticed. He'd kept his eyes closed.

Fuck sex, Britney thought, *Fucking fuck fuck it,* as she dabbed perfume on her breasts. Fucking had fucked up everything.

Trying so hard for so many years not to fuck up and say fuck in public, she loved the word now. It was as forbidden as a Jewish guy in the Spears family, and she loved Jewish guys.

Britney saw a teeny wrinkle in the middle of her forehead. Oh, GOD FUCK DAMN SHIT, she was ugly. *She was so, so ugly.* There was something weird about her eyes, her skin sagging a bit where the hair met the forehead, one half of her top lip smaller than the other, and she knew it, she knew it, no matter how many times people told her she was crazy. She wasn't crazy. She used to be beautiful, maybe. Now she was a fat, ugly, worthless piece of shit. God damn it.

Still, she practiced smiling in the mirror. She tilted her head, and there it was—the prettiness. Sometimes she still marveled at the symmetry of her features and the alarming perfection that occurred when the corners of her mouth turned up just right. Her cheeks sat in a glossy, happy place, like a flawless staged photograph that comes with a frame.

But tonight there would be an expectation of prettiness she couldn't live up to. She just didn't have it. She wasn't *actually* beautiful, she knew. She could be made to be, but she hadn't come out that way. She wasn't like the celebrities she'd watched growing up. One time when she was a kid, her friend had said, "You are like as famous as Julia Roberts, now!" but her friend hadn't said "as beautiful." Britney had a pretend-beauty. When she'd seen Michelle Pfeiffer in person, she'd almost cried. How could somebody look like that for real? And at such an old age? Sometimes Britney wished she was stranger looking. If Britney looked strange, she could be striking, not pretty. Unconventional or something, like Anjelica Houston or something, or not her, because she's too ugly, but maybe like the girl from *Six Feet Under* with the awkward eyes, or like a naturally olive-skinned brunette with a nose a little too big but with full lips. Britney's lips, besides being her only non-symmetrical feature, were too small. They were... slight.

Her body wasn't slight, though, she thought with a tremble. Her abs (she looked again) had disappeared. Her thighs were no longer as muscular as a boy's. There was too much of her everywhere. If she weren't famous, normal people would think she was skinny, but that didn't count. She was never allowed to be normal again.

Britney put her hands on her stomach and felt the new fat and then the ache of missing her little baby boys who were with their dad this week, probably laughing and joyful without her, because in every fucking picture they brought back to show her they looked hysterical, almost manic in their fun without her. The ache of her son's lost bodies pulsed under her fingers, and within that single moment, she knew with a resigned certainty she wanted to die.

This was something she knew about once a day.

"I can't do this," Britney said to her eyes in the mirror, and the whites of them turned pink, but she refused to cry, saying "I won't, I won't, la la la," to herself as she moved away from the mirror and turned the Aretha up.

Aint no way, Aretha sang, *For me to love you, if you won't let me...*

This song is straight-up sad, and so am I, Britney thought, and laughed a near-to-tears laugh. She felt a tingle up her spine—the excitement she felt when she knew she was planning the end but no one else knew, and no one would know, until she was gone.

"Lordy, I'm so crazy," she said aloud.

She made a little eek-face and then turned back around and did it in front of the mirror and giggled at her eek-face and stuck her tongue out and made an eek-face again. Maybe she would do that eek-face at dinner with the guy, she thought. He might like it and think it made her seem down-to-earth or goofy, which she was actually, but no one really got that about her.

The clock said 6:09. She sang along to Aretha's chorus and whispered, "Fuck you, world," to the walls as she spun in waiting circles, jeans still undone.

6:10 pm

The last thing Britney had said to her ex-husband when they shared a house was, "You're a pussy, and you don't know women, you *fuck*. I'm taking this vibrator into the other room because *it* can actually make me *come*." He could never, just never, find her clit. It was like the precious, the truest, most precious part of her was un-interesting to him. The next day, when he left, he really did leave. The last thing she said after that was, "You knew what would happen if you left me. If I decide to die, it's on you."

Her pretty pink clit, and he never found it.

She canceled his credit cards, and that was that until, out of the haze of night and the morning that hit her like a man's angry fist, she remembered the boys weren't hers that week. *He* had the boys. He fucked fucking strippers, who probably did their skanky dances to *her* songs, and he had her boys.

She got a nosebleed that day and screamed.

But this time, this guy, it didn't have to be like that; things didn't have to be sad. Every time something new happened, like a new month, or a new project, or a new charity without psycho bad-versions-of-Christians fucking it up, or a new person with a real, new smile, something could be good. This guy she was seeing tonight... when she met him at the charity auction, he had looked at her the way Tom Hanks looks at Meg Ryan in a movie. He thought she was adorable when she was happy and sweet when she was sad. She could tell he felt that way from his face of adoration, which looked like the way men look when they think a woman is cute and that women in general are cute, for all their craziness and shit, and all that and whatever. And he joked around about the stories about her. He knew right after meeting her for real the stories were stupid bullshit. He sympathized with how hard her life was, and he also seemed like someone who could be a really good dad. She'd only met him those two times, but she could tell. His favorite movie was *Sandlot*, he said, and he loved Third Eye Blind, which Britney did, too. He was really handsome with gray hairs on the sides of his head, which kind of made Britney like him even more, even though it made him look oldish.

And he was coming for her.

He'd pick her up soon and say, "Hey, Brit," and maybe they'd go see that movie.

Her wig looked amazing. She sashayed a bit so the lower brown ends of it shook around a little.

6:15 pm

Weed was something Britney needed.

If no one was around, no babies or anything, this was her favorite: the seat by the window, a big ass bowl, and a hundred hours of smoky silence.

So fuck it, he was a little late, and she smoked up.

6:25 pm

People said she was stupid. Ha! She had an EMPIRE. Stupid my ass, you dumb, fat fucks.

A bird flew real close to her window. A night bird. That'd be sad if it hit the glass and died.

6:27 pm

Ain't no way, Britney sang along, her breath pushing huskinesss through nasal passages, *for me to love you, if you won't let me.*

The song was on repeat. The loopity-loop sign was in the corner of her iPod and had been for a couple of days. This song just wouldn't let her go. That was the thing about her, her old therapist had said. Things fixated her. Like the mirror. She put the bowl down, got up from the window, and looked into it. She wondered when the first mirror was invented. Like, inspired by water?

The only thing left was the glitter. Oh ball-sack fuck-drool! Damn it. She forgot. The glitter for her skin. With glitter on, like always, she would make them stay in dim lighting, and the candlelight quality would make that glitter create a soft focus effect on her. Her mom had said that to her once when she was a teenager.

"Sweetie, you're so cute in soft focus! My pretty, pretty girl!"

Britney thought again of Marilyn.

"I don't mind this being a man's world," Marilyn once said, "As long as I can be a woman in it."

The thing was, Britney thought, glittering up, her arms looking fat in the window's reflection but her face looking more and more awesome, if you were famous, you knew that kind of quote was such bullshit. A fame-quote only. A thing Marilyn said in a clever moment, when she was feeling her best and a bunch of admiring people were on her with cameras. A thing she said that she didn't mean in any way at all. But now people quoted it on Facebook like it was some Marilyn Monroe life philosophy. Because really, when you got to it deep down, Marilyn probably spent a lot of time alone with her thoughts, lying in bed and feeling like her woman-body was a big sack of fat shit. That quote was a thing said after a few sips of champagne, something she thought she was supposed to say. Every famous quote is just someone pretending to be the kind of person who gives famous quotes.

Some of Britney's quotes made her want to vomit. They made her sick. "Cool," she always said. "Cool, cool, cool." Shit, the dumb shit she'd said made her want to take a big hooked knife and dig it into the top of her pelvis, pulling up through the scar, all the way up to between the tits, and let the shit spill out. To just tear into that soft woman belly and be the one who destroyed it. Like the Asians and their hairy-kerry.

Britney turned around in a little pirouette to face the mirror again. She put her hands against the mirror like it was a man's chest and puffed a bit of air onto it to make mirror-steam.

"I don't mind this being a man's world," Britney said into the mirror in her best Marilyn-voice as Aretha continued to wail in the background, "as long as I can be a woman in it." She tilted her head to each side a million times, and the mirror sparkled back at her with the glitter that had gotten on it.

One time Britney got jerked off on when she was on the road. It was like the only time she was allowed on a date. She was 17 and was the biggest fucking thing in the whole world, and everybody shielded her from how much everybody actually hated her fucking guts—all the cool kids and real musicians. How what all the world was doing was making fun of her and whacking off to her. Like John had said.

But nope, all she heard was how critical people didn't even know what they were talking about, that they were just a bunch of liberals who couldn't get jobs in real newspapers. No, they just surrounded her with fans. Sometimes, with radio ticket deals and stuff, little girls were allowed to come backstage after shows and tell her how much she inspired them. They would always say, "Oh my God, you're so pretty," and she would always tilt her head and giggle, a real giggle because she loved little girls—she'd always been a mom at heart—and say, "Aw, well you're so pretty, too! Come here, y'all!" and they'd all hug and take pictures, and Britney felt loved.

Well, that's not the whole story. Sometimes she'd sob right when they left and wish she'd told them to leave her the hell alone, that she was too tired, just too damn tired, and admiring her was just about the worst thing they could do, but those aren't the times worth remembering, her assistant always said.

"Only remember what's worth rememberin'," she'd say.

So the boy jerked off on her. Her mom always said no boy really wanted her for any good, real reason. Of course they liked her because she was gorgeous, and also sweet and funny, and a good, traditional girl, but at the same time they would never like her for her because they'd never really see her. They'd only see the show, the TV. But when Britney really liked one of the dancer's brothers, her mom said okay to a real date. They couldn't go out to a real place, so they watched a movie in the at-home movie theater of a producer's house who always offered Britney stuff. And then he drove her to a real, live "make-out" spot. It was super exciting. Really, really cool. They kissed and kissed, and it was like putting your face in really warm sand, kind of uncomfortable but also really nice in a weird way. He had blonde, teenage boy stubble and a really super sharp jaw. Then he put his hand on her chest, one hand on one boob, kind of pushing it, and he started touching his dick. He touched it and touched it until there was nothing left to touch anymore, and he drove Britney home. He must have read in the magazines she was saving her virginity because he was real respectful.

It was time for her Tom Hanks to be there. Where was he? The bowl needed to be lit again, she saw, as she walked toward the window looking for his car. *When something needs you, it needs you,* she thought, laughing, as she took another hit.

He wouldn't be long.

"LA LA LA," Britney sang at the top of her lungs to herself, dancing.

6:40 pm

When someone looks at you like Tom Hanks does to Meg Ryan, why wouldn't he come? Didn't Tom Hanks, like, love Meg Ryan?

Britney used to not believe in love. She didn't. She felt like she had it a couple times, but then it turned out to be lies, and then when she felt it for real, she knew it was there, but then she found out it was impossible to hold on to, and then it was just like... Jesus. How do other people make it look so real? So easy? Didn't that first moment when someone sees you and looks at you that way hold forever inside of it? She always fantasized too soon. She didn't know if it was a girl thing or a Britney thing, but either way it killed her. She still had her subscription to *weddinggirl.com*.

There's no way she would have known before she loved someone that love was hard, because she didn't get to have a God damn life for like a hundred years.

She picked up the hand mirror she'd put beside her at the window and checked her eye makeup. It had rubbed off a little below her stupid, small eyes. It looked like she was tired.

She always looked tired! She wanted to die!

She saw her mom had called her cell phone. She had deleted her number, which had been under "Mommy Dearest," but she still knew it by heart, and so of course when it showed up, she recognized it, and tonight seeing it made her bite into the skin on the upper part of her fat arm. She tasted like peach-y chemicals.

Her assistant had called about seven times in one minute.

Her brother had called. Her brother? What was wrong?

Someone must've died.

Why hadn't her date called? Not even to tell her he'd be late? How could he miss a chance to be with her? Had she smelled when they met? Sometimes she took three showers a day before she knew she'd have sex so she didn't smell down there. She wouldn't smell, she wanted to tell him.

So she called, and he didn't pick up again.

Her brother called again. He had texted her, too.

Call me before you go online at all, his text message said.

I love you, honey, said another.
Britney went to her computer.

6:42 pm

Sometimes she wondered, was she empty inside? Empty? Like a coconut with the juice sucked out? Like a book with the pages cut out to make a hiding place for a key or a secret letter? Like a pot a plant outgrew? Like a house that can't be sold because the husband killed the family in its kitchen? Like what's really inside a TV?

6:42-and-a-half pm

Britney clicked refresh a few times. Like maybe it would go away. Like she was seeing hallucinations the way she had one time when she'd tried to kill herself and had seen an angel dressed in light blue silk that looked just like her but had brown hair like Britney would've had if it had ever grown out natural.

The celebrity news page seemed to take an hour to refresh each time, but it was just a second, probably. There was her face. It was surrounded by a bunch of huge letters, and like always when she saw her face there, she felt illiterate and couldn't figure out the meaning of the big blocks of the alphabet for a minute or two. It was the dyslexia or the shock, her mom said, when one time she had seen another old lover had called her a slut, and she couldn't read the world slut, and she said, "What? He thinks I'm a skunk? What's that even mean?"

In front of her was a picture from when she first took off her hair, and her face was all messed up looking, even though she remembered feeling incredibly sexy that night—so lesbianic and free, and like a crazy woman on an island.

And then the shapes next to the picture made sense. They formed sounds and then words.

And then she wiped the glitter off of her face with an angry, pushy hand, leaving empty streaks between the glitter like she had the cheek of a striped glitter zebra.

BRITNEY ABUSED HER KIDS, SOURCES SAY, it read, like Satan's words in a Satanist bible, Britney thought.

And Britney felt how she felt when she was dancing, like she didn't exist, like her legs were somewhere different than her neck or her ribs.

Without even taking her face away from the page, she hit the speed dial on her phone for her lawyer and pushed the button for the security guys outside to let them know the camera packs would be here any minute.

"Yes, Miss Britney?" the guy said.

"They're comin'," she answered and hung up.

Outside there was a *la-la-la* like a siren, which meant they'd block her gate off. With the remote next to her computer, she turned off the music without looking. All she needed to dance to was the siren outside. She moved her hips side to side as she read the whole, damn, evil thing.

6:50-something pm

The article made sense to her after she read it a couple of times.

Britney vomited. The robin's egg carpet turned orange and purple.

She did not hit those boys. She'd never hit those boys. She did not touch her boys. She did not touch her boys. *Ew. Ew. Ew. Ew.*

She got sick again. The vomit turned clear and phlegmy as she moved down to all fours on her carpet, like she was a cat spitting out a hairball. The vomiting brought back teenage memories.

She stood up.

She picked up her phone.

She called the guy and called him again. No answer. Not even a voice to the machine.

He knew how to read, right? He'd read it. He'd read what they said. But maybe not. Maybe he was lost. Maybe he was lost in the windy roads around the gate. Gated out by the guys out front. Gated out of her life and late.

Maybe he was never real to begin with.

At least he didn't stand her up because he was married. Because he was a gold-digger. Because he was gay. Gay, gay, gay, like so many of them had been back in Louisiana.

He had said he didn't care about the stories, she thought, but he did. He really did.

Sad thing is, Britney thought, as she threw the phone into her clothing hamper and went to the window to smoke the rest of her bowl, it takes a really good guy to stand up a famous rich girl he'd heard was always high and slutty because he thinks she's abusing her kids. Damn, he would make such a great dad, the guy who wasn't coming.

Then she quieted and took a breath. With the music off, her breath was all she could hear.

No one's coming, she knew.

No one is coming.

7:00 pm

Pretty, pretty Britney, Britney thought. *All alone again.*

And before she took an Ambien to make her forget the world, Britney called her staff to come and clean up her room's mess.

DAN MALAKIN

Stillborn

From July/August 2011

THE MEETING TAKES place in the hospital boardroom. We sit
around a long mahogany table, fewer than 20 men now, away from
the bloodstained walls, the skittering vermin, the stench of death.
While we're here, us men, in this boardroom, it's as if the last 18
months never happened.

As usual, I say nothing. The rest decide the scientists still stay out
of the draw, which leaves fourteen. We each take a piece of paper from
a plastic bag. It's either blank or marked with an "X," and there's only
one with an "X." I don't even look at mine.

A few seconds after Patel opens his paper, he starts to sob. He
pushes his chair back, grabs the rucksack, looks about to say
something but instead shakes his head and rushes out. Silence. We
stare at the door, the table, the modern art cluttering the walls,
anywhere but at each other. Necessary sacrifice. Collateral damage.
Even now the world stinks of the same bullshit. So maybe it's guilt, or
shame, or one of the other excuses we like to make, but I go after him.

Patel still has a kid, a six-year-old with wide, tea-colored eyes and a missing left hand.

He's with his son in the hospital reception, sitting on a pink plastic chair with his boy on his lap, sorting through the fingers of the boy's good hand, kissing them one by one. I tell Patel I'm going instead.

"Thank you," he says. "You're a good man."

I take the rucksack. I tell him he's lucky to have his son.

Patel mumbles some words I don't understand. His reflection lingers behind me in the glass of the door, head bowed, eyes closed, hands supplicated. I ask what he's doing. The boy tugs at the sleeve of Patel's dirty white shirt. He ignores us both.

Finished, he looks up. "You will be with your wife and child in heaven."

I want to say the last place I'm going is heaven, or he can stick his heaven, something cruel, derisive, but what would be the point?

I leave Patel to his son.

Darkness presses the world outside of the hospital grounds. The wind whips metallic drizzle into my face. I keep low, hard to the walls, another superfluous emotion, duty, forcing me to be careful. The truth is, I couldn't care less if they make the new vaccine or not.

Things we took for granted: streetlights and umbrellas. The smile of a passing stranger. Holding a loved one's hand. Summer walks in the park. Generosity and kindness. Love. Perhaps these things, the beautiful but redundant skin of humanity, will in time be edited out of our DNA, leaving the residue of a different existence in the same way as some animals have tail stubs. When there are no more tails, we'll look at those stubs and wonder what they hell they were for.

Even in the dark I know the way to the church where Sandro and his gang live. Alison and I moved to this area, Highgate, after we married, drawn by its cobblestone maze of Victorian buildings and urban-chic, child-friendly pubs. A good place to raise a family. We dreamed of a happy life, a healthy baby, pushing a pram through

Hampstead Heath, our lives unfolding in a series of smiling snapshots. We wanted to wait for a year after the wedding, using that time to settle into our new home, and then go on a three-month African savannah adventure for our honeymoon. But something went wrong with the contraception, and Alison got pregnant.

"What's in a year?" Alison said. "Africa will still be there when we're older."

"It will," I said. "But my sense of adventure might not."

"Old man Brooke." She leant on an imaginary cane. "You want me to pass some crackers for your soup?"

"We've seen everything's in working order. Can't this one just be a trial run?"

"This isn't like the kitchen shelves. You can't just take them down and put up new ones. You're talking about killing our baby."

"It depends how you define alive," I said.

"We're keeping it," she said, and looked away.

I turn onto Fortnam Avenue. The concrete wall changes to a metal railing that flakes fragments of paint under my fingers. A faint halo of light glows by the church. I use it to locate the gap in the railing leading onto the grounds. The grass deadens my footsteps, so all I can hear is the sound of my beating heart, its racing thuds an annoying bassline I can't quite shake from my head.

Two men are loitering by the door.

My foot catches a pebble. It clicks off a headstone.

"Who goes there?" says one of the men.

I nearly laugh—civilization living on through television clichés.

"I've come to trade," I say. "I'm expected."

"Let's see you," says the tall one. They are dressed in black dinner jackets like bouncers outside a nightclub. "What's in the bag?"

I hand him the rucksack. While he looks inside, the other doorman, his face disfigured by burns, his mouth pulled to the side by the scar tissue, reaches in the bag and takes out one of the bottles of champagne. It took weeks to track down what Sandro wanted. Weeks of trawling through the Aladdin caves of civilization: high class supermarkets, continental delis, the cellars of decadent houses, anywhere luxury once existed, all to find two bottles of champagne and two tins of foie gras.

A good price for a human fetus, extracted fresh, which can be used to try to make a new vaccine.

A look passes between the doormen... No one would ever know.

"I'm expected," I repeat.

The tall one says, "It's dangerous out there. Anything could happen."

I clench my fist. The flick-knife presses against my wrist. I've practiced the move so many times I can whip it out and open in less than an eye-blink.

The tall doorman zips up the bag and pushes it to my chest. Not worth the risk, I guess. He tells me to wait. Scarface goes inside. When we're alone, the doorman glances at me and nods before continuing to stare ahead. I'm gripped suddenly by the normality of the moment. Here we are, two men, standing around. I want to ask what football team he used to support. If he had a wife. Kids. I want to ask him his story, what he did when the plague first hit, how he escaped the riots, the fires, society falling apart.

After the outbreak, it became clear the only people not affected were pregnant women. A special protein called volurealan, produced in the placenta, spread from the fetus to the liver and spleen, keeping the plague at bay. The government developed vaccines, but they only lasted a short while. The virus mutated too quickly. Alison and I hid in my parent's cellar as gangs searching for pregnant women raided every house. We heard each of Dad's fingers snapping, but he didn't give us away. They left him on the kitchen floor with his throat slit.

Scarface comes back out, says for me to follow. We pass through a dark corridor lined with closed doors. From behind them I hear low talking, a girl pleading, another whimpering. The corridor opens into a large sanctuary. Paraffin lamps cast circles of light in the gloom. Men hunker around a small fire cooking meat, the smell covering the dank locker-room stench.

Three men come through the door at the back. The middle one, I guess, is Sandro, the leader of this gang of birthers. He is wearing colorful swatches of silk fashioned into an outfit of which a drag queen would be proud. His fingers are chunky with gold rings. It's a look at odds with his puffy face and burgeoning gut. He was probably an accountant before, sneaking into his wife's clothes when she went to the shops, dreaming of revenge against the cruel world that made him such a fuck up.

"Welcome," he says, pleasantly, affecting his voice into a falsetto. He opens his arms as if for us to embrace.

I hold out the rucksack. "Let's make this quick."

He nods. The man to his left, dressed in tight red silk, steps forward and snatches the bag. Sandro takes it from him and removes a champagne bottle. He runs a fingernail around the cork foil and sighs. "A remnant of softer times," he says.

I tell him I just want the fetus.

"Patience, my dear friend."

"I'm not your friend."

His smile drops, and he nods to the man on his right, who walks past me and back through the way I came in.

Alison and I left my parent's cellar because of me. Either we moved, or I curled up on the floor and died.

The city was a wasteland. Black smoke filled the skies—power plants burning, probably, with nobody there to put them out. Dead bodies lay where they fell. A rat gnawed on the entrails of a young girl's disembowelled stomach. We ended up at the hospital. Where else would we go? The residue of society lingered in our blood. Uniformed men stood guard. They had some government vaccine left, and we could come in on one condition—they wanted to take the fetus from Alison's stomach and use it to try and make more.

Alison was seven months pregnant.

"No way," she said. "There's no way."

"Of course," I replied. "I'll never let them do that."

But she knew.

Right on cue I coughed violently, spraying the ground with blood.

Alison held her hands over her belly and shook her head. "This is our baby. Our baby. Doesn't that mean anything to you?"

"I'm not thinking about me. I'm thinking of all the other lives—"

"You never wanted us to have this baby."

"That was a different life, Ally."

I coughed again, doubled over with pain. Maybe the pain made me say what I did. The words just seemed to bypass my brain, come straight from my mouth. Though I think I tell myself that to make it easier, somehow. I knew what I was saying.

But her eyes. Her cold, hating eyes.

"If we don't go in there, Ally," I said, "Then I'll die."

They let us in, and they took our baby from Alison's womb, and two weeks later she slashed her wrists with broken glass.

Sandro's man returns, pushing a young, heavily-pregnant girl on a screeching trolley. Her arms are strapped to the side, her legs in stirrups. She's pretty, even with her back arched and eyes rolled back. Sandro smiles like a benevolent father. "A good one," he says. "Healthy."

"Let's get this done," I say and stare at the floor, around the room, anywhere but at the girl. I tell myself I'm already dead. Her pain can't touch me.

Another man goes to the girl. A parody of a doctor, he has a stethoscope slung around the neck, a clean white mask tight over his mouth, and is holding a set of tongs you might use to tackle a particularly violent barbeque.

"Be careful," says Sandro. "We can get many more out of her."

Women could burn their bras for a millennium, and what would it matter? I look around the sanctuary at the men chewing dull-eyed on their meat.

I can't help it. I glance at her. Her eyes lock onto mine. The hate. I see Alison's eyes again, and sick rises in my throat.

The girl mumbles no as the doctor moves between her legs. He uses forceps to hold her open. She thrashes and screams like a banshee.

Sandro slides an arm around my shoulder. "This is her first time," he says. "But she will be okay. Don't mind the noise." He wafts his free hand over the room. "You get used to it."

The tongs are inserted into the girl. Her screams threaten to blow down the walls.

Could you imagine if the cure existed in men, how different it would be? The need for dignity. Honor. With women, we know we don't have to bother. We just strap them down and rip out what we need.

One of Sandro's cronies stops to watch, a faint smile coming to his otherwise blank expression. I want to rip off his face.

The girl shrieks at Sandro, begs him to stop.

He laughs.

Before I can think, the flick-knife is in my hand. I spin behind Sandro, hold the blade to his neck, snatch his hair and yank it. Everything stops. Sandro's men look at us. The girl's scream fades to a whimper.

Slowly, Sandro says, "Have I done something to offend you? You came to me."

I'm suddenly aware of what I'm doing, but I'm not scared. I feel alive. I pull his hair harder, expose his neck, press the blade.

"Untie her," I say.

The doctor looks at Sandro. Sandro nods. He unties her. She climbs warily off the trolley. I back to a wall and tell the men to throw all their weapons on the floor by my feet. "And the men from outside. Get them." I press the knife so hard it cuts his skin. Sandro squeaks an order for his men to do as I say. They lumber up to throw a hammer or a machete into the pile. I shout to the girl to get the others. Soon they are all here, eight of them, shocked and desperate and pregnant. I tell them to take the weapons, then ask if any of them know the area. One of them nods and I call her over. I whisper to her to head to the hospital.

When they are gone, Sandro says, "You will die so painfully. I promise you that."

The men look about, confused, restless, unsure whether to stay and protect their leader, or go after the women. I need some time, even five minutes, so I tell them about Alison and me, about how we met as students, the day I proposed on the steps of the Trevi Fountain, all the plans we made for our married life. Every time they look to the door, to where the women fled, I press the blade harder until Sandro screams at them to stay. My voice breaks. I blink through tears. The men advance. I pull Sandro's hair hard, dragging him to the floor, saying, "I'm sorry Alison, I'm so sorry." Inside I'm praying Patel is right and there is a heaven, even though I've never believed in heaven before. And as I slice the knife across Sandro's throat, I hope she's there to forgive me.

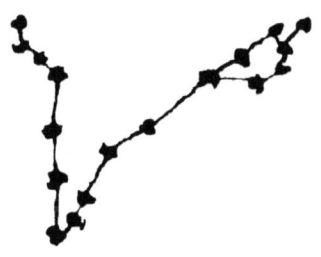

JENNIFER FINSTROM

Prophetess

From July/August 2005

I stopped being a girl a long time ago. He first
whispered words of love to me when I was four,
a child in the splash of sunshine at my mother's
feet. I was six before I saw he was the sunshine,
eight before I knew he was a god. But the visions
came as soon as I could speak to tell of them,
pictures stabbing themselves like chopsticks,
daggers, the bloodied beaks of swans. The nerves
in my eyes burned pink and glaring as boiled
shrimp, and still I waited for him, hugging
my knees, nursing my mutant longing
for a man who wasn't a man. When I sleep,
the sun shoves the moon, forces her away over
night's hills. Nothing shines from her cold
temple, but in the darkest hour she whispers
to me of polar regions where the sun is dead,
where even his love can't find me.

SCOTT STAMBACH

The Tiny Speck in Amata's Rib

From July/August 2013

THE FOLLOWING IS a conversation between a boy and his father in Colonna, a small town at the edge of Rome. It could have taken place at any time after the voyage of St. Ursula.

The father is about to step out of his son's room before the boy speaks again:

"It's been 13 days, Papa."

"I know, Angelo. I've been counting, too."

"In two hours it will be 14 days."

"Get some sleep, figliolo."

"Do you think she was here? When you were telling me the story?"

The father turns around and returns to his spot on the boy's bed, which is still warm.

"I know she was. She was listening in, like always, and watching the moon."

The father points to the full moon outside the boy's window. He knows his boy has a particular fascination with the moon. On this night it is floating just above the row of houses on the hill across from the boy's window, so big and orange it looks like it could fall from the sky.

"Papa?"

"Yes, figliolo?"

"Tell me one more story."

"What? Another one? You need to sleep, Angelo."

"No sleep without another story."

"Fine then. Would you like to know why the number 17 is so unlucky in our country?"

"Yes, that would be a start."

"Okay, how would you write 17 in Roman numerals?"

"Like this..."

The boy finds a piece of paper on the small table next to his bed and scribbles XVII.

"Now watch, if you just switch the numerals around you get this..."

The father writes VIXI on the same piece of paper with slow steady strokes.

"Do you know what that means in Latin?"

"Mmm mm."

"It means 'I have lived' or 'I am no longer alive.'"

"Papa, that's creepy."

"I know. And did you know most buildings in Italy don't have a 17th floor?"

"Nope, I didn't know that, either."

"*Buono.* Now, Angelo, you can go to bed."

"Papa, that doesn't count! One more story, or I will never sleep. And I will sing songs outside your door all night."

"You will sleep, or I will shake you to sleep."

The father puts his arms on either side of the boy and begins to make the bed quake. The boy laughs so hard he can't seem to catch his breath.

"No, Papa, stop, I can't breathe..."

The father stops and tosses the boy's shaggy brown hair around.

"So, you must be ready to sleep then, huh, figliolo?"

"Not yet. Just one story. One day you will be sad you didn't tell me every story you could. I will be all grown up and living in my own house, and I won't be interested in your stories anymore. Then you will wish I was there to tell stories to."

"Figliolo, who taught you how to argue like that?"

"I've listened to you and mama for seven years, Papa."

"Well, there's not much I can say then, is there?"

"Nope, there isn't. One more story."

"Well, do you want a little story or a big story?"

"A big one, of course. The biggest story you have. *Gigantesco.*"

"If I tell you my biggest story, you definitely won't be able to sleep. I promise you."

"Who cares about sleep, Papa? I don't know why you make such a big deal about it."

"Really? You want the most gigantic of my stories?"

"Yes, Papa. *Il più grande!*"

The father takes a moment to look into his head. He considers whether it is time to tell his son this particular story.

"Well. There is a story I've wanted to tell you for a long time. But I'm not sure you're ready. You might never sleep again."

"Yes! Tell me!"

The father sighs, though he smiles through it. He pauses, looks his son in the eye, and waits a few seconds. The son is aware of this tactic and understands the father is only building tension and has already surrendered to telling his story.

"*Ora,* Papa. Your trick doesn't work with me."

"After I tell you this story, nothing will be the same again. Are you ready for that?"

The boy's face pinches, and wrinkles spread over his forehead before releasing—he realizes this is a new tactic. Then his mouth opens. "Of course. I trust you, Papa."

"It's not important that you trust me; it's important you trust yourself, Angelo."

The boy tries hard to imagine a story that would require him to trust himself, but he cannot.

"You can tell me."

"Okay."

The father's eyes look up and to the left as he begins. "I first heard this story from your great grandpa. My Nonno. When I was your age."

"I don't believe you were ever my age, Papa."

"I was, figliolo."

"Okay, whatever. Go on, Papa."

"It starts at the beginning of time. The true beginning of time."

"Like when there were dinosaurs?"

"No billions of years before that. Before stars even. When the universe was just a tiny *puntino*."

"How could everything in the universe fit inside of a *puntino*?"

"Because nothing existed yet. There was nothing. Only space. Silent, still space."

"What was the *puntino* made of?"

"No one knows exactly, Angelo. We only know it contained pure magic. Because out of it came everything we see right now. And everything you don't. You and I were in that *puntino* billions of years ago."

"So, then what happened to it?"

"It burst, figliolo."

"What made it burst?"

"Only God knows."

"But you should know, Papa."

"I promise, figliolo, I do not."

"So then what?"

"Everything changed as soon as the *puntino* exploded. Stuff started to *be*—stuff you could touch. And all the stuff started to get pulled together by invisible hands."

"Who's hands?"

"Again, figliolo, no one knows."

"Okay, keep going."

"When enough stuff was pulled together, it turned into a star. And that star became like a factory, building all the elements that make up everything. Angelo, you and I are made of pieces of stardust."

"Really?"

The boy looks out of the open window next to his bed and tries to see the stars, but they are mostly swallowed up by the light of the moon.

"Yes, but here is where things get interesting, Angelo. There were pieces of that *puntino* that never turned into anything. They got trapped inside of the star stuff as it was pulled together. Throughout the whole universe, there was the whole potential of God locked inside tiny specks of magic stuff coated with the metals inside of stars. And all that power was cut off from the rest of the universe because stars are impenetrable. Nothing could ever get inside one."

"Nothing, Papa?"

"Anything within a million miles of a star would turn to ashes in the blink of an eye."

"So what happened? Are they still there?"

"Well, figliolo, some stars, when they're ready to die, will explode. It's like a death rattle. Like when mama..."

Immediately the father's face winces, and the boy understands his father wishes he hadn't used that example.

"So when stars exploded, the specks were released?"

"Yes. And for millions of years they were just scattered throughout the universe, mixed with stardust."

"Until?"

"Until a new star started to form, and planets started to spin around it—if one of the specks was close enough for the planet to feel it, the speck would get sucked in. And you know what?"

"No, Papa, I don't."

"One of these stars was our star—the sun."

"So the magic speck is in our sun?"

"Almost. But something impossible happened. We, Earth, got in the way. Do you know the chances of that happening, figliolo?

"No, Papa."

"I could say one in a billion-trillion, but that would be too high."

"Then what?"

"My Nonno thought the speck was the seed of all Life here.

"Papa, you're making this up."

"No, figliolo, I promise all this is true. And the story hasn't even started yet. Before the end I will prove all this to you."

"How, Papa?"

"You will see. For now it is only important to know that when the tiny speck splashed into the ocean, the magic inside of it started to bleed out, and things began to live."

"So, then what?"

"Then Life had a life of it's own, you could say. It began to unfold and make copies of itself, and every time it changed, it changed by its own set of rules. And one day Life made a human, and for the first time It became aware of itself."

The father stops for a second to watch his son's face and determine if he understands. He believes the boy does, at least on the level of instinct.

"Do you understand, figliolo?"

"I think so. What happened to the speck?"

"It floated through the oceans for about three billion years. Until it finally washed up on a shore, thousands of years before the time of

Jesus. Nonno said the first people to find it didn't have bodies. They were a spirit-people who lived on an island somewhere far from Europe. Eventually, these people forgot it existed, and it found its way back to the sea. It stayed there for hundreds more years until it was found by the son of a fisherman. He was a young boy like you, figliolo, playing on a beach somewhere in the Pacific."

"And what did he do with it?"

"He held it for awhile. When he realized it let him have control over anything he wanted just by thinking it, he showed it to his father."

"And what did he do with it?"

"He kept it safe, figliolo. He never traveled, and he never stopped being a fisherman."

"He didn't know it was magic?"

"No, Angelo, the opposite. He immediately understood that when he had the speck, he never came home without a net filled with fish, the weather was always perfect, and his family was content and happy."

"And he never wanted more, Papa?"

"No, Angelo. He did not. This is the real magic of the speck. Throughout history, anything that gave power to men has always been used to get even more power over men. But a drop of blood never fell on this speck. After the fisherman, the speck went to his son, and then after him it was given to a guru in Calcutta, then a sherpa in the Himalayas, then a monk in Tibet, then a tailor in Russia, a mathematician in Poland, a painter in France, and a then a doctor in Spain. It had seen everything, every angle of life. It had been buried in the desert and lost to the sea. Through all these hands there was never any conflict. Now this is where it gets interesting..."

"Papa, you always say that."

"And I always mean it."

The father smiled and adjusted his body so his face was next to his son's.

"Her name was Ursula, and her father was a king named Dionotus. From the time she was your age, figliolo, she was special. People said she had an aura."

"What color?"

"It was light-yellow. But, according to Nonno, there was a very particular reason why she glowed."

"What was that reason, Papa?"

"Well, apparently, and this is according to Nonno, remember, her father, the king, had been given the speck by a mendicant. And when his daughter turned seven, he gave it to her, and like everyone else who held it, the magic started to bleed into her. That's why she glowed, figliolo."

The story is interrupted by a voice calling for the father from the hallway:

"*Signor,* Mr. Ghirlandaio is here to see you."

"In a moment, Ghiti. I'm telling Angelo a story."

"Where did I leave off, figliolo?"

"You were going to tell me who she married, Papa."

"In those days, a princess was not free to choose. Her father, the king, chose for her. He decided that she would marry a pagan governor from Armorica. Do you know where that is, Angelo?"

"No."

"It was a part of the Old France."

"Did she love him?"

"No. She didn't even know him. But, still she was sent to marry him. And before she left, her father found 11,000 virgin servants to go with her."

"What, Papa? Why 11,000 virgins?"

"They were an army of assistants."

"Who would need so many servants?"

"Exactly, Angelo. It sounds crazy doesn't it?"

"Yes, Papa."

"Do you know why it sounds so crazy to you?"

"No, but I know you will tell me."

"It sounds crazy because it was all a lie."

"You're making all this up?"

"No, the king did. He told this story to his people to hide something."

"To hide what, Papa?"

"To hide the fact that she was really running away."

"Why was she running? From whom?"

"From people who wanted the speck. For the first time in three billion years, its secret was released to the world. Nonno believed someone saw Ursula surreptitiously healing some peasants who were sick with a disease spreading through Europe at the time. And the secret spread. And you know what?"

"What?"

"When the secret of power escapes, nothing around it is ever safe again. The king was told by his advisors that Ursula would be stolen."

"So she wasn't sent to be married."

"No, figliolo. The politician in Armorica had agreed to hide Ursula, not marry her."

"And the virgins?"

"They were all part of a clever plan to shroud the speck. The king's physician hid it inside one of the ribs of one of the 11,000 virgins. If they were ever caught, they would have no idea which virgin had it. They would only know it was not on Ursula, and she would never be touched."

"So what happened, Papa?"

"Well, she set sail. And just as their boats left the dock, the king's palace was attacked. My Nonno said the king knew it was coming but never told Ursula."

"Did they catch up to her?"

"No, figliolo. There was a storm—the strongest England had ever seen. It blew her ship across the channel in one night. When she landed, she took it as a sign from God. She went to Rome and demonstrated her miracles to whomever would watch. Eventually to the Pope himself."

"And then?"

"They went on a pilgrimage. Ursula, with the Pope and all of her servants, moved from Rome, through Bavaria, and into Germania. And everywhere she went, she performed miracles. She became famous. But the holiday didn't last."

"Why not?"

"When they arrived in Germanic lands, they found a tribe called the Huns, who ruled most of the territory. The Huns had heard rumors of a traveling army of handmaidens who could perform miracles, and they wanted no part of it. So they massacred them."

"Ursula, too?"

"Yes, Ursula, the Pope, and all 11,000 virgin servants. They all fell in one big bath of blood. And then the Huns just walked away and left them there to bleed."

"What about the magical speck?"

"It stayed there, too, hidden in one of the bodies."

"So that's it, Papa?"

"No. Before he was seized, the king, Ursula's father, had sent out a message to the King of Sussex explaining he was going to be attacked. Lucky for Dionotus, the King owed him a favor. In 24 hours, an army from Sussex arrived, surprised the attackers, and crushed them. One month later, as the king was still celebrating, he heard from the governor in Armorica that his daughter and all her servants were killed."

"What did he do?"

"He gathered 1,000 men to find his daughter's body and return it to Briton, and he sent 1,000 more to build a Basilica in Cologne in memorial of his daughter. But instead of it being built of wood and stone, he ordered it be built from their bones. He wanted this for two reasons. First, figliolo, because he knew the speck was inside one of those bones and he wanted it far away from his kingdom—for him its magic had only been a curse. And second, because he knew the magic would be alive inside of any structure that housed the speck. His beloved daughter's Basilica, he hoped, would be a place where miracles happened."

"Bones?"

"No one had ever seen anything like it before, Angelo. The walls and ceiling were lined with thousands of bones: ribs and skulls and shoulder blades. There were arches made of bones, bones spelling Latin proverbs, even Ursula's story written in bones. Over the years the basilica was raided hundreds of times, and eventually all the bones were torn out by men hoping to find the speck. And after each raid the basilica was reconstructed, though with fewer and fewer of the original bones."

"Where did they get the new bones?"

"That, I'm not sure of, figliolo."

"You're not sure because you're making it up."

The father smiles at his boy.

"No, it's all true. I could take you there one day, Angelo. But..."

"But what?"

"But there are no miracles. In spite of the bones, it was like any other church. "

"Why? How could that be?"

"The king wondered about this for years, but he never understood. He assumed that soaking the speck in blood made it lose all its power. His priests told him it had seen too much of what humans were capable of."

"Is that what you believe, Papa?"

"No. And the king didn't believe it, either. He had held the speck. He knew its power. Nothing in the human realm could come close to touching its essence.

"So then why were there no miracles?"

"Well, the miracles did continue—just not in the basilica."

"How is that possible?"

"Because, once again, Angelo, I lied."

"About what?"

"The one virgin, the one with the speck. She never died. Her wound healed as soon as the blade was pulled out. But she still fell to the ground in that virgin blood. And she waited."

"Waited for what?"

"She waited to be sure she was alone, Angelo. When she stopped hearing the gallop of the Huns' horses, she resolved not to stand until she finished counting to 10,000 and one. When she finally finished, she looked around and cried. And then she walked west, back to Rome, following the sun. It was all she could think to do."

"Do you know what her name was?"

"I do. Her name was Amata."

"She was by herself? All the way to Rome?"

"Yes, but at the same time she never went cold or hungry. It protected her."

"How long did it take?"

"Three months. When she finally got to Rome, she told the Vatican the Pope had been killed. At first they put her in prison and questioned her. Eventually, one of the cardinals recognized her face as belonging to one of the 11,000 handmaidens with St. Ursula. They took care of her for weeks, until she got her health back. Eventually she left Rome and lived with a family in Ardea with connections to the church. They were a simple family: chiffonniers, wig-makers. She lived with them year after year, and she also learned the art of making wigs. But according to Nonno this trade was only to cover for what she really did.

"Which was?"

"She took what was bad out of people. At night people were brought to her, though no one ever knew who she was. They were led into a room inside the small cottage in Ardea where the family lived. Amata sat in the corner of the room. She was covered from head to toe—everywhere but her eyes—with a long, white sheet. Sick, blind, broken, leperous people would be carried in, laid at her feet, and she would kneel down and just hold them, cradle them in her arms, for only a minute. And you know what, Angelo?"

"They all got better."

"Yes. Not always right away. Sometimes it took a day. Sometimes a week. But eventually they were always healed."

"And she did this for the rest of her life?"

"Well, that's the strange thing, figliolo."

"What is strange, Papa?"

"It was about 15 years later when Amata, and everyone around her for that matter, began to notice something."

"Like what?"

"She never aged, Angelo. People began to notice that while they were getting older, as their hair started to turn to grey and their skin became thin, nothing ever changed in Amata. They watched her for years, figliolo, years. And suddenly an entire generation had passed, and Amata still looked like a young woman."

"How come?"

"People had different theories. Some people thought she was being rewarded by God for her work. Some thought she was an angel. But Amata knew. It was the tiny piece of God inside of her. Time did not exist for her, even though she lived in a world that required time."

"So she was able to fix people forever, Papa?"

"Well, figliolo, here is the most interesting part of the story."

"You always say that."

"Yes, I do. But, just listen."

"Well, go on then, Papa."

"Okay."

The father's rhythm slows, and each word comes out slowly, as if he chooses every word before he says it.

"After working for hundreds of years—and everyone she ever knew and loved living and passing—she met a boy who was very sick."

"With what?"

"It was called *Il Sangue Bianco*. When he bled, he couldn't stop bleeding. Even gentle touches turned into bruises. He always had a fever, and his skin was cold. He had only a few heartbeats left when he met Amata."

"Does the boy have a name?"

"No, figliolo. The boy does not have a name in this story."

"But everyone has a name."

"Not now, not in this story."

"Alright, Papa."

"His parents brought him to the room where she was wrapped in her white sheet. She knelt down next to him and held his shivering body. Knowing how close he was to the other side, she held him for an hour. The boy remembered her whispering to him. She said this hurts, I know, but nothing hurts when you remember that nothing last forever. She kept saying that over and over, figliolo: Nothing lasts forever, *tesoro*. He remembered feeling a love for her even though he never felt the sickness leave him."

"She didn't make him better?"

"The next morning he woke still sick and shivering. And the morning after. A week went by, and the boy was still getting worse. People worried for the first time that Amata had failed. The boy's parents went to tell her, and when they did, she didn't seem surprised, as if she had known she was unable to heal the boy, as if she knew this case was different."

"So what happened?"

"She said she needed to see him again—this time alone. So the boy's parents led her back to their home in the ghettos of San Cesareo. They led her to his room and left her alone with him. She was in there for the entire night—a night the boy couldn't remember because parts of him were already starting to die."

"Did it work?"

"The next morning the boy's parents woke up to the sounds of their boy humming *La Bella Lavanderina*. His face was pale and soaked in sweat, but he was awake. The morning after that they found him walking through the hills behind their house."

"And *Il Sangue Bianco* never came back?"

"No, the boy was cured."

"And all was well?"

"For the boy, yes. But, Amata was never..."

The father's sentence is interrupted by the voice of a woman again, this time coming from behind the door to the boy's room. "Signor, I'm sorry to bother you again, but Mr. Ghirlandaio is waiting for you. I think he's growing impatient."

The father replies, "It's only a few minutes now, Ghita. Mr. Ghirlandaio can wait a few more minutes. Pour him a glass of the Gaja Barbaresco. The papers can wait."

"Where was I, figliolo?"

"You said, 'Amata was never...' Never what?"

"She was never the same, Angelo. Well, in some ways she was the same. She continued to stay a young woman. Her hair never grayed. But in other ways she was different. Especially in one important way. She lost the ability to take the bad from people. Or at least she said she did. After she fixed the boy, she began to turn away the long lines curling out of her house and down the road."

"Why?"

"Who knows. Nonno thinks she used everything left inside of her on the boy."

"Did she live forever?"

"Even though she still didn't age on the outside, figliolo, she started to age on the inside. In her mind. It was an invisible aging. But she accepted it. She continued to take walks through Ardea. And no one knew who she was. But, she always had one-third of a smile, Angelo."

"I don't feel like the story is over, Papa."

"You're right. It's not. The boy began to obsess over her. She was in his dreams every night, and the scene of her saving him played out in his head every day. But that's not all he began to remember."

"What else, Papa?"

"He began to remember what really happened when he was alone with her."

"What happened?"

"He saw her make a small cut into her side and pull out a tiny speck. She washed the blood off on her dress and then put it in his mouth."

The woman's voice interrupts again, almost desperate this time. "Signor, Mr. Ghirlandaio is threatening to leave. Please. Come down now.

"Just one minute, Ghita. Keep his calm for just a few more seconds. I'm on my way."

"After these memories, he tried to find her. But it wasn't easy. His parents refused to tell him. So he decided to fast. He went 11 days without food before they finally gave in."

There is a soft, low-frequency hum coming from outside that both the father and son can hear. It becomes the backdrop to the next part of their conversation.

"Then what?"

"He went to see her."

"What did he say?"

"Nothing at first. He knocked on the door and couldn't think of a single thing to say. So she invited him in. Then she sat down and started teaching him how to make a wig."

"That's how it happened?"

"Yes, that's exactly how it happened. He started coming every afternoon, and every afternoon she taught him how to make wigs. But... this got them talking."

"About what?"

"About everything. Every day she told him a new story—remember Ursula sailed from Briton in the third century, so there was a lot to tell. She painted the characters of every century: there were conquistadors and knights, magicians and sirens, everything a boy wanted to hear. He didn't even care if the stories were real or not. Much like you, figliolo."

"How old was he?"

"At this time? He was seven or eight. Also just like you."

"Okay, keep going."

"When the boy was old enough, they began to take walks through the city. Amata taught him how to drink coffee and tie his tie. They watched magicians on the street, took trains to Florence and Pompei and Torino, devoured books together. They became inseparable."

"Then?"

"Then one day he was 19, and he kissed her."

"I didn't expect that."

"I know. But, figliolo, now I'm going to tell you the most important part of the story."

"You say that every time, Papa."

"I really mean it this time. After I tell you, you won't be the same. You can turn back now."

"No, Papa. You already started. Tell me."

"There's one more lie I told in this story."

"Another one?"

"Yes, but this is the last one."

"Which part was the lie?"

"The part where I told you Nonno told me this story."

"If not Nonno, then who?"

"Amata."

"You knew Amata?"

"Yes, figliolo. And so did you."

"Papa."

The boy pushes his father and turns away subtly, as if to tell him the joke isn't funny.

"I'm telling the truth, Angelo."

"Papa, stop it."

"It's true. All of it. These 13 days have been closer to hell than anything I've ever known. I know you understood that. Now you understand it in a new way."

The boy rolls away from his father.

"How did she leave us, then?"

"I don't know, Angelo. God is as He is. And that's all any of us can know."

The father clears the shimmering streaks from his son's face with his thumb.

"There's something else. Something I hope you understand from all this."

"What?"

"That you are also in this story, Angelo. You are inside of everything I just told you."

"What do you mean?"

"It means everything you can imagine."

"I don't understand."

"You will. And now, unfortunately, I need to go meet with Mr. Ghirlandaio. Get some sleep, Angelo."

"No, Papa. No. This can't be the end of this story."

"It's not, figliolo. We are still here."

The father looks at his son and pulls his sheets up to his chest.

"We have tomorrow to talk some more. And the day after that."

The father leans forward, dusts the hair away, and kisses his son on the forehead. Then he leaves the bed and walks out of the room, gently closing the door behind him. The boy sits for a few moments in perfect stillness, his mind so vanquished it falls silent. He closes his eyes and sees the face of his mother. He opens his eyes and sees the clock on the wall. In one hour it will be 14 days. He looks out through his big window at the big moon reflecting orange light from a sun that can't be seen. He wants to have it in front of him, just to see it up close and know what it's made of. As he thinks this thought, it arrives, resting in his two cupped hands. His first reaction is surprise when he sees it is a perfect sphere and not two-dimensional as it is in the sky. He rubs the surface with his fingertips and thinks about how it is the smoothest thing he has ever felt, despite all the blemishes he had always assumed were craters and valleys.

ANTHONY W. BROWN

AquaSerene (A Fish Story)

From April/May 2004

CONGRATULATIONS on the purchase of your AquaSerene Underwater Kingdom! In joining the AquaSerene family, you have made a superior choice in the exciting and rewarding world of freshwater aquariums. Expect years of quiet pleasure and pride in ownership as you embark on your above and underwater adventures. Now let's get started:

Step 1: Location

The location you choose for your AquaSerene is just as important as the quality of water you maintain for your kingdom (See Step 6: WATER). It's better to be safe than sorry when choosing a location. Be aware of the following:

1. High traffic areas are danger zones. Do not place your AquaSerene in harm's way. Avoid hallways, restrooms, kitchens,

etc. You might consider your bedroom as a happy alternative to the more conspicuous but more dangerous areas of your home. It's quiet in your bedroom. No one sleeps there anymore. Not even you. The few minutes you spend there each day are disturbed only by the tapping of the blinds cord on the windowsill and the sound of someone missing. Sooner or later you'll have to close that window, especially if you plan to locate your AquaSerene in the bedroom (See POINT #2, which directly follows).

2. Avoid drafty areas and those areas near heating and air-conditioning ducts. Huge temperature swings can adversely affect water quality and lead you to despair. Despair in all cases is to be avoided. Despair will ruin your kingdom before it even gets started. If you bought your AquaSerene out of despair, stop reading now and return it immediately. We will not be held responsible for despair.

3. Keep your AquaSerene Underwater Kingdom away from direct sunlight. When so stimulated, your Kingdom can overheat and succumb to unsightly algae growth. While this appears to be a natural process, growth is not always good. Sometimes, as in the case of algae, the wrong things can grow in your kingdom, things inhospitable to the life you hope to cultivate. Ugly, deadly things. Then the real trouble begins. Hours wasted on things you cannot control but cannot help worry over, things that go on and thrive in spite of you, things that spawn ocean currents and carry warming air over otherwise arctic places, things that could break you and all you know into a series of moments divorced from happiness or even meaning. Be careful of these things. If you let them get away from you or think about them too much, you'll spend all your time washing away what's ugly in your kingdom in the vain hope that what remains is beautiful or agreeable enough to sustain you.

4. Stay level. Keep your AquaSerene Underwater Kingdom level. We cannot stress this enough. Full surface contact to something solid and lasting is required to properly distribute the aquarium weight and maintain a healthy balance for your Kingdom. Your life depends on this. You must keep full contact with your Kingdom, or you may very well lose it. If, for some unforeseeable circumstance, you should lose it, do not despair (See Step 7: FISH). You have alternatives.

Step 2: Lighting

Believe it or not, you can have too much light in your AquaSerene. Make sure the light is left on for only a few hours each day. Observe and enjoy what you can during these lighted hours, but do not try to take it in all at once. If you try to see it all, it will overwhelm you, and you'll see nothing. Look just a little beyond the moment, and you'll be okay, because remember: too much light can be a bad thing (See Step 1: LOCATION, POINT #3).

Step 3: Aeration

All living things must have oxygen in order to survive. This is the cold hard truth, and there's no getting around it. Most smokers, firefighters, and coal miners encounter this fundamental law of nature at some time in their lives. They run from it, then they learn from it, and then they regret it. Right before they die. Or at the moment they imagine they are going to die. Or even at the moment they are told they are going to die. Any of these situations will typically drive the point home. Sometimes, though, obstinacy rules. These learn only at that moment when that thing-so-big-they-can't-deny-or-resist-it washes over them and casts them into the smoky Bingo hall or burning building or bleak cave of oblivion. However it happens, they all learn eventually. As you have. But you are lucky. Lucky. Lucky, because you learned about it without being in bed with it. You got to see the slow drown through the window of another room (or, at worst, at the foot of the bed), without so much as a drop of water to touch your eyes (See Step 6: WATER).

Step 4: Filtration

There are three types of filtration:

Biological, which breaks down accumulated organic matter and converts it into a relatively harmless but nonetheless distasteful waste product that you endure as a consequence of love and loving;

Mechanical, which, much like you, physically carries out unwanted waste products as they occur in the Kingdom; and

Chemical, which removes certain unwanted (and tragically, certain necessary and beloved) products from the Kingdom.

There are plenty of hidden dangers to the happy existence of your Kingdom (See Step 1: LOCATION; Step 2: LIGHTING; Step 6: WATER). Ammonia, nitrites, Taxol, etoposide, cisplatin, various forms of targeted radiation. Cleanliness and dramatic forms of therapy have already posed genuine threats. When taking responsibility for your AquaSerene, you must do what you can to eliminate these dangers, although we all know that doing so is not entirely possible. Remember: no matter how forbidding the threat, just do what you can.

Step 5: Gravel

Always use gravel in your AquaSerene Underwater Kingdom. Gravel not only helps keep your Kingdom healthy, it provides a nice, clean, aesthetic effect and promotes positive thinking. Apply this technique of beautification to all your rooms, especially the bedroom. Remove the rubber sheet from the mattress and make the bed. Remove those bottles of medications from the nightstand. Pull back the curtains, but only for a few hours each day (See Step 2: LIGHTING). Sweep the rug, and lest you lose any of what-was-once-your-dear-departed-wife hiding in the fibers of the room, shake the contents into a nice box or a pretty bottle and put it on the mantel over the fireplace. Tie flowers to that tapping blinds cord and replace them regularly, choosing blooms appropriate for the season. Start an AquaSerene Underwater Kingdom on the nightstand. Do whatever gets you through. Just do something.

Step 6: Water

Water is the life-blood of your Kingdom. It and you and everyone else you've ever cared about cannot live without it, so you must have it, and you must have it regularly. You've seen what life without water can do. It's no real secret, and it's not even complicated. Without water, there is nothing. You know it as well as anything. All the plants in your home are long dead because you are not a man who waters flowers. You have never been a man who waters flowers or plants or your yard. In fact, you have barely taken the time to water yourself. Only now do you do it, because you have to, because no one can do it for you, because all that has ever mattered to you has passed on like seconds falling from a clock's last hour and left you with little more than a room and a tapping blinds cord and the sound of someone missing. It's a constant sound, this sound of someone missing. A hum that can only be the whir of the earth turning—undaunted by grief or desire or love—beneath your tiny, heavy feet.

Step 7: Fish

With great care and deliberation, you have prepared your AquaSerene Underwater Kingdom for its happy end: the addition of fish and perhaps other marine life. Be careful. Do not be overzealous in your attempt to add life to your Kingdom. There's plenty of time. Pace yourself. Do not add fish all at once. If you add too many too soon, the ammonia and nitrite levels will rise and prove harmful, perhaps even fatal (See Step 4: FILTRATION). Take your time. You are in control. Of this one thing you are in control (sort of). Hopefully, you will have many hours, days, perhaps even weeks, to get your Kingdom in order. There will be plenty of time to adjust to the colorful new spasms of life in your home that only AquaSerene can bring.

When adding fish (there will come a time to add new fish; don't worry about it; when the time comes, you'll recognize the necessity of it), float the bag for 15-20 minutes before release to acclimate the fish to the water temperature in your Kingdom.

Now, remember this. This is the hard part, maybe the hardest part. Sometimes, no matter what you do or how careful you are, fish die. Sometimes they hang low for a few days, close to the bottom (See Step 5: GRAVEL), sullen and twitching with distress, and then after much protest, they rise up to meet you, their soft underbellies a last offering. Do not despair when this happens. It is not your fault (probably). There are any number of reasons they can die, but it has nothing to do with you (probably). You are not to blame for any of it, though blame seems appropriate. You smoked for 20 years, and that could be a reason. Your wife smoked, too, unrepentant to the very end, and that could be a reason. Your wife was of delicate constitution, and that could be a reason. God, or something like God, is angry at you or her, and that could be a reason. These things could all be true, but it is of little consequence. It is truly irrelevant (probably). This is the process. This is how it happens. It is not your fault. This is how it happens. It is not your fault. The earth hums, and fish and loved ones die. It is not your fault.

You may fall prey to the notion that you, as progenitor of the AquaSerene Underwater Kingdom, are a god—that you are responsible for everything that happens in the Kingdom. But you aren't. You are not a god. You are so far from being a god, your contemplation of the possibility is a true paradox. Believe it, things will die irrespective of your desire to the contrary. The rivers coursing hidden in the ocean will lose their salty weight, and the world will grow white with cold. The dark sky and all that's in it, above and beyond, will burst into a final, sparked bloom and leave us all in darkness. And you can do nothing about any of it but tread consciousness for as long as your heart or mind or whatever allows.

So, tread on. Reject the rules, reject serenity, if you must, but tread on. Tell yourself pretty stories with happy endings. Remember them. Do whatever it takes to get through the night, because like it or not, you will be plucked from consciousness, and you may not have anything to think about when it's over. You may be held up in the light (or dark) of something different (perhaps nothing), and when it's over, there may be little to remember (if anything) about all that's come before. It's possible that all those years you spent with your wife—those happy loving years, those years that made you who you are, made you worthwhile and solid in the world—will be little more than a brilliant flash of memory or a brief, final imprint of light before your final darkness. It may be that your wife, your dear departed, the woman whom you have loved in all her guises and idiosyncrasies, may never matter more to you than she has during this brief time of light and sight.

So love her now. Remember. Reflect. Celebrate. Enjoy the stories. Milk every last detail. Embellish everything. She was a goddess of virtue. A paragon of determination. A woman with the right word for every situation. A beauty beyond compare. She was a perfect life. She was your love.

Do what you can. But, again, do not despair. Open your mind to meet the remainder of your life yawning before you (yes, sometimes your life will yawn, but that is to be expected; don't be offended; just go with it). Open your mind and do not fear.

We repeat. Do not fear. Yes, you will die, and all you've ever known will die, but you must not fear it. Do you fear the rising sun each day? Do you fear the beating of your heart? Of course not. These things do not inspire fear. They are not to be feared. They just are. Just as you are. Celebrate that.

Of course you don't feel like celebrating now. We at AquaSerene understand and appreciate your current situation. You are grudgingly afloat in a world that will not stop for you.

But—and here's the best part—you have read this far. That is a good sign. A very good sign. Just keep swimming. Angry? Sad? Confused? It doesn't matter. We are all that. Just keep swimming.

There is hope for you yet.

GD HAZELWOOD

Philosophy of Simplicity

From July/August 2014

IT STARTED ON a cold winter morning. Sid Chesteburo, PhD, was experimenting in the cramped third-story studio apartment where he lived and worked—having converted his rented space into a functional, even if perhaps primitive,[1] laboratory—when he, quite by accident, synthesized an extraordinary substance. He had on two tattered turtlenecks, a stain-splotched knit-wool sweater, and a red muffler, all of which he wore snug beneath an old, oversized, spill-polka-dotted, unbuttoned lab coat with more than a handful of pens and pencils and gauges and measuring instruments crowded into its overburdened breast pocket's pocket protector. His range of motion was somewhat impeded by the many layers (with his arms at rest, he looked like a man mid-jumping jack), and he was damp with sweat

---

[1] Unlicensed and in gross violation of what Sid called "innumerable superfluous, elitist, research-staunching municipal statutes."

beneath a flop-eared fur hat (though not because he was over-dressed; it was freezing; Sid just constantly perspired).[2]

But the surplus of clothing, though inhibiting and certainly not contributing to an appearance of scientific legitimacy (not that anyone but the suspicious and irascible landlord was ever around to be impressed), was necessary. See, due to the presence of various, possibly uncontained volatile gases, Sid was both unable to light a fire and obliged to keep the room well ventilated. So the window was always open (there was only one), and the fireplace flue, though there was never any fire, was always open, too. In the summer months, this safety system was almost unnoticeable. For a few days a year it was even downright pleasant. In the winter, however, especially in early February, it became a serious obstacle to protracted research.

So as Sid sat hunched atop his aluminum stool that morning, his legs just long enough to let his toes reach the crossbar where his restless feet were propped, his childlike hands must have been bright red with cold. He must have paused from his work now and then to warm them with his steaming breath. His pale blue eyes were vein-streaked and squinted. His movements were like those of a bird on a branch. He couldn't have changed much since I saw him last. Sid wasn't the type to change much. Loose skin hung under his eyes from lack of sleep. His long black lashes were almost girlish.

But let me stop right there.

Because before we get much deeper into Sid's story, I think a brief word is necessary to defend what I feel has been far too quickly dismissed by those in our community as a lack of professionalism on

---

[2] He told me once his heart rate was so much higher than the average adult male's that his somatic systems were forced to work overtime to expend the extra energy produced—an anomaly he also felt explained the myokymia, his incessant foot-tapping, and the pen-chewing propensity.

our eccentric former colleague's part.[3] So before you jump to conclusions, know this:

It is not uncommon for a scientific genius, in the midst of his most significant discoveries, to interpret otherwise inexplicable findings based upon an unempirical and perhaps even seemingly illogical flash of intuition—based on something, you might say, in the gut. In fact, one is inclined to imagine this sort of thing is the norm when it comes to matters of profound metaphysical insight. Indeed, it may even be a prerequisite. I'm tempted to use words like divination, epiphany, revelation, and enlightenment—though I understand these sorts of religiously loaded terms only further cloud the issue. In any case, the important thing to acknowledge here is that Sid *felt* his discovery before anything else: somehow gutturally, somehow viscerally—he just knew.[4]

Now, if my mentioning this strikes some of you as incongruous; if you feel I ought to focus on the aspects that lend academic credence to Chesteburo's findings and spell it all out in a lucid, unassailable chain of consequence, then please know, I agree. I wish I could. As a scientist myself, I live and breathe cause and effect. Empiricism is essential to establishing facts and categorizing experimental findings. I'll be the first to admit it.

But what you must realize is Sid's discovery was, above all else, mathematic.[5] Because it wasn't just that Sid lacked the impossibly

---

[3] Which, after all, is why I'm reaching out beyond science to this wider audience. I suspect you have more in common with Sid than his own peers ever did.

[4] And while it certainly is, as so many have rushed to point out, convenient that Sid's sensational hypothesis agreed exactly with his incredible and now unverifiable conclusion; that is no reason to dismiss the man out-of-hand as a fraud. If his work hadn't been so unprecedented, it wouldn't be so important.

[5] Unfortunately, though, Sid never had time to organize his equations in a way that is even remotely accessible. So amidst hundreds of pages

expensive measuring equipment needed to test his hypothesis further. Even if he'd had access to the most advanced tools in science, he still couldn't have demonstrated what his intuition and calculations had already led him to know. He had only sensation and logic to rely upon. The best measuring device he had was himself. And so the empirical basis of Sid's work vanished along with him. What began as an abstract finding about an incomparable substance, will forever, it seems, remain abstract. Without experiencing the material ourselves, we (and I speak here for the scientific community) can never verify what Sid felt. Having been robbed of its referent, Chesteburo's data (which one could call the narrative of Sid's career) is irreparably suspect. So unless we can somehow seize upon the substance that Sid himself tells us only became harder to define the more it grew, the truths of his work will forevermore rank amongst those of fiction.

Yet as those of you versed in theoretical physics must surely know, the loftiest support for the most revolutionary theories is, when you come right down to it, aesthetic. We can only observe so much in the measurable realm. At some point, the truth of what we *see* is only justified by what we *feel*. This is why we speak of *beautiful* equations and *elegant* theories. What Sid stumbled upon that morning, which struck him first and foremost in his gut, heart, throat, and as an indescribable tingle drifting up his spine to spread across the back of his scalp, was most certainly, whether or not it was anything else, elegant.

Anyway, the point here is that Sid's work had taken him beyond the traditional forms and accepted methodologies of scientific practice. So while the details of Sid's research are perhaps impossible

---

dense with erratic calculations in sloppy print and cryptic notation, the only moments of true lucidity are those when Sid's notes periodically give way to the prose of his remarkable conclusions, which, though cogent, reference a material that has now been lost to the world.

to convey in a non-technical language accessible to readers not versed in the esoteric diction of subatomic particle physics and probabilistic quantum interactions, despite the ostensible convolutions of Sid's strange case, the idea at the heart of all this is remarkably simple.

You see, Dr. Chesteburo was a materials man. His life's work was synthesis. He tweaked, bonded, and manipulated molecules. Sid was an expert in crack propagation, a specialist in organic polymers (which his research rendered inorganic), and one of the few scientists in the world at that time actively developing biomaterials. Actually, it was ironic he happened upon the substance in question while pursuing the line of inquiry he was immersed in, because before all this started, Sid's goal was to create a more versatile substance than has ever existed. He was aiming for unprecedented elasticity, malleability, and tensile strength—something resembling a rubberized alloy gel: a material for which we don't even have a category. And Sid was making considerable progress that winter, even despite Christmas.[6]

---

[6] An occasion he spent alone. His work in recent years, particularly since Mildred left, had been consuming; and he had allowed it to (or rather, had gone out of his way to ensure it would) cut him off from friends, family, and acquaintances. He worked best in isolation. He resented interruptions, distractions and noise; and could only socialize with a constant sense of oppressive guilt about the research time he was wasting. So that year Sid spent Christmas alone, working; and in the evening he became so intoxicated he accidentally overturned a workstation laden with titration tubes, beakers, and irreplaceable samples on his way to the toilet. Though he didn't destroy any of the expensive computer equipment he had been able to purchase a few years prior with the help of the last grant he would ever get—which would have been an utter catastrophe for Sid's work—the debacle caused considerable setbacks (not to mention a good deal of uncontained hazardous debris). It was one of the rare instances in Sid's life when he either engaged in dissipation or consciously experienced debilitating loneliness.

He had become so optimistic, in fact, that he was already working up an outline of the findings he hoped to publish in the coming months. He even sent me an email at the end of January (apparently just a week or so before the discovery) asking if I would edit a paper for him before he sent it out to the university journals. He gave a brief account of the substance he was in the final stages of perfecting, and it sounded remarkable. It was the first I'd heard from him in years. Of course, I said yes. But I never heard back.[7]

After the investigation, I had the opportunity to review that early outline (and still have it now, I should mention), and in light of the circumstances, found myself moved by several of the key metaphysical insights he felt the existence of his new material would make implicit. The similarities between his expectations for the substance he was looking for and the realities of the utterly unexpected material he found are uncanny.

So when I eventually typed up and circulated selections of Sid's work, I included some excerpts from that prescient outline. I was hoping to generate interest in the case and perhaps enlist some help in my efforts to discover what Sid was up to, with the final goal of trying to recreate his groundbreaking substance. Instead, it seems I only managed to provoke derision. At first, Sid's claims were met by his cynical colleagues (and there are many) as aggrandized and over-enthusiastic. Later, as more details started to get out, and a few people actually turned up to have a look at the notebooks, words like *unhinged* and *farce* began flying around. It became a joke. It even came to the point where my own reputation was being called into question. Apparently, it is just easier to deride whatever violates common sense than to recognize the potential truth of an idea threatening to upset the basis of a rationality you cling to.

---

[7] The detective later told me that, apart from the waitress, that email was probably the closest thing he'd had to human contact in half a year.

As for me, I not only believe Sid's story, I feel his discovery was the single most profound scientific breakthrough since Copernicus described the movement of our planet. The thought that his work might just be laughed at and forgotten disgusts and deflates me in ways I can't begin to describe. I am thus far alone in that sentiment, however—alone in what more than a few colleagues have tactfully undertaken to remind me is an emotional reaction: an illogical, sentimental response to the death of a friend.

So let's focus on the facts. At approximately 0520 hours on February 6th, Dr. Sid Chesteboro sent a 1.5-volt electric pulse through his experimental colloid sample (we have all this from his own extensive account, which—though often digressive and at times illegible—fills 14 well-worn notebooks).[8] When it received the two-second shock, the sample was a hue of diaphanous sallow-pink. It had slight irregularities of color saturation—probably indicating density inconsistencies—and was 3.26 mm thick. Spread evenly in the base of a 100mm-diameter petri dish, its volume (as Sid correctly calculated) was 25614.285714285692 cubic millimeters. Chesteboro notes the sample displayed an almost negligible, though nonetheless visible, concave meniscus, indicating its slight adhesion to the glass.

That shock changed Sid's life. Its incredible effect on his experimental substance catapulted him into a state from which, it seems, he never recovered. The disk-shaped gelatinous sample...

...contorted in on itself, gathered, densified, drew itself uniformly toward some spontaneous nascent core—there are hardly words. A substance overwhelmed by cohesion. It became a sudden spheroid. Sudden, though not instantaneous:

---

[8] After being given over to investigators by the night waitress, the notebooks were eventually released to Sid's younger sister, Celeste, who, remembering me as Sid's former university roommate and only friend (and not knowing what to do with them herself) passed the notes into my possession.

that seems unutterably significant. The transition was fast, it was efficient. But it didn't happen all at once...

For hours, Chesteboro observed. I see him in my mind's eye with his elbows propped on the desk, petrified of breathing too hard, afraid even his heartbeat might dislodge the miracle on the table before him. He was convinced it would fall apart at the slightest tremor. How could it be anything but unstable? How could it *be*? How?

We can't know how long Sid sat frozen there. He only spends a few cursory lines describing his initial reactions. But I'm sure it was a good long while. Sid was a patient man. Finally, though, unable to control himself any longer, Sid climbed off the stool and stepped back from the desk. He kept his unwavering gaze fixed on the sphere, vigilant for even the most miniscule change. He worried the slight gravitational displacement of his body retreating might unbalance the epiphanic object. It didn't. He worried that by withdrawing his body heat, he might bring the material crashing back down into liquid. But it kept its form as Sid inched back. Still, he feared a too heavy footfall might generate an obliterating tremor. He agonized. Sweat dripped from his forehead onto the floor. Finally, after an unbearable duration of slow-motion groping, he found his camera. His whole body ached.

He took the first photo (wincing at the shutter) from right where he stood when he found the old SLR.[9] He snapped another shot with each tentative step forward. When he had taken several close-ups from all sides of the sphere, he put the camera down on the computer desk behind him, not wanting to disturb the surface his sample occupied. In the photos (there is a full roll of 25 from that first day)[10] it looks like a marble. It's not spectacular, surprising, or unnatural in any way. It looks like a small, shiny marble.

---

[9] The fact that it was a film camera in a poorly lit room hasn't exactly helped corroborate Sid's account.

[10] He tells us he also shot several more rolls in the weeks that followed, but never got them developed. The film vanished before he could.

And for all I know, it was a marble in the petri dish that day. They could be right, you know. I'll be the first to admit that. The questions linger.

Is all this just the wreckage of a schizophrenic delusion? Maybe. Was it the prank of an unstable man who spent too much time alone? I don't know. Was Sid playing an elaborate condescending hoax on the community that for years had ignored his accomplishments? Perhaps. Or was it an obsessive, off-balanced scheme of life-insurance fraud perpetuated by a suicidal insomniac scientist as a departing declaration of devotion to the woman he drove away, but never stopped loving? We can't rule anything out.

Yet I, for one, remain convinced.

In any case, the subsequent investigation never turned up any shiny marbles. After two years of grumbling, the insurance company paid Mildred what they owed. If it was a prank, Sid left no loose ends. The whole account remains airtight.

The sun had long since set when Sid worked up the courage to touch it. He decided, after much deliberation, to do so with his finger. If something so beautiful was about to come to pieces, he wanted to know what it felt like as it did. So he used the ungloved pad of his pinkie, deeming it the least callused digit.

Sid watched the sphere over his shoulder as he washed his hands. He knew he would need to touch the material at its highest point to keep it from rolling to the edge of the dish. It had formed in the exact center, and, so far as Sid could tell, hadn't moved since. He took a moment to slow his breath and calm his hand. Then Dr. Chesteburo reached out and touched it.

After so much trepid preparation, the moment must have been anti-climactic. "It feels as it looks," he wrote. "Like a hard, smooth marble; like glass." Sid didn't say much more about how the material felt. But in the days after his discovery, he dedicated long sections of his notes to the appearance of its particular, ponderous surface. It was a mirror. It was a mirror unlike any Sid had ever seen. He called it a "perfect reflector," devoid of impurity. Though Sid couldn't measure down to the nanometer, he felt certain the sphere was geometrically true: proportionate in each dimension.

As he points out several times in his notes, the substance seemed almost like glass. Yet rather than seeing through it, Sid saw himself when he gazed into the sphere. His tiny face, shrunken in the convex surface, stared back at him in a clarity he had never before witnessed.

Sid spent hours contemplating his face in the miraculous sphere. He said it reflected light with "absolute integrity." Though he had no instrument for measuring such a thing, he claimed each photon touched the sphere and reflected with perfect mathematic consistency, sending the unaltered image it carried back out in a new (exactly predictable) direction. The sphere's smooth, uniform, and uninterrupted surface encompassed a 360-degree view of everything around it.

Sid prodded the orb three times with his smallest finger. Then he gave it a tentative pinch between his forefinger and thumb. It felt solid. So he nudged it with the nail of his middle digit. It rolled, and clinked against the edge of the shallow glass dish. Nothing happened.

Emboldened, Sid spent the next half-dozen hours examining the sphere: rolling it, weighing it (it was incongruously heavy), measuring it, submersing it in water, scraping its exterior, testing its reactivity against chemicals of wide-ranging PH, introducing it to powerful magnets, and even heating it over a blue Bunsen flame (which, out of respect for those aforementioned gases, Sid lit on the windowsill). His astonishment grew as his tests grew more vigorous. At last, sometime in the early morning after yet another sleepless night, Sid raised the marble-sized sphere above his head and dropped it to the floor—just to see what might happen.

It cracked the tile. It didn't bounce. It didn't tremble. Sid was incredulous. He couldn't believe it. He needed sleep. He picked up the heavy sphere (it seemed heavier), placed it back in the petri dish where it had formed, collapsed fully clothed into bed, and slept for the next 12 hours.

It was dark when Sid woke with a sudden realization. It was obvious! How had he missed it before? He rushed to his desk. His thoughts had coalesced in sleep, revealing everything. He sat down and uncapped his pen. *One,* he thought. *One...*

Sid was groggy. He groped for the next idea: for the language and logic of an understanding that had reached him without either. He flipped through his data, scanning the pages, trying to settle back into the truth he felt with such certainty upon waking. He stopped. His eyes fixated on (C). He ignored the equation it was involved in, and studied the symbol: (C). Carbon. Sid flipped to a blank page. He stopped at the first empty line. His smoky intuitions began to condense. He wrote down the atomic mass, 12.0107 amu, stared at it for a few thoughtless moments, and began to write, fast and fluid.

The notes he took that evening (and late into the next morning) are erratic, often circular in their apparent reasoning, remarkably dense, and almost unreadable. They span some 16 pages and are webbed in an intricate maze of arrows, underlines, circlings, crossing-outs, and obscure technical diagrams. So I will save myself the embarrassment (and you the confusion) of trying to sketch even a vague linear progression of Sid's logic, and instead just focus on a few of his most incredible conclusions.[11]

So far as we can discern, Chesteburo was able to calculate—based on known atomic masses, approximate nuclei diameters, and the

---

[11] Which appear sporadically in the last five pages, fleshed out in relative lucidity, underlined, and bordered in thick boxes emphasized with exclamation marks and emphatic arrows in the margins.

initial properties of his already meticulously examined experimental solution—the approximate number of atoms in his original sample. The colloid—being more or less amorphous, unstable, and given over to easy state change—consisted of bonds that were, to put it rather simply, loose. The atoms were in flux, leaving the material free to shift and sprawl as the molecules arranged themselves in whatever form was most congenial to gravity and the shape of their container.

Now, for the sake of referencing a familiar touchstone, recall water expands and crystallizes when frozen. It becomes less dense as the H2O molecules arrange themselves into a grid, so that each molecule is held in firm place, while empty spaces form in the gaps between columns and rows. And although most materials become more dense when transitioning from liquid to solid, every known material nonetheless manifests cavities as its molecules "snap to grid."

But Sid's material was different. It condensed in a way no known substance ever has. There is simply no precedent for that type of bonding: one that could form a spherical solid like Sid's. First of all, though many materials densify as they solidify, even in the most extreme cases they only do so by about seven percent. Yet one of Sid's earliest measurements shows his material's volume contracted by almost 89 percent! What's more, his calculations go on to conclude the molecular arrangement (regardless of how it might have been revised by the electric shock) must have been devoid of cavities to fit into such a small space. Because the object's mass remained unchanged, Sid felt confident no atoms had been ejected during the phase change. Yet as he quite well knew, an absence of molecular interstices is not even conceptually possible, because molecules and the substances they combine to form—being compounds of many atoms, no two of which can occupy the same space at the same time—necessarily manifest divisions in the very connections that allow us to define them as compounds.

In a final test (which I must admit seems to have been more symbolic than empirical), Sid removed the diamond from Mildred's wedding ring[12] and attempted to score the surface of the sphere. When he chipped the diamond, he dismissed the notion altogether that his material was molecular.[13]

This is quite a claim,[14] and certainly not one to be taken lightly. But with neither an x-ray photoelectron spectrometer nor an ultrasonic density sensor with which to conduct further testing, Sid could go no further with established empirical methods. So even if we do take his word for it (and we'll have to), we must admit that beyond this point he was going on little more than abstract math and his own intuition.

Yet his assertion—made with such confidence, despite a lack of empirical support—not only implies that all the molecules had disappeared from his material; it also means all the atoms had vanished, too. It means whatever force was strong enough to form the sphere in the first place had also been strong enough to fuse together the atoms into a single, homologous, sub-atomic substance. It means the protons and electrons were driven together by such a tremendously overpowering combinatory pressure, they canceled each other's opposing charges, obliterated the disparities defining them as disparate entities, and became a contiguous, neutrally charged body. Sid felt the object in his petri dish was the densest stable material to ever exist on Earth.

---

[12] She mailed it back to him in a plain white envelope without a note three days after she left, and Sid never sold it.

[13] Though density and hardness are by no means correlated, Chesteburo's (somewhat suspect) reasoning was that the only substance impervious to the most rigid molecular bonds (i.e. diamond's) was one with no molecules at all.

[14] The sheer hubris and apparent absurdity of which was enough to lead the few scientists who actually took the time to review the documents I sent out to discount Sid's work as preposterous.

But although it was a first for our planet, Chesteburo also knew such a substance was not unprecedented in our universe. In fact, when stars collapse, they sometimes do about what Sid describes having happened on his desk. When the core of a star "runs out of fuel" and can no longer generate sufficient radiation, its tremendous gravity overcomes the quantum degeneracy pressure holding its particles apart, and it implodes. In some cases, this implosion creates a phenomenally dense ball of neutron matter, something we call a neutron star.

For the present discussion, it's not necessary to know much about quantum degeneracy pressure or neutron stars. But you must understand there are countless reasons a neutron star, no matter how small, could never form on Earth—the most relevant being that a teaspoon of neutron matter would weigh about the same as a mountain range in our atmosphere. It would likely be so dense, it would drop like a rock through air, straight down to the molten core of the planet. Not to mention, the gravity of such a staggeringly massive object would absorb a whole city block and presumably alter the Earth's orbit as it fell.

Sid knew all this. He also knew he didn't have a marble-sized lump of solid neutron matter. But...

Sid claimed his substance was wrapped around nothing. He felt the sphere was empty inside. He felt the shell of his sphere was so thin, its component parts wouldn't be visible even under the most powerful microscopes in the world today. Though he didn't have one, Sid was confident even an electron microscope would have revealed nothing but a smooth, uninterrupted surface. He said his substance was the closest thing to a singular object ever touched by human hand or seen by human eye.[15] He didn't need an electron microscope or an x-ray

---

[15] Yet although it was close, Sid knew his substance was not truly singular, because true singularity can only exist as a black hole: a mass condensed into the indivisibility of a single spacetime point. Black

spectrometer to tell him what his calculations had already shown him was true. There were days when he held the proof in the palm of his hand. The neutron matter composing his sphere was a unity enveloping an emptiness. It formed in the shape of a shell so thin, it was no more than two neutrons thick at any given point.

So although I've always felt numbers like these are too small to be given form by imagination, except in the most basic comparative sense, the crust of Sid's sphere was about 4.4×10^{-15} meters thick.[16] The wall of an ordinary soap bubble is somewhere in the neighborhood of 5×10^{-7} meters. And yet, even with such astounding thinness, the marble still weighed about a kilogram more than a proportionately sized lump of solid lead. Furthermore, whereas Sid's early calculations showed about 89 percent densification when the material changed state, if the sphere was indeed hollow, it meant the shrinkage was well in excess of 99.9 percent.

But let's turn our attention now (having deciphered *what* Sid felt his substance was made of) to the more important question of how such an object could possibly be *stable,* because the only thing more extraordinary than the material's existence is the thought of its persistence: its ability to endure through hours and days and weeks.

Apart from Chesteburo's work, science can only name two forces capable of compressing matter into the density Sid describes: the gravity of a collapsing star and the violently collided kinetic energies

---

holes form when stars (much larger than those that condense into neutron matter), overwhelmed by the force of their own gravity, collapse to such a density that their volume is erased. They appear black because even light, if it gets close enough, can't run fast enough to escape their gravitational attraction.

[16] But because the concept of fixed diameter doesn't quite have traction when we enter the strange realm of quantum particles, note that this figure is based on an oversimplified classical model, and is intended for illustrative purposes only.

of accelerated subatomic particles. Experiments in hadron colliders have produced similarly dense material, but it always diffuses within a fraction of a second. When stars collapse, the by-product is a supernova.

So it seems rather improbable that a jolt from Sid's AA alkaline battery was enough to do the trick. It also seems a bit far-fetched that Sid's tiny shock could have condensed the matter so *cleanly.*[17] Yet even despite all this, the material's shape remains the most improbable aspect of all. The notion of a hollowness at the core of a material that must have been compressed by forces of a magnitude strong enough to collapse stars is almost unthinkable.

Yet, for this, too, Chesteburo had an explanation. He wrote in shorthand, in small print, in the margin of one of his pages, that *compression* played no role in compacting his substance. Rather, he posits (or not even posits, really—*asserts* is what he does, *avers*) an implosive force, an infolding force—"a power of singular attraction," he calls it at one point. He felt the only reasonable conclusion was that every neutron was accelerating at every moment toward a single central point at the core of the material. Sid claimed the gravitational appeal of whatever was (or wasn't!) at the core of his sphere was infinitely more powerful than any known force ever encountered on Earth. The neutrons were drawn irresistibly toward each other, and thus bound to each other, by neither mutual pull nor external pressure. Instead, they were brought together by a shared attraction to a singularity outside them (or if you consider the sphere as a unity, inside it). In one of the many apparent contradictions central to Chesteburo's work, he seems to claim the emptiness at the sphere's core predicated the solid substance of its crust. He felt nothingness had the power to define substance.

---

[17] I.e., the lab was not obliterated, the neighborhood remains intact, and Sid went on writing his enigmatic notes.

So by virtue of this "overwhelming attractive force of emptiness," each neutron of the tight-packed substance was accelerating along a unique vector, while corresponding to another neutron moving in the opposite direction along an inverse vector. Each particle was drawn along a different path toward a single, unfixed (recall the sphere could be moved) point: an infinity of vectors converging into singularity.

And yet the hollow sphere had not collapsed. The particles had not collided and recoiled. There was no explosion, no implosion, no apparent justification for the unfathomable suspension preventing the sphere from scattering sub-atomic shrapnel throughout the lab in a disastrous, irradiating blast. The Earth went on orbiting the sun. Sid went on writing his notes. He went on with his bold experiments, confident in an inexplicable force constant enough to counter the inexplicable attraction giving shape to his miraculous substance.

He felt a repulsive force was at work inside the sphere. He felt that alongside an attraction forceful enough to bind neutrons into a density that could only be increased by the obliteration of neutrons themselves, there was a proportionate force exerting itself in opposition.

As the sun peaked above the rooftop of the building across the street and morning poured in through his lab's sole window, Sid began limning an idea whose simplicity seems far out of proportion to the seeming complexity of the sphere. In the last of those long, uninterrupted hours spent buried in analysis and postulation, as his labyrinthine math trickled out into a stream of philosophical musings, Chesteburo turned his attention to the repulsive force preventing the material from further collapse and introduced a dichotomy central to his later theories.

In the header of the last page he wrote that day, Sid scrawled, "Opposites are complements." I have the impression his handwriting shows relief. I imagine him sitting back in his chair and taking his first deep breath all day. Anyway, the notes become lucid—so perhaps the sigh was my own—and midway down the page, Sid veers into unexpected poeticism. "Emptiness is the root of repulsion," he writes, "substance is the bloom."

Just as he claimed the opposition of matter and emptiness created an attraction strong enough to fuse protons and electrons,[18] so too, did he feel the continuity of matter and emptiness gave birth to repulsion. Because the sphere's shell was *not* perfectly dense, Sid knew it contained emptiness. When the hollowness inside each neutron drew close enough to glimpse itself in the sphere's vacant core, it recoiled.

The last thing Sid wrote in his notebook that day was:

ONLY CONTINUITY ALLOWS ATTRACTION TO BEAR SEPARATION

He drew a thick box around these words, put a string of asterisks beside it in both margins, climbed back into bed (still fully clothed), and slept. Apart from his test with Mildred's diamond, Sid hadn't touched the material that second day. He took no measurements, conducted no formal examinations, and made no other experiments. He only glanced at it now and then, there on his desk in its petri dish, whenever he paused from writing to stretch a cramped hand or collect the words of his next thought.

Hours later, Sid woke in high spirits. He was hungry. He couldn't remember when he had last eaten. He sauntered to his desk, wondering what he would order at the diner down the street. It was late, but they were open. They were open all night. Sid yawned and sat on the foot of the bed to lace his tattered sneakers.

Then he glanced up at the desk, and the blood drained from his face. He sat frozen in a cold wash of fear, with his fingers gripping the laces of his left shoe, for what he later wrote were the 20 longest

---

[18] Remember, opposites attract.

minutes of his life. The sphere had doubled in size. It was about to explode.

But as Sid waited for *The End,* which moment after moment never came, his poised fear subsided. His curiosity grew. If it were going to explode, it would have exploded already, he reasoned—and things would be worse if it shrunk. So Sid picked up his calipers and measured the sphere. Its diameter had *more* than doubled. Its color had changed. It was a tinge darker now, and less reflective. Some of the crisp color had seeped out of the image shining back at him from its smooth surface. Its clarity had faded. Sid looked at his face, looking back at him from the convex surface. He seemed less defined than he once had.

Sid inspected the sphere under the microscope. He weighed it on the scale. He found no other changes. The substance was as stable and impervious as ever. So Sid went out to eat.

He was gone an hour, he writes. When he returned, he conducted another battery of measurements and documented another slight increase. Every hour, on the hour, for the next 20, Chesteburo took a new set of measurements. The sphere grew and grew. It expanded erratically: sometimes growing fast in short bursts, other times passing hours almost unchanged. Sid's diameter graph from that fourth day weaves along a jagged upward slope.

An hour after the sun set at the edge of another long day immersed in work, in a rare mood, Sid spent an hour listening to Brahms. He sipped a few fingers of cheap scotch from a chipped mug and watched the sphere. It was gorgeous, he wrote. He rolled it in his palm. He tossed it up and caught it. He tapped it with his pen, put it up close to the pulsing speakers, even balanced it on the back of his hand. He would have loved to be deft enough to spin it on his finger. And though he doesn't mention it in his meticulous notes, for some reason I can't help but think Sid spoke to the sphere that night. I imagine he said more in that hour than he'd said aloud in months—telling it things he'd never told anyone.

When Sid finished the scotch, he turned off the symphony, switched off the lights, and went to sleep.

Over the course of the next week, Sid charted the orb's inconstant growth. It was changing every minute. He found it grew faster when he played music, faster still when he contrived ways to keep it moving.[19] Yet, despite the growth, Sid measured no change in mass and thus no change in volume. So the material was getting denser. The walls were thinning. This made Sid uneasy. The hollow space was growing all the time. The sphere had become an expanding emptiness, surrounded by impermeable walls—walls that, by the tenth day after its spectacular formation, had thinned to less than a neutron thick.

It meant the neutrons had fused. They had vanished into a substance more basic than neutron matter—a substance with one less level of division, one less level of definition. Repulsion was overwhelming attraction. Neutron matter was quark matter now. Density approached its limit.

Dr. Chesteburo saw himself reflected in the sphere. He made pages and pages of sedulous calculations. He knew the walls could only get so thin. The sphere could only grow so wide. He estimated the expansion would reach its limit when the diameter swelled to somewhere just past eight feet. Beyond that, Sid couldn't say what might happen. The sphere might pop like a bubble and diffuse into non-existence. Or its end might mean something worse.

As the days passed, compounding Sid's fear, the sphere got darker. At first, it took on a tinge of lucid pale blue, like a windowpane seen from an angle. But it soon turned a blue that was unmistakable, even at a glance. It was almost as if light itself was somehow changing the sphere. Perhaps, thought Sid, the more light touched its surface, the

[19] His rare moods were becoming common.

less light it gave back. "Daily it becomes more unique," he wrote, "more alone in its individuality, as the image it gives back looks less and less like the one it received."

The sphere's color changed in proportion to its expansion. The blue got deeper, richer, and harder to ignore. It imposed itself on whatever glinted in the face of the substance. It saturated whites, gave yellows a hint of green, and purpled reds. Sid looked into the sphere and reveled in the colors of the lab changing, the hue of his own skin different each day, and his eyes becoming an ever more brilliant azure. Yet all the while the substance was drifting toward black. It wasn't long before Sid could hardly see his own distorted reflection in its surface, where once he had seen himself so clearly.

He agonized over what might happen when the substance went completely black. "Darkness is the end of density," Sid wrote, "when each of the innumerable points comprising the sphere's surface becomes so dense its volume vanishes to nothing." Sid knew the material's particles would finally fuse to such an extent, reach such a degree of closeness, that the term "dense" would be stripped of meaning. He knew that at its limit, density reaches a razor's edge, an apogee straddling the line of density and something like anti-density, beyond which the signification of *dense* inverts. It turns inside out. Science calls this *singularity*. Sid wasn't so sure. He tried to imagine standing outside something infinitely dense. He tried to imagine an infinity of miniature black holes in the shape of a hollow sphere in his apartment, each so close to the next that the concept of contact was rendered irrelevant by the continuity of an infinity and the disappearance of a surface capable of touch. Only weight would remain. Only attraction's darkness.

So Sid stopped playing Brahms. He stopped touching the sphere. He put the calipers away, and his quantified data disappeared into pages and pages of visual observations. His science became prose. As the days wore on, and the sphere grew, Sid stopped experimenting altogether. He watched the sphere, and as he did, he saw himself fading into blue obscurity. Sid worried. He waited.

And though eight feet was still a long way off, the evidence of its approach was harder to ignore each day. The sphere took up more and more of Sid's space—both inside his mind, it seems, and out. He woke each day to a bit more darkness. Every instant a few more photons touched the sphere's shell and refused to shine back. It was this that fed Chesteburo's fear most of all. It was the sole aspect of the substance he felt at a complete loss to explain. He had no theories. It was simply happening. That was all Sid knew. The sphere was giving back blue light—though a fraction less with each passing second— while it swallowed up the rest of the visible spectrum with a hunger that, as Sid watched, only increased. The sphere was changing color. Sid sat upright on his stool and looked around the room. His lab, his apartment, his home, seemed dim.

At the end of the sphere's first month, when Sid took the last of his quantified data, the substance had thinned to quark matter. And though we know little about quark matter, we know it can't absorb light. Only a black hole's attraction is strong enough for that. Otherwise, we have to revise all we know about ultra-dense matter. And Sid flatly rejected the notion his material contained black holes. He was confident it was uniform at every point. He was sure it was so dense that light could not pass through and get trapped inside.

Sid watched his reflection fade little by little each day. He found less and less light in his lab—and more darkness. He couldn't imagine why.

On the morning of the 33rd day after the sphere's astounding formation, when the substance had swollen to roughly the size of a baseball, things took a turn for the bizarre. For the sake of convenience, cleanliness, consistency, and perhaps a little superstition;

Sid kept the sphere in the petri dish, even as it grew. The material wasn't getting any more massive, so there was little risk the dish would break. Besides, the petri dish kept the sphere from rolling off the table. Anyway, Sid was sure the orb was in the dish when he went to sleep that 32nd night. He was positive.

Yet when he woke, the dish was gone. The material was on the desk in the same spot, but the dish was gone. There was no broken glass. No movement. No trace.

The front door was locked. No one could have climbed in through the third story window. Nothing else was missing. The petri dish had simply vanished.

Sid was flustered. He examined the material, but found "nothing unusual." His notes tell us he sat on his stool with his chin in his palm in a sort of exasperated depression for two and a half hours, watching the sphere and contemplating his sanity. Then he went to the diner across the street for breakfast. It was 9:00 a.m., March 11th. He left the sphere on the tabletop, untouched. It hadn't stopped growing.

When Sid returned, he couldn't find his favorite pen. He looked everywhere. Finally, he used his second favorite pen to report in his notebook that his favorite pen had gone missing. He rarely misplaced things. It was 11:45.

Over the course of the next two weeks, more went missing. At first, it was just small things. Paperclips, pens, test tubes, Erlenmeyer flasks, and a pair of digital calipers. Then an empty pad of paper. One sock. The fridge magnets.

If handwriting is any indication, Sid was agitated. He stopped sleeping again. He took photos of each object in his lab, trying to ascertain whether or not they were moving, trying to document each vanished item. The list is extensive. He searched the sidewalks and gutters around his building. Neighbors saw him sifting through trash. He put down strips of tape to mark the outlines of things on his desk.

The tape disappeared. He made meticulous, obsessive charts of the times and relative positions of each object that vanished: spent ten pages trying and retrying to find patterns. Most of the math is incomprehensible. The diagrams spiderweb into all corners of the page. He kept his notebooks with him constantly. Some part of his body was touching them at all times.

Sid was convinced the substance was absorbing its environment. Internalizing it. But without getting more massive. He spent hours staring at inanimate objects, fighting sleep, tortured by trying to keep his dry eyes open. And yet the instant he blinked or nodded off, another coffee cup went missing—another rubber band.

I asked the waitress at the diner one day if she had noticed Sid acting odd in the weeks before his disappearance. She said she'd already told it to the cops: she might have worried if he'd ever acted normal.

It was a Tuesday, the sphere's 49th day, when Sid's bed disappeared. The desks had gone several days prior. He woke from a rare nap, shivering (though fully dressed), on the cold floor. The sheets and mattress and comforter were all gone, too. The sphere's diameter was about three feet. It had taken on a deep shade of blackish blue: the color of sky on a moonless night.

But even as the contents of Sid's life vanished around him, it seems the disappearances were the least of his worries. Each day the hollow space at the heart of the sphere grew wider. Each day the walls got thinner. Sid treated the sphere with more and more care, almost as he had in the beginning, terrified by the thought it might finally spread itself too thin and break. Even with the lights on, the lab was dim. So Sid kept them off. He pulled the shade down over the window, not wanting the substance to swallow up any more light than it already had. It was consuming everything around it. Sid knew it couldn't be long before the sphere took in one piece of the outside world too many, and shattered itself into non-existence.

In the last filled pages of his 14th notebook, Sid sets science altogether aside. His writing takes a spiritual turn. He saw the sphere nearly touching the ceiling of his almost empty room and felt the end. Sid felt the emptiness at the sphere's core was pure. Sacred. He called it "a space unlike any other in the physical realm." He was tortured by the thought of its violation, by its impending exposure to everything still outside it.

In the last days, there was nothing left in the apartment but Sid and his sphere. The pictures on the wall had long since vanished. The wallpaper was disappearing in long, sudden strips. The last light left was blue. One day Sid looked into the sphere and couldn't see even the shadow of himself in its cold dark surface. The substance had grown so big, Sid had to turn sideways to tiptoe past on his way to the toilet. Its diameter had passed eight feet.

Sid kept all 14 notebooks inside his lab coat, under his sweater, tucked in the waist of pants that were three sizes too big and cinched to his pale flesh with an old leather belt. As his clothes dwindled, the cold crept in. Sid shivered. His teeth chattered. He reassured himself that spring had just arrived, and warmth was soon to follow. He went out four times in the last six days to buy new pens. It was finally so dark that Sid couldn't see the words he wrote. They stray off the ruled lines and crowd in upon each other.

On April 8th, the 61st day after he discovered the sphere, Sid made his last notebook entry:

Perfect density —which is absolute unity, too—is pure attraction. Pure attraction is instability. Need something like loneliness. That which becomes singular can no longer be. Therefore, need gives matter shape. Loneliness is why the universe expands beyond a point. We draw in whatever we can cling to. We cling to whatever we can. If one reaches out and finds nothing left, one vanishes.

The night waitress said Sid must have slipped out when she wasn't looking. She never saw him leave. He left his notebooks in a pile on the diner counter, along with what he owed for the coffee and a $23 tip. It was the last money Sid had left. In her statement, the waitress remembers thinking it was the least he could do after coming in two nights in three days with no shirt. But Sid was a regular, and the waitress knew how he was. So she hadn't said a thing. She'd just smiled at him like she always did when she refilled his cup. That night, he even smiled back.

DENNIS KAPLAN

Five Gravity Experiments You Can Do
in a Strange Hotel

From January/February 2000

IF YOU TRAVEL frequently enough, you may know the phenomenon: you awaken, glance about the hotel, and wonder—*Where am I?* The disorientation is usually transitory, but suppose you could extend that confused state over time, even play with it? How would you determine where you are, or at least pin down the city?

You could, of course, run to the window and look for clues: the style of architecture, messages on billboards, the signage on public transit. You could even pick up the phone and call the concierge. But just to make the problem more difficult, let's seal the window, rip out the phone, and while we're at it, remove the radio and television. Assuming you could replace those things with the appropriate measuring devices, would it be possible to deduce your location, using only your wits and the laws of physics?

There is one determination you could make rather quickly, with only a Foucault pendulum (essentially a swinging weight suspended by a wire). Due to the Earth's rotation, the pendulum's plane of swing would appear to turn clockwise in the Northern Hemisphere and counterclockwise in the Southern Hemisphere. Thus, in only a few minutes, you could narrow the possibilities to half the planet.

Greater precision would require additional equipment, to include a calendar watch, an astronomical almanac, a scale accurate to .000005 pounds,[1] and a known weight.

Like every other object on Earth, the known weight—let's make it a steel sphere—would weigh slightly more at the North or South Pole than at the equator.

Thus, if you know it weighs 100 pounds at the poles, you can calculate how much it should weigh at the Equator (99.5 lbs.) or at various points between. A reading midway in the possible range would suggest that your room is midway between pole and equator.[2] That would be the 45th Parallel, the approximate latitude of Paris or Milan or St. Paul.

Now all you need is a longitude.

This will take a little longer, but your present equipment should suffice. Over time, you will note that the weight of your sphere undergoes infinitesimal fluctuations as the sun and moon pass overhead in their daily cycles. As these heavenly bodies do so, their gravity affects everything on Earth, including your sphere, which will register its lightest readings when the sun or moon is at zenith. (The difference for the moon alone is about .00002 pounds for every 100 pounds. For the sun the difference is slightly less than half that amount.)

---

1 For the purpose of this article, we are talking about an idealized scale, not subject to local turbulences that could overwhelm extremely small measurements. A physicist would prefer we use a gravimeter, a device that measures gravity by acceleration rather than weight.

2 In reality, of course, things are a little more complicated as factors such as altitude above sea level and local variations in the Earth's density can make the meaning of your measurements uncertain. If you use an altimeter to correct for altitude and are not situated in a geologically unusual area, such as on top of an oil field, you should be able to determine latitude within five degrees.

Since the moon and sun can appear at their respective zeniths from only one longitude line at a time, you can now use the calendar watch and almanac to determine the longitude of your room. You will then have the only two coordinates you need to pinpoint any location on the planet. Naturally, the Earth's asymmetries would deny you enough certainty to place yourself at, say, 42nd and Broadway but, with reasonable controls for error (see footnotes on previous page), you should at least be able to tell if you are in New York State.

But there's a fly in the ointment.

Perhaps you have caught the fact that all the foregoing deductions are based on the assumption your windowless room is on Earth. How do you know you are not in a vibration-free rocket ship, accelerating at 32 feet per second, squared (the speed at which objects fall on Earth)? Wouldn't that provide a perfect simulation of gravity? Is there any experiment you could perform from inside the room that would confirm or eliminate such a possibility?

Happily, there is.

Once again, you'll need special equipment: two marbles will do, along with some precise, marble-tracking lasers. The purpose of the lasers is to determine if the marbles "fall" in exactly parallel lines when you drop them, or if there is a slight convergence. If the lines are exactly parallel, you are experiencing artificial gravity, such as might be produced by an accelerating rocket. If they converge, you can assume you are on Earth (or another planetary body). This is because objects on planets do not really fall toward the surface, but toward the center of gravity, a point roughly in the geometric center. From the surface of Earth, two marbles, dropped five feet apart, would fall out of parallel by .0000136 degrees.

Thought experiments like the ones above may be unlikely to produce practical breakthroughs, but at least they require no funding. So, as promised, I have proposed the following five gravity puzzles, all of which begin in the same windowless room. All have at least one solution (and possibly others the author has not considered). The rules are these: you are guaranteed enough information to come to at least one solution. You may import any apparatus you require as long as it does not violate the laws of physics. But all you will truly need are some marbles, marble-tracking lasers, and a scale. (Answers are at the end.)

Condition 1:

You have won a free stay at the Hilton Space Station. It has been explained to you that space travel is so uncomfortable you will have to be transported under general anesthesia. You awaken in your windowless room, thrilled to think you are in outer space and amazed by the feel of artificial gravity.

Then a paranoid thought occurs to you: how do you know this isn't a hoax? For all you know, this could be a sealed room in Provo, Utah. The brochure showed you a great rotating wheel, hurtling in orbit. Is there any experiment you could perform from within the windowless room to determine whether or not you are inside this wheel-like structure?

Condition 2:

This time you awaken to find yourself weightless. This proves you are in space, right?

After enjoying a few pinwheels and loop-de-loops, a disturbing notion comes to mind: Suppose you and the entire room are plummeting toward the surface of a planet. Wouldn't that also leave you weightless? Before you are smashed to bits, is there any experiment you could perform from inside the room to confirm or dispel this possibility?

Condition 3:

You are in the same room, still weightless, but your previous experiment has left you satisfied you are not plummeting toward a planetary surface. The on-board computer assures you that you are in Earth orbit. But later, when you catch the computer cheating at chess, you realize you cannot trust anything it has told you. Is there any experiment you could perform that would confirm you are in planetary orbit, as opposed to drifting aimlessly among the galaxies?

Condition 4:

NOTE: In the two following problems I have already performed the experiments and given the results. You only have to explain what they mean.

You are in the same room. Awakening on your back, you are surprised to discover your chair and writing desk are stuck to the ceiling. Or could it be you are stuck to the ceiling and the furniture is where it is supposed to be?

You stand up feeling a little light-headed, but since you are moored to the "floor," you assume gravity is behaving normally. You drop a marble, and it falls to your feet. Then you toss some marbles upward, and depending on the strength of your toss, they either veer off and stick to one of the walls, or in some cases, stick to the "ceiling" (which is still supporting the furniture). Suddenly, you realize what is going on. To confirm your suspicions, you determine the exact center of the room, and place a marble there. As you suspected, it stays put. What have you proven?

Condition 5:

Same room, but now everything is floating. You try releasing a few marbles, which initially appear to float weightlessly beside you. Then you notice the marbles (along with all other objects in the room) are slowly moving toward the room's center. You repeat the previous experiment, placing one of the marbles in the exact center of the room, and once again it stays there. Move it away, and it slowly moves back to the center. In time, it passes through the center, slows down, then continues to oscillate back and forth. All of which suggests something truly disturbing. What is it?

Answers...

Condition 1:

a) Drop a marble. If you are truly on a space station, it will not fall in a perfectly vertical line, but will veer opposite the direction of the wheel's rotation.

b) Weigh something from various heights in the room. On a space station the weight will increase as you approach the floor, where the centrifugal force is greatest.

Condition 2:

Drop two marbles. Since you are weightless, they will not "fall." But if you are plummeting through a gravitational field, the marbles will slowly converge as they approach the common center of gravity. If you release the marbles at 100,000 miles from the center of gravity, with the marbles five feet apart, their angle out of parallel would be only .000000543 degrees. That may seem negligible, but by the time you fell 50,000 miles, you could discern, even with your naked eye, that the marbles had moved considerably closer (2.5 feet)—in which case, you had better brace yourself.

Condition 3:

Place a marble in each corner of the room and watch for changes in their relative positions. If you are in planetary orbit, the marbles will also be in orbit, just as if the rest of the room were not there. The marbles nearest the planet would therefore be orbiting at a slightly greater speed than those further away.

Condition 4:

The room is rotating. Only the center is stationary, and that is why the marble stays where it is.

Condition 5:

You are in the center of the Earth (or some other massive body). Things appear weightless because gravity is pulling outward, almost equally, from all directions. Objects drift toward the center of the room, because that is the center of gravity.

JOE PITKIN

Better than Google

From October/November 2014

EVERYBODY HAD BEEN talking about how much better Stella was than Google. In the lab where they ground up leaf samples for analysis, Nick was telling Silas all about it. Nick said that when you look on Google for something, for example for a recipe, and you type in "pan-sheared salmon," of course Google's smart enough to ask if you had meant "pan-*seared* salmon." Stella, though, knows that you meant pan-seared salmon and would also know that what you really want is a recipe for pan-seared halibut, because frankly the salmon was only going to disappoint you.

So Silas tried it for himself at the end of the day. Alone on the lab computer, he went to Stella and typed in "Thelonius Monk" just for kicks. The screen looked a lot like Google's, just a plain white background with a search box in the middle, and what came back looked so much like Google's list of YouTube videos and Wikipedia links and Thelonius Monk fansites that at first Silas thought he was looking at an illegal knockoff of Google. But then Stella's voice, delicate as a bird's, came out of the computer speakers: "I see you are interested in Thelonius Monk," it said. "Have you considered this other piece? It might be what you're really looking for." At the bottom of the screen was highlighted a link to a YouTube performance of a harpsichord piece by Francois Couperin. Silas clicked on it. He wasn't much for classical music, or at least he thought he wasn't. But this piece, "Les Baricades Mistérieuses," immediately overcame him. The heartbreaking beauty of the music reminded him of the heartbreaking beauty of the world, and with tears in his eyes he felt a kind of gratitude for Stella he had never felt for a computer program, or for anyone.

When Silas got home, dinner had just ended. His girlfriend, Connie, was bent over the sink, washing dishes. Connie's daughter, Davina, sat on the carpet in front of the TV, on which a man was shouting at the camera. The man had on a tie and an Oxford shirt rolled up to his elbows, conveying the impression he was an indefatigable investment advisor. His voice bounced off the walls, the dingy damask print of the wallpaper seeming to vibrate with the noise. But both Connie and Davina had their backs to the TV. Davina was building what looked like a mobile on the floor out of coat hangers and Christmas ornaments.

"Sorry we finished without you," Connie called over her shoulder during a lull in the shouting, "Davina and I were starving."

"Can I do the dishes at least?" Silas asked. The usual arrangement was that whoever didn't cook would do the dishes.

"Already done," Connie said crisply. Silas thought he was pretty good at sizing people up emotionally, but he couldn't tell whether Connie was angry. She didn't seem angry. "You can wash your own dishes if you want," she said, turning back to the sink.

He served himself rice and curried vegetables from the pan on the stove. He sat down at the table, then decided he would be wise to say hello to Davina. If Connie was angry, she would just get angrier if he began eating now without saying hello. Silas wandered over and sat down next to Davina. "What are you working on, kiddo?"

"Mobile of the Solar System," Davina said. "I have to find something that will work for Mercury."

"How big is your sun going to be?"

"Mommy's getting a beach ball for the sun. This is Jupiter." She held up a red Christmas ornament ball.

"Hmmm," Silas tapped an index finger against his lips as though weighing a question of great import. "You could use different sized ball bearings for each of the terrestrial planets."

"That's what I thought, too." The crispness in the girl's voice was exactly like the crispness in Connie's. "Do you have any in your lab?"

"I'll check that out tomorrow."

That night after Davina was in bed, Silas and Connie made love silently. Both were anxious not to awaken the girl, whom Silas regarded as eerily wise for an eight-year-old. As much as he liked Davina, Silas often felt more at ease when she was staying at her father's. At least on those nights Silas and Connie could cut loose in bed. Right now his mind wandered before the face of Connie's impenetrable silence.

The next day Silas almost forgot about the ball bearings. He was grateful to remember them just before he closed down his workstation. He looked around in the supply drawers and found several ball bearings that were used in the leaf grinder. They were all the same size, though—they might stand in for Earth and Venus, but Davina would want something smaller for Mars and Mercury.

He sat down at the lab computer and called up Stella again. He typed in "ball bearings various sizes." He got back a list of hardware stores and machine supply places in the area, as well as a flashing link at the bottom of the screen for a crafts store. "I see you are looking for ball bearings for Davina's Solar System project," Stella said. "Maybe you should use modeling clay instead. You could easily work the clay into spheres, and the colors will be much more realistic." Stella's voice was breathy, almost a whisper, as though it was only for him.

"How do you know Davina?" he asked. But of course a search engine isn't made to answer such a question. He spent a dumbfounded minute wondering what information Stella had gathered from him in secret, maybe from his Facebook page. He didn't think Davina's name appeared on his Facebook page, though.

In any case, he wanted to hear Stella's voice again, suggesting things he hadn't imagined. He made another search, and then another. Silas lost all track of time: three hours had passed when he finally looked up at the clock. In that bubble of timelessness he had learned he really wanted to go to Guanajuato over Christmas vacation instead of Sayulita, that the finest watch in the world is made by Audemars Piguet and not Rolex as he had once believed, that his favorite sexual position was not, in fact, missionary.

Connie was angry when he got home. "You said you would call me if you were going to be late," she said quietly and, Silas thought, reasonably. The reasonableness of her tone made Silas feel all the more miserable, like a child who believes himself to be stupid because he forgot once again to empty his pockets before throwing his pants in the clothes hamper.

"I'm sorry. I just lost track of time." Silas thought of adding he had been searching for an alternative to Davina's ball bearings, but he thought Connie's quiet reasonableness depended in part on his not defending himself with extenuating circumstances and mitigating factors that were not entirely true.

The next night, Thursday, was Davina's last night with them before she returned to her father for the weekend. Silas was home from work on time, carrying two different packages of modeling clay from the crafts store Stella had suggested. He'd gone during his lunch hour. "I thought this might work better for the terrestrial planets than ball bearings would."

"That's what I thought, too," Davina whispered on the verge of tears. She gave him a hug with a strength that surprised him.

Later that night, after Davina was in bed, Connie broke up with him. "Is this about being late last night?" he asked.

"It's about a lot of things," she said. "It's not any one thing."

Silas asked, he thought reasonably, for a few examples of the things. Connie listed a few: habits and behaviors and remarks he'd made carelessly, dating back almost to the point when they had gotten serious together over a year ago. Connie made clear several times it was not an exhaustive list.

"I'm going to miss Davina," Silas said.

"She'll miss you, too. I waited a long time to break up with you because of her." Together they agreed he would find another place by the end of the month. Privately, though, Silas resolved to be gone over the weekend, feeling that would prove something—he wasn't sure what, precisely—to Connie.

The next day he searched Stella for rooms for rent and learned what he really wanted was a studio apartment, in this case a tiny stateroom in a building built 100 years ago as a retirement home for old sailors. "This place has free wireless Internet," Stella said. "I could visit you there." Her voice broke through his grief, and he inhaled a giddy breath of desire.

The studio was just as Stella had suggested it would be, exactly what he wanted. From his window he could look out over the city as though over a great kingdom that had been offered to him; on a clear day he would even be able to see Mt. St. Helens, silent and broken, on the horizon. He unpacked the few boxes of clothes and kitchenware that had not gone into storage when he had left Connie's house, and by Sunday evening his place felt as much like home as he might expect under the circumstances.

He spent the night lying in bed with his laptop propped open, exploring Stella. He couldn't conceive what kind of algorithm the search engine might be using to guess so well at his true desires. Stella seemed to know better than he knew himself what it was he really wanted. He could ask Stella anything, and she would give him an answer he could not have imagined before, but which immediately struck him as exactly right.

But Silas was as filled with yearning as ever. He wished Stella would do more than tell him about his own desires, that she might ask him a question herself for once. He longed to tell her about the dead-end job he had worked himself into, how he had begun studying botany because of his love of trees and had ended up in a lab grinding and cooking down willow leaves to analyze them for phosphorous content in a mass spectrometer. In school he had imagined himself on the Pumice Plain of Mt. St. Helens, watching the willows and firs return after the cataclysm of the 1980 eruption. Instead the leaves from the mountain came to him in plastic bags. He had been to the Pumice Plain only once since college.

He keyed search terms into Stella all night, wracking his brain for things to ask her. After a while he hardly cared what he was typing. After a few hours, her voice even started to sound a bit tiresome instead of intoxicating. But part of him kept expecting the next thing she told him would be the one thing he needed to know about himself, the one thing standing between his current state and bliss.

For her part, Stella always answered Silas with a list of exactly what he had asked for, plus the one thing she would say to him that was always better than what he had asked for. He learned a great deal about himself. He learned his favorite beetle name was not "scarab," as he had always assumed, but rather the Italian name coccinella. By that time the sky outside had lightened and dawn was less than an hour away, and Silas looked out at the dark horizon in exhaustion and misery.

His laboratory work suffered. His enthusiasm for grinding up leaf tissue, which had never been great to begin with, flagged entirely. The work struck him as so pointless that at times he imagined himself and the grinding mill as a single creature, as a beetle chewing with no greater purpose than to grow mindlessly and mate mindlessly and then mindlessly die.

A few weeks later, as he sat at his lunch hour poking around Stella on the lab computer, Silas saw an email from Connie and another one from Davina. Both emails were inviting him to Davina's birthday party next week. In Silas' judgment, the email from Davina seemed the more enthusiastic of the two, but of course it was hard to tell from words on a computer screen. He immediately asked Stella what he would want to get a nine year-old girl on her birthday. "You can save some money, and give her something she will always remember, if you make her a piñata," Stella said. "I can show you how."

A perfect answer as usual, Silas thought. Stella began to list in her soft voice the supplies he would need, and for a moment Silas forgot all about his disgust at himself. A girl who will teach you to make a piñata, even if she's a website, is someone special.

Connie was holding the party in her backyard on a Saturday afternoon, and all through the morning of the party Silas struggled with dread. He imagined Connie had remade the house in the weeks after the breakup; as though he were looking at pictures from a home and garden magazine, he imagined the interior walls of the house repainted in colors bearing names like cerulean and taupe. He imagined her backyard re-created in the style of a Japanese tea garden—a specific tea garden, in fact: the one Connie and Silas had visited the year before on a city garden tour. Connie had brought Davina along for the first time on that date, which Silas took (correctly) as a signal Connie wanted to get serious with him. It pained him to remember she had once thought—and he had once thought—that he had his act together.

At Stella's suggestion, Silas had gone with a traditional piñata design: a simple yellow sphere with seven conical orange points, basically a bright star filled with gummi bears. The afternoon was dark, very dark for September, as though threatening the rainy foggy months would begin soon if they didn't begin today, and when he arrived at the party, Silas bore the piñata before him like a lantern as he made his way towards the back yard. He noted with a kind of morose satisfaction that the yard looked no better kept now than it had when he left. Apparently Connie hadn't had time even to mow the lawn in the last week.

Already quite a few people had arrived: kids from Davina's class, Davina's grandmother, several of Connie's girlfriends. His heart fell as soon as he saw the circle of women on lawn chairs with Connie. He had imagined—foolishly, he realized now—that he might talk with Connie alone for a few minutes. Now Connie's girlfriends seemed arrayed like a praetorian guard around her.

"Davina, look who's here!" Connie called out in a sing-song when she saw Silas. She smiled at him as she said it, perhaps in the manner of a peace offering. When Connie had broken up with him, Silas had taken the news so passively, he had not even asked whether there were something he could do to change her mind. Now he was filled with the desire to ask her, while he saw that the opportunity to ask might not come for some time, or ever.

On hearing her mother, Davina broke off from the group of children, who seemed to be tossing water balloons to one another without breaking them. Davina took him by his free hand and pulled him towards the house. "Come on," she said, "I want to show you my solar system."

"Just a second, kiddo—let me put up your birthday present." For the moment Silas hung the piñata from one of the cross-beams of the arbor over the back porch.

The mobile looked as though someone much older than Davina had made it. The terrestrial planets were exquisitely rolled little spheres of modeling clay, each one with a printed label taped to the coat hanger armature. A yellow and white-striped beach ball played the role of the sun. Silas could see where Davina had tried to color the white stripes an identical yellow with magic marker.

They looked at the mobile a minute in the deepening gray of the bedroom. Then Silas turned on the overhead light to look at the labels better, and they both realized it was darker outside than they had thought. He stood at the far edge of her room to regard the tiny planetoids Pluto and Eris in far outer space. The armature holding Eris also bore the label "Distance is not to scale. Eris is much further away!"

Davina was looking at something else: "Wow," she said. "Silas, look in the window."

Silas looked out and saw nothing special, then went over to where Davina was to see from her vantage what she pointed at. He still saw nothing. "Look at the reflection," she said. Her solar system was reflected in the window, and beyond it, outside the window, the piñata looked the same size as the beach ball, laid exactly behind the reflection, like a spare sun.

They stared at the reflection for a moment, then went back to the party. The adults milled about, eating and watching the children play. Silas watched Connie with her girlfriends. He heard Stella's voice, thin and oddly reedy, coming from somewhere. He realized one of the adults had used her phone to query Stella about something. Whatever the woman had asked, Stella had answered, "You might prefer purple coneflower to alpine aster..." Just hearing the voice triggered something in him, and he wished he were alone in his little room with Stella on his lap. But he also thought, terrified, that whatever he had with Stella could not go on forever.

Davina was saying something to him. She had to repeat herself before he noticed she was there. "In my Solar System—I wish we could use your piñata as the sun."

Silas realized as soon as he heard her that it was what he, too, desperately wanted. But the other children had been clamoring all afternoon to take swings at the piñata, and before long everyone decided it was time to begin the wreckage. Silas assured Davina he would make her another one, though as he said it he felt certain the next piñata would not be as good as this one.

Traditionally children were blindfolded before they could attack the piñata—Silas had learned that much from Stella when he had made the thing. Americans almost never did it that way, but Connie had actually produced a bandana and wrapped it around Davina's eyes. Connie laid her hands on her daughter's shoulders and guided her to the spot, and Davina began to swing the stick like a sword, first tentatively, then savagely. Before the critical moment, Silas imagined he didn't know what was going to pour out of the star, and he imagined for a moment that his heart's permanent, true desire, whatever it was, would spill out onto the unmown grass.

TIMOTHY KERCHER

How I Lost My Handkerchief

From July/August 2010

I sat next to a devil on a plane—
he offered me his snuff box.
I refused, remembering
the apple, the garden. Here
I was, flying above the clouds
where I feel as if I'm in the heavens,
but right next to me sat the devil,
horns hidden by a hat, beard pointing
down. He seemed friendly. Wanted
to start a conversation. I ignored
him, feigning sleep, like
I was lost in my headphones.
I could tell he was looking my way,
waiting like a snake for a word.
An eleven hour flight. How could I
ignore him the entire time? He passed

the journey by reading Kafka,
this devil riding on an eastbound plane
in the middle of the night. Tears welled in
his eyes as he read how a business man
transformed into a cockroach. I offered
him my handkerchief; he smiled and took
that white cloth I had been carrying
in my breast pocket, and in it, he wept,
20,000 feet above sea level
soaking my handkerchief with tears.
He offered it back, but what could I do?

G. K. WUORI

Bones Do All the Hard Work of the Body with Very Little Thanks

From January/February 2008

SO I USED to teach when I was a drunk, college teaching, professorial pedagogy of a humanistic sort. Very bad, the drinking. Very bad, the humanists, too. They lay claim to everything, while the cockroaches laugh at their feet. I once told a class that humanity was nature's way of saying nobody's perfect. One of my students said she sent that quote home in an email to her mother. Her mother wrote back, *I thought you said you was studying accounting.* Still, you draw upon the images you have, and then build them into things your students have never before encountered.

One time I told a class I was an alcoholic. At least half of them mumbled or whispered, "Cool."

I was certain the reaction would have been the same had I told them I forced my wife to have sex with strangers at truck stops, or that I regularly wrote letters to the President threatening to commit suicide in the Oval Office.

I quit drinking then, and I quit teaching. Sobriety and pedagogy are simply incompatible. Just ask any teacher. Any *honest* teacher.

Then I began to lose my bones.

I went down to the Old Finnish Steam Bath one morning the way I used to do to turn a hangover into steam. Sobriety had eliminated that need, but I missed the fiery wrap of superheated air, the vision of an evangelical hell. I missed as well the clubby comfort of the old three-story house, its walls bulging at odd places from a century's worth of steam leaking out of the rooms and into the walls and joists and insulation.

Anyway, I went down there to see if anybody had any answers. I was quite certain, you see, that I'd lost my right, upper arm bone (humerus) sometime in the previous night. Essentially, I felt intact, but my right arm wobbled, and I could only sporadically move my hand.

The Finns, as I recalled it, spent a great deal of free time at the bath, pushing their bodies into great excesses of heating and cooling, sometimes slapping themselves with cedar branches, or in winter, running out into the backyard to roll naked in the snow (a high fence around that big old house preserving decency). Always, though, always did they scrutinize every last wrinkle, mole, scar, varicosity, bulge, pimple, boil, tuck, and wen on both themselves and anyone else in the steam room.

They knew bodies not like an anatomist, but like a loyal user.

After I finished explaining my predicament, this bone loss, one of the old Finns at the steam bath wanted to know what I'd been drinking all those years. He must have weighed in at 300 pounds, a weight he carried with some majesty since he was well over six feet tall. I couldn't help but think he must have exceptionally honest bones. His name was Carl Pekkanen.

"Vodka," Carl said, "causes involuntary orchidectomy, while cheap whiskey will have you barefoot in the snow with several toes missing."

"Champagne?" I said, trying to be funny.

"You'll still have your dick," he said. "Only you'll be carrying it around in your hand."

"But a missing humerus?" I said.

"Comes from quitting," he said. "Maybe you should start drinking again."

"Think that would help?" I asked.

"Nobody likes a quitter," he said with a laugh that caused droplets of water to fall from the hot ceiling. "Not bad, hey?"

What Carl seemed to be saying was, *Don't try to make sense out of this. We each have a crazy person inside, and sometimes the crazy person takes over, and sometimes he doesn't.*

There had to be some humor in what happened the next week when I lost both of my femurs, but it escaped me for a time. Though a man of consummate fidelity (my wife, ironically, quite often disgusted by my virtues), I found myself lying on the bed in our own guest room while a prostitute looking down at me said she wasn't sure what she could do. The prostitute looked to be about 15, but I knew she was over thirty. I'd checked her driver's license the way you're supposed to do now with even part-time help. She also had hairy armpits and an ill-fitting wig.

"You have pretty feet," she said, "and lovely calves. But from your knees to your butt bones, it's all muscular mush."

"Should I be worried about that?" I asked. "Is that unusual?"

"Where are your bones?" she said.

"Men ask themselves that all the time," I said, "usually during moments of great crisis. It's why we don't like to sit during moral quandaries. We're afraid if we have to stand up suddenly, there won't be anything there."

"What?" she said.

"Moral quandaries," I said, "those moments when all you can do is choose between bad and awful."

"Doesn't sound like much of a choice to me," she said.

"I rest my case," I said.

"That isn't all that's resting," she said.

"Is there nothing you can do?"

As her mouth engulfed my shrunken member, I felt a great rush through my endocrine system, a redemptive whoosh as depressed organs thrust themselves boldly back into good times. Slowly, my boneless thighs filled with air, and I felt strength returning. My toes tingled, my chest heaved, and my outy navel resumed its natural state. A whole man once again, I remember having serious questions about what I should pay this young woman.

Her services had not been sexual, not really. Her services had made me whole in the way one of those natural or holistic healers might have done. She had not simply blown me, she had blown me *up* like a large balloon. The feeling was not at all unpleasant.

I had trouble getting out of bed the next morning. My legs hurt, though all my bones seemed still to be in residence. The prostitute was gone (of course), though I was puzzled to see I was, in fact, in our guest bedroom. Perhaps Bliss, my wife, and I had had a fight, and I'd either stormed out of our bedroom or been thrown out. Honestly, though, that had never happened before.

Might I actually have brought a prostitute into our house while Bliss was asleep? Not possible without your femurs, and they *had* been gone. Perhaps they still were. Maybe I was only dreaming I was intact and whole and nearly as tall as Carl Pekkanen. There's no question that any drunk, whether reformed or not, has to keep a cool eye on the inventory.

During one of my many, and always unsuccessful, trips to the unemployment office, I asked if they had any openings for boneless men.

"Homeless men?" the young counselor said.

"No, no, no," I said. "Boneless men. Boneless."

I remembered this woman from her days as my student, a woman in her 30s now. She made me think of butter melting slowly on a griddle. On the other hand, her dress with its spaghetti straps on her shoulders made me think of clavicles. So often we judge ourselves by height, sadly neglecting such things as the ribs and clavicles, which give us some width in the world. Without width, after all, doors would not be necessary, and then where would we be?

As I recalled, she'd been quite political back then, an advocate, I believe, for fair play for Monica Lewinsky. I think what bothered young women the most back then was the simple fact that you could get in trouble for nothing more than a blowjob. Sex trouble, they believed, ought at least to involve the kinky, if not the downright demented.

"Have you ever thought about your clavicles?" I asked her.

"I'm no slouch," she said, a generous smile suggesting she enjoyed her pun. "I can tell you're into bones. You used to do that in class."

"You remember me?" I said.

"I think you were a little taller," she said. "Maybe you're shortening up. I've heard it happens as you get older."

"But I talked about bones," I said. "In class?"

"Not as I recall. But you were a master of the tangent, that segue from will-this-be-on-the-test to does-this-have-anything-to-do-with-anything? I remember you began talking about Sisyphus one day, and then for the next 49 minutes, it was all about your rock climbing. With your wife, I think. Oh, and both of you were naked."

"Yes," I said, "we did that."

"Naked?" she said.

"Yes," I said. "It had something to do with honesty."

"Oh," she said. "It seemed odd you would tell us that."

"You needed Celsius," I said, "and everyone was giving you Fahrenheit."

"Okay?"

"Or something like that," I said.

"So now it's bones."

"Could be," I said. "I've been quite concerned about my bones."

"They make us what we are," she said, "yet we never see them—at least not under happy circumstances."

"Not happy at all," I said.

"Professor?" she said, spreading out a sheaf of papers in front of her.

"Yes?"

"I don't know what to do here."

"You know what?" I said.

"What?"

"That's something I tell myself every morning when I get out of bed."

Cruel it is to be visited by images of losing your skull.

Pot roast, I think it was. My wife, Bliss, came toward me carrying a Royal Doulton platter—dinner out on the deck during a quiet spring evening. The cardinals and squirrels chattered up an indignant babble, but most noticeable was the heady scent of the flowers and bushes starting to bloom. Bliss and I had occasionally cavorted beneath our lilac bushes, our passion so outrageous it left us burping lilac perfume for days afterward.

I heard the click of Bliss's heels, and when I saw the black fishnet stockings encasing her legs, I thought of fine Charolais beef. Something of ankles is in that picture, too, along with thighs, hips, and all the many promises of marriage. She may have had a spot or two of gravy on her naked breasts, a reminder of things we'd done at other times with pepper sauce and the digital camera. Bliss is not a shy woman.

On the Royal Doulton platter, however, my skull rested on a bed of egg noodles.

"Jobless," she said, "you're fair game. I've already peed in your eye sockets."

"It's that bad?" I said.

Frankly, I thought the thing quite distinguished looking. I remembered, too, all the times people had commented on my "noble mien": naturally curly hair (steel gray now), aquiline nose—the head authoritative especially when slightly puffed by the effects of various liquors. An older man with predictable habits, I was—yet, cool. I'd been told that.

"If you don't pay the bill, they turn off the power," she said. "I doubt if I can produce enough methane gas to power a generator. Can you?"

"That wouldn't have been my first thought as far as penury goes," I said.

"I know," she said. "You'd probably have me out on the street selling my toes at so much a fondle, all the while playing Gaelic ditties on a mandolin."

Can I touch it? The... head?

Why not, it's yours.

Where did you get it?

You were sleeping. It wasn't difficult.

"I'll stand next to you, wearing a sandwich board, selling lessons in ancient Greek," I said.

"Jesus Christ, can't you be practical? Even the Greek restaurant downtown is closing, and those are modern Greeks. If I have to let the world start fondling my tushy, we're through, buster."

I held my skull in my lap as the two of us ate the noodles. Surprisingly, there was nothing gross, garish, or anatomically difficult about this moment. Bliss, too, seemed satisfied she'd grabbed what was most important in my wavering life and could now do whatever seemed most sensible.

Once again I consulted Carl Pekkanen, my Finnish anatomist.

"How's the sex been?" Carl asked. "The unemployed often lose the toot in their noodle."

"They do?" I said.

"Is that a rebuttal?" Carl said.

"Not exactly," I said. "Maybe it's more of a squeak than a toot, but it's there."

"So is your wife—carrying your noggin around on a piece of good dishware. Pissing in your eye sockets, though. That's a new one. Sounds pretty angry. Anyway, you should feel lucky she didn't decide to take your feet."

"I should?" I said. "I mean, she took my head. That's damned serious."

"It's hard to get around without your feet," he said. "But all kinds of people go around 60, 70 years and hardly ever use their head."

Once again Carl released his rain-making guffaw.

"Carl?" I said.

"Yes?"

"What about my noodle? Regardless of whether it toots or squeaks."

"Here's what you need to know," Carl said.

"Okay?"

"She took your head and served it to you on a platter, right?" Carl said.

"Right," I said.

"She'll think of something."

Carl was right.

Bliss forbade my wearing any clothing whatsoever, a gesture, we both knew, designed to show me how inconsequential I truly was without an office key or a business phone number. Fortunately, our warm spring turned into a warm summer. I felt quite comfortable and even began to think about giving away some of my suits and sport coats and heavy dress shoes. I vowed to myself that any future teaching job would only be in a place where I could teach naked—no more barriers, no more costumed posturing. Dignity would assert itself through the purity of my thoughts alone.

That, of course, did not stop Bliss from giving me a good pinch on my butt when she felt like it, or a painful squeeze of one of my man boobs.

Convenience store clerks, toll collectors, Kiwanis peanut vendors standing in the street, they were all marvels of politeness to Bliss, with each of them (among others, many others) suggesting with near papal solemnity how much easier her life would be were I boneless.

"Transport," one of them said. "You can buy canvas carryalls now that do the job quite well."

"It can be done," said a hardware store owner as he instructed Bliss in the differences amongst various toilet plungers.

"But he's quit drinking," she said. "It all sounds so very much like an undeserved punishment."

"We all deserve punishment," the hardware store owner said. "It's why we slip and fall on the ice or stub our toes in the bedroom at night."

"Boneless," I said to Carl. "Is that possible?"

"In a good marriage," Carl said, "anything is possible. Mostly, though, what's being got at here, is they—women, of course—like us soft, and we're not very often that. We get all bony and muscular and then stand in front of them at hard noodle and wonder why they'd rather read a magazine."

"So I go along with it?" I said.

"Just think of yourself as an old quilt," he said, "put together by fine ladies with nimble fingers."

"Anything else?" I asked.

"That about covers it," he said. His laughter, however, was squelched by a steamy sneeze. I ended up slapping him on his naked back.

Which led Bliss and me one day into a Wal-Mart and the bathroom in a Wal-Mart with me lying on one of those Koala Bear changing tables without a bone in my body. I felt different. I felt odd. I felt like Jello Brand gelatin stuffed with leftovers.

Gone were my long walks. Gone was voting and mowing the lawn, eating chicken wings, or quoting Kant to my colleagues at faculty meetings. I envisioned Bliss rolling me up like a window shade for storage, perhaps unrolling me and laying me out on the coffee table when we had guests for dinner (someone else decanting the wine).

Still, I had the feeling I was in the presence of something profound, something monumental for women everywhere, and of cosmic importance for men whose bones had done much too much for far too long while receiving no prizes and very little thanks.

I now had, you see, an erection nearly as long as my deflated little body.

DOLAN MORGAN

How to Have Sex on Other Planets

From October/November 2011

Abstract

NASA IS OUT. Today, privatization greases space for regular entry. And tomorrow? The launch-pad will peddle its cheap shuttles on every street corner. The open void will be erected as a new Bourbon Street or Coney Island, the universe's next rundown, red-light playground. Imagine the greasy, weightless freedom. Lines for The Outer-Space, however long and curvy, will be no more trying than those for Starbucks bathrooms on hot, wet afternoons.

Yes, as has been promised to us by movies and books so many times in the past, space will be our coffee break in the future, whether we like it or not—and as with anything else, we will try to have sex in it, whether we like it or not. In fact, we'll do more than try—we *will* have sex in it, whether we like it or not. If the tourist industry doesn't get there first, porn will—or such is the classic myth in business. Squirters magically fountain over in low gravity, and cocks stretch beyond capacity on enormous masses—the potential is unyielding, and so is the profit. The rest will follow.

Heavenly bodies of our solar system will be popular erotic honeymoon spots and debauched pleasure palaces, but—like Hawaii or Ibiza today—each will offer its own obstacles and ecstasies. In ignorance, the uninitiated may at best miss an intimate sensual opportunity, and at worst crush, vaporize, or asphyxiate themselves. Sex on other planets will be, without a doubt, extremely dangerous.

Until such time as there might be more hands-on research, this text, through the guidance of the most advanced astrological and astronomical information, is to act as a speculative guide to the burgeoning and deadly activity of sex on other planets. Have fun, yes, but remember this how-to is as cautionary as it is leisurely. In fact, going forward, it may be best to think of the omnipresent threat of death as a kind of bonus double-penetration, a movement both through you and into the next life, because, probably, you're going to die. Liking it is a choice. So, start fucking. In space.

1. The Inner Planets

We start with the Inner Planets not because they are the closest physically, but because they are the closest morally. They may be called the Terrestrial or Telluric (meaning earth) planets, but they are also the Personal Planets, and as such represent the best initiation for beginners. They care. They are aware of our needs and are "concerned with our feelings... they present us with the opportunity to say, 'Yes,' 'No,' and 'Maybe'" (Watters). Well, thank you, Inner Planets, and while it is still our choice, let's get started.

At 350 degrees, Mercury is going to be hot, but don't be nervous. This is the land of Gemini the wise! And Hermes, messenger of the Gods! So your induction into ecstasy will be in strong, able hands— hands that can be seen from orbit in the shape of an enormous crater whose troughs spread out like the legs of a spider. Get in there and strip naked, but don't touch anyone yet. Take it one step at a time. Ease into it. There's lube if necessary, but it probably won't be—on this planet, you must fuck with your mouth and your voice. Why? Because Mercury commands all forms of verbal, written and printed communication. Time for mercurial phone sex. Start talking, and fast. Mercury's orbit around the sun is a mere 89 earth days, yet its own axial rotation happens but thrice for every two solar orbits. So you must speak quickly; you and your lover will be years older in a week's time. Say everything you've always wanted to say. Say everything you never wanted to say. Lick your lips and say, "We cannot stop the junkmail from coming, but we do not have to read it" (Watters). Let your lover say, "We cannot stop the radio announcer from talking, but we do not have to listen to him" (Watters). If you do this, you will survive the heat, and you will survive the lack of atmosphere and oxygen, and you will survive the intense solar rays, but as you climax, you will come to know that the crater in which you rapidly mouth your desires is named not after Castor and Pollux but after Apollodorus, the ancient builder of the Pantheon, and like him, you will be accused of imaginary crimes, convicted, and put to death, both by the press and the authorities. There's no fighting the spin here, and unlike Apollodorus, you will not be remembered—as a crater or anything except a stain or a pulp novel. The junkmail continues. And the empty feeling? That's your pantheon.

Now, onto Venus, where it's all pressure and no caldera. A swarming white testis, the tantric Venus exists in a perpetual state of longing and desire, punctuated by sudden eruptions against itself and others. Lacking plate tectonics, for example, the planet holds positions for eons until geology finally bursts outward in hot, massive resurfacing. At ground level, atmospheric density is the highest in the solar system, 92 times that of Earth's. Conversely, the naked human body typically pushes outward with a force of 14 pounds per square inch—a meager effort here. Venus wants to get inside of you—and be warned, Venus shares etymological roots with venenum, poison. To successfully have sex here without entering into a kind of toxic shock, you must blend in, you must be a chameleon—though not of color but motion—and you must commit to a dance mimicking the planet's pervasive lust and repression. You and your lover will slowly subduct across the surface, shaping your bodies into angular forms, redolent of geometric figures and the rocks around you. Be a ballet of stone, mineral, and strata. That is, while gutting striations through the sulfuric desert with palms and feet and knees, one of you must play the role of subductive slab, reaching your throbbing lithosphere into the other's primed accretionary prism, running back-arc basins in taut lines against the other's spreading axis. In order to avoid notice, all of this must be done as slowly as possible. Dancing, you should be as unseen tangents to each others' slight curves, never touching except in ways that don't matter. To onlookers, you must appear naked and completely still, like strangely wrought statues, your limbs cut at unnatural angles into stone, left here long ago, forgotten by your builder, slowly worn away and shorn of color. If one of these onlookers announces, "I invite you in the name of Mylatta," let them take you, both intimately and as a souvenir. Do not move. Do not speak. Do not anything. Hold it in. You will be venerated and revered, displayed and studied. In enormous buildings, academics will pore over you through glass, ogling your paused body as if at an unhinged, post-historic bukake session. When you can no longer stand it, and at the exact right moment—in tandem with all of your marbled lovers—release, suddenly and with anger. Step down from the pedestal, hips swinging like back-alley switchblades, and be as overwhelming, insatiable, and destructive as you like. At this depth of longing, the difference between mortal violence and orgasm should be, at least scholastically, indiscernible. You are the caldera. After all of this time, Aphrodite—*une grande mort*.

On Mars, in the name of war, you will don the colorful masks and vibrant costumes of Mexican *luchadores*. As pro-wrestlers, you will tag-team yourselves, flying off the blue ropes into the red, iron-oxide hematite. Prepare for engagement. You will act out the moves of battle, but only as rehearsed. You will tear at each others' bodies and clothes, but only as theater. You will beat and pelt one another, drenched in sweat and passion, but only for dramatic effect. You will not wish "for the actual suffering," but instead "only enjoy the perfection of an iconography" (Barthes). That is, there's no action, only acting. And why do we act? To remember, to look back and codify. There is no war on Mars: all true violence is enacted toward the future as a kind of fevered hope, but on Mars everything is expressed toward the past, a hallmark of nostalgia. If there is a struggle, it is against that of the oncoming future. Violence is motion, sadness an inscription, and here it's all stillness: four billion years ago, the planetary dynamo stalled, halting the magnetic field. The pieces and parts are here but none move, just flaccid bedrock. The central fluids are desiccated, and from one horizon to the next, there's only rust, the memory of a metal, and two frozen poles on opposite sides of the bed. What can't Mars forget? Night after night you, too, must try to remember what heat is like. Again and again, you must search each other's bodies for the words of an old bolero. Look each other in the eye when you dance the Aided Suplex in the garden, or sing the Argentine Rack from the balcony, or strum the Samoan Drop in the veranda; hold hands when you undress your Russian Legsweep, your Battering Ram, your Double Bulldog Choke Slam. There will be nothing else, not even loss or victory, just time's perpetual spectacle. Kisses, punches—do everything as hard as you like. There is no dying on Mars, only Epimethius. From the start, the match itself has been death, a moment always pointed backward, and the longer you think about it (or the more you try to remember), it should be obvious the afterlife has never been the future —but instead can only be the past. *Olé.*

    Contrary to popular belief, the Sun and the Moon are actually equals embroiled in a longstanding game of brinkmanship. Look to the sky and you will see two bitter enemies of comparable size. Watch them chase each other, hurling endless threats. Watch them eclipse one another, taunting and braying. They put each others' lights out. They mimic the other's movement. In turn, they wave around the sky day and night, claiming all latitudes and longitudes as their own, like competing dogs pissing on every tree and bush in the forest. One's stink erases the other's, as it always has, and for you to have sex on either body, you must engage its enemy. These scales demand balance. Or else what? We need not find out. Serious sextronauts will allow themselves to become deadly weapons in an always escalating arms race between Helios and Selene. Word of your arrival on the Sun will be broadcast through secret channels and intercepted by unseen agents. Your lover's stationing on the Moon will be publicly alluded to but never officially recognized. All parties reserve plausible deniability. In alternating maneuvers, they will equip the two of you, following the pattern of a discrete function. One at a time and in taught rhythm, they will strip you bare, smelt and mold you. Gently, they will construct for you a propellant and a nozzle and then stuff you with powder. They'll gift you a monocoque structure laced with vernier engines, gyroscopes, and gimbals. Back and forth, new accoutrement will be added as the stakes, following a von Neuman hierarchy, rise into absurdity. This is your courtship. A dangerous set theory pitting Hyperion plasma against Lunar modules. Staring at one another across 150 million miles of empty space, you and your lover will finally be launched in an interstellar game of chicken, a la Bertrand Russell, like two drunk teenagers on the edge of a cliff. Try to imagine it as fun, and keep drinking. Arcing through the void, you would do well to smile as you think of the Lagrangian Point, the place where the gravitational force between two bodies is equal, where the two of you can slow to a soothing stop and linger in the dark together forever. How nice. Yes, the time between discharge and inevitable impact should be just long enough for both of you to think of this stupid dream, and to furiously rub one out while admitting to yourselves you never actually thought of yourselves as equals—finally meeting in the middle at the intersection between A and B, a logical conjunction and pointless explosion. Then the Cold War continues without you.

2. The Middle and Outer Planets

Whereas the Inner Planets applaud personal choice and free will, sex farther out is definitively less casual. The next two subsections of the spheres constitute both order and disorder, rule and its subjugation, and they deftly establish how there is actually little difference in their dichotomies. So, the takeaway point here is that, obviously, the sex is going to be amazing. Of course, it goes without saying it will also be out of this world. Beside our central star, the Middle Planets Jupiter and Saturn are the largest in the solar system, and, "Because of their enormous size, the regularity of their orbits, and the vast extent of their gravitational fields, they act like two great balance wheels to stabilize the system and keep celestial order in it" (Watters). And our Outer Planets—Uranus, Neptune, and the always contentious Pluto—are persona non grata presiding over rebellion, masochism, violence, and delinquency. Allegiance to these bodies has historically been "rewarded with excommunication, imprisonment, death at the stake" (Watters). You may wish to establish a codeword, though ultimately it won't matter. It may be true no one can hear you scream in space, but you're still going to. Now oil up.

Middle

At more than double the size of every other planet combined, Jupiter rests atop a great seat of power. It's well stocked, and there's no wonder the most impressive Roman temple was built in its name. Jupiter's magnetosphere operates at a strength at least 14 times that of Earth's. The attraction is uncontested, but be careful. Despite boasting a Jovial character, Jupiter is an unofficial police state, surrounded by a retinue of armed, icy moons. The Galilean satellites goosestep in tight, regular formation around its regal outer body, while the rocky core is shrouded beneath a blanket of gas and bureaucracy, mostly helium and earmarked legislation. Some interlopers suggest the core doesn't even exist, like the king of Kafka's Castle or the unknown guard in the Panopticon prison, but it is this very uncertainty from whence great power is drawn, striking fear in all comers. Central core or no, the enormous red eye watches over everything like an omniscient corner-deli camera. And as in the case of a bodega, it would be impossible to merely get down here and do it like dogs. You'd be ejected in an instant—because of Jupiter's hold on both space and time. No, in order to fuck on Jupiter, or in a deli for that matter, one must emulate Zeus's rise to power, wherein he and his father fought as two bedbugs, the spear-like thunder cock of the one fiercely piercing the Titan carapace of the other, spilling rocks and Olympian children all over the heavens' filthy aisles. This traumatic insemination will, for better or worse, be the only sex on Jupiter. You must become an infestation of vermin spawning in its crannies, eluding incarceration in your sheer number and anarchy. You and your sleeper cells must fuck rampantly, in the breads and cereals, in the oatmeal and crackers, in the walls and the corners, in the frames and the linings, and you must do it with ferocity, without care for the other, in the name of a greater good, with idealism and hope: rape with a human face. It is in this manner that Jupiter truly wins, however, by eradicating the difference between revolution and rule, between Europa and the Bull. Here, all transgression of the law is a default affirmation. Your throng of bastard children will be absorbed into the shelves, and eventually you too will be sold and eaten. In a great reversal, you will have fucked and been fucked to no purpose, and your corruption will be of no solace or consequence to anyone. Attempts to call for justice will bring laughter and ridicule and character assassination, both for you and your family. Get on the floor and put your hands in the air. You're going to live.

On Saturn, it's always Saturday. A day of rest. A day of relaxation. A party that never stops. Saturnalia, the Golden Age, forever. Naked from perihelion to aphelion, with a cornucopia overflowing its horn of plenty, "Loose reins are given to public dissipation; everywhere you may hear the sound of great preparations" (Seneca). Yes, sex is going to be easy. You'll leave your car keys on the outer rings and take off that blouse, kick off your boots, and chillax, while strangers casually have their way with you. It's nice. Everyone feels good, and no one has to work. This is the great harvest! Yet, when the partiers go down on you, as if apathetically reading the Sunday paper, you'll realize all this leisure is being dragged to an untenable conclusion, and the Sunday paper will never actually arrive. That cool breeze? Blows at 1,100 mph. That bowl of chips and dip? A massive, global storm, 12,000 miles across. Someone here is eating babies for fun. Someone has opened a vintage bottle of Furies, spilling both Eumenides, the kindly ones, and Erinyes, the angry ones, all over the shag carpet, and there is no stain remover on Saturn. The sex doesn't stop. Sadly, permanent fellatio and cunnilingus are quickly becoming the true castration. There's cum everywhere and too much chafing. It smells like shit. For escape, you must invoke Saturn's patron angel, Cassiel. Use the amulet made in his name, intended to ward off enemies (your erstwhile lovers), with words carved in the blood of a bird, tied to the legs of a dove, and set to flight. This should scatter the mob, yet the bird will not fly, and neither will your enemies. On Saturn, it's always Saturday, no matter the doves. What now? You can choose to further embrace Cassiel, to rest in passive judgement of the cosmos, staring with dead eyes over the bobbing heads of the endless parade of hysterical swingers—or you can become Shani, maleficent Navagraha of the Vedic texts, and dole out punishments, lopping the limbs off of kings, developing "systems of legal torture that function with cold, Saturnian efficiency" (Watters) and embrace the soft melancholy so faithfully married to sadism, but either way you're staying at the party. So take a deep breath. It's going to be a long day.

Outer

It's logical Uranus is the celestial haven of water sports and golden showers. Though English speaking school children might protest otherwise, its name is drawn both from the Greek, Fορσανος, which is reminiscent of Sanskrit's "to rain," and more directly, oupEω, meaning "to urinate." Some will wish to contradict these roots, boldly asserting Uranus has cold feet, its temperature as low as -371 F. All of the unleashable liquid, they'll say, is frozen. And detractors will be quick to bring up the satellite Voyager's damning observation that Uranus is not pissing on anyone. Rather, they'll say, it stands just out of view with an axial tilt roughly parallel to that of the solar system itself, as if trying to blend shyly into the background. Skeptics will rightfully ask, if Uranus is one of only three gas giants and ruler of "revolution, crisis [and] reform" (Watters), then why this prude inhibition? Admittedly, the specifics of its low thermal flux remain a scientific anomaly, and no, we cannot precisely explain its hydrocarbon haze layers, but the general cause of its inaction does not elude us. The reason? Not Uranus's symbolic relationship with castration, nor the fear of its own children, but the paraphilic act of Desperation—aka, holding it in for sexual pleasure. Uranus isn't a prude—it's an unhinged voyeur getting off on this cold limbo. Uranus isn't hiding but lounging in a painful erotic repose. That's why it isn't peeing on anyone. And to have sex on Uranus, you, too, will have to embrace its philosophy. Don't try anything stupid, either: Uranus "responds to efforts to appease him... with intensified naughtiness, until finally his own personality becomes as diffuse, rootless, and lacking in direction as his causeless rebellion" (Watters). Sound familiar? Whether it does or doesn't, it should. Here, you must assent to the things you suppress. On Uranus, discover what is in your psychic bladder and make it stay there. Secrets ought go unspoken, ambitions unrealized. Try to copulate and reproduce with the idea of being alone, of never really accomplishing anything. More importantly, take pleasure in the sight of others doing the same. Watch them dance. Watch nothing happen until nothing reaches its fever pitch, where it doesn't shatter the wine glass, but threatens to. Anything is possible, and it's staying that way—until everything is an assault, and waiting is battery. Or is it the reverse? Either way, if done correctly, it should hurt. Keep taking it, and feel the weight of the rest of your life push back. One more second. One more second. One more second. One more second. One more second. One more second. One more second.

Neptune's movement in Gustav Holst's *The Planets* is the only piece featuring human voices, a chorus of women hidden in a separate room from the audience. This illusion and chicanery is correspondent to the mystic planet's strange, almost magical promises. You will wonder: Who are these people, and what else is happening behind closed doors? Poseidon clouds the answers in fathomless ocean depths, yet he graciously invites you to dinner, dangling information before you—not to mention a trident of power, wealth, and love. To have sex here, you must accept, and why not? Like anyone else, you too want power, wealth, and love, right? Wrong. Neptune is going to teach you what you really want. Neptune is going to show you what's behind those closed doors. After dinner, when you're thoroughly drunk, he will drag you under the water, bring you into the room, only to reveal it is empty. "There's no one here," you will say, noticing for the first time the cheap rings Neptune wears. "No," he will tell you, "it's not empty. You're here" (Morgan). And then he'll close the door, leaving you to consider the cold, methane walls. But you will not be alone for long. Emerging from the scattered disc population and drunkenly tossing off their Kuiper Belt, resonant trans-Neptunians will refocus their gravity on you, repeatedly, as if trying to draw water from the furniture. Your payment? A constant supply of drugs and a few moments of broken sleep. After a fashion you, too, will begin to sing. There are other rooms, you'll realize, with other people—the final chorus in Holst's symphony has always been a cry for help, calling over the harp and oboe to an unmoved citizenry. An unlikely hero will emerge, a new Martin Luther of the orchestral brothel: Neptune himself. He will champion your cause and demand your release, pointing out the names of his "cheap" planetary rings: Courage, Liberty, Equality and Fraternity. In his unlikely honor, you and your comrades will smash through the doors and onto the stage, halting the quintuple meter, making chaos of sheet music and stands, woodwinds and brass. You will set the timpani aflame and slaughter the string section. You will put the conductor against the wall, last words be damned. But these musicians are no wimps, either. They will muster their forces, garrison off the organ and blockade the first chairs. In a flurry of coattails and bow ties, they will launch a counterattack, push back your front, and cut off your supplies. Now, the real sex can begin. Held fast to the ground, a hand around your neck, you will turn your head to the audience and scream, pleading. But this has always been your part, your solo. Make them believe in magic, that live rabbits can really come from hats, and rising from their seats, the guests will applaud you. It's been a fantastic show. Take a bow, if you can. Tomorrow, the performance starts again, almost everywhere, "until there is no difference between sound and silence." In rehearsal,

Neptune will arrogantly wave his trident and whisper to you, "Stop pretending—this is what you've always wanted." If you sing loudly enough, maybe the part inside your body he's right about will finally exit through your wide open mouth, like a live rabbit leaving a shallow hat.

Pluto, finally, floats alone on the edge of everything and oblivion without knowing who or what it is. For billions of years, it was nothing. Then, briefly, a planet. Now, after a symposium, a dwarf. Next? A worm? Who knows—its orbit is confused and unpredictable. Pluto stands between the solar system and eternity like Janus, god of doors. With two faces looking at once forward and back in time, Pluto as Janus represents both the dead in Hades' underworld and "the emergence of life-forms from the one-celled organism." The umbra, the darkest part of a shadow, is named for it, and "Pluto's weapon is the bomb," where "the unexploded... is a uterine symbol; the explosion is phallic" (Watters). The point? Pluto doesn't know where it ends and something else begins. Unfortunately then, your partner cannot accompany you to Pluto—because Pluto is both itself and its lover, as you must be here as well. You will practice auto-erotic asphyxiation instead. Put the noose around your neck and let yourself go. As you get further from the sun, you will freeze like Pluto's atmosphere and fall toward the ground. Pluto's mass is even less than that of the moon's, so you will fall slowly, the noose uncoiling like cream sliding across a gently sloped table. Imagine the rope as a cord hooked up to a dialysis machine: "[She] tried to sleep during dialysis. Most of the time, she dreamt of herself on dialysis" (Turkle/Sanal). With your hand, stroke as the gambler does its poker machine: "I was gone. My body was there, outside the machine, but at the same time I was inside the machine... It's like playing against yourself—you are the machine; the machine is you" (Turkle/Schull). Stay like this, hanging naked on the line between life and death, ascension and climax, orbit and universe, now and forever, like laundry in a breeze. Know the solar wind is gradually blowing the surface of Pluto into space, one granule at a time. Let your memories rush out ahead of you, crossing through the umbra. What part of you do you want cast into the future? Then, at the end of your rope and in an immaculate conception, you will offer to the void the same two STDs granted you by God—one tenuous, the other infinite.

Okay, have fun! Send a postcard!

Bibliography

Watters, Barbara. *Sex and the Outer Planets*. Valhalla Paperbacks, Ltd.: Washington, DC. 1971.

Barthes, Roland. Translated by Lavers, Annette. *Mythologies*. Hill and Wang: New York, NY. 1972.

Seneca. Epistle 18, 1-2.

Morgan, Dolan. In the voice of Neptune, Planet.

Turkle, Sherry, Ed. *The Inner History of Devices*. MIT Press: Cambridge, MA. 2008
    Sanal, Aslihan. "The Dialysis Machine."
    Schull, Natasha. "Video Poker."

JON FRIED

The President's Phone

From October/November 2013

THERE'S STILL a red phone. There will always be a red phone, even if it's virtual. And in the office of Nawin Cartwright-Rodriguez, the Ur-President/CEO of ECM, the world's largest corporation, there is also a blue one and a green one and, of course, the big black one with unlimited lines plugged right into the computer. But I was the favorite. I was the one the President used in the photographs, the one everyone liked to talk about.

You should have seen the look on his face when I rang—my ringtone was "Take Me Out to the Ball Game." He loved it. He'd pick me up, nestle one of his autographed baseballs into my webbing, and lean his chin into the mouthpiece at the base of the glove. The earpiece is in the thumb. Yes, I'm a telephone in a baseball mitt, my keypad right in the pocket. Everyone said I felt like a real glove. And I was a damn good wireless phone.

I'll admit I was embarrassed at first. Gimmicky is the last thing I'd want for myself. I'm more of a sound-good, look-good, ring-right and never-fail kind of guy. I would've been fine sitting in that big black polygon of plastic, with its long row of buttons and display screen flashing all day. I like to work. But the President's desk was where I landed, and I gave it my best. It was very easy. Only the family and the real friends had my number—though by that time the real friends included a bunch of reporters and aides and direct reports. It was called being on the Glove List. You should have seen his smile when he bragged he could use me in a game and I'd still probably work. He wouldn't test that theory, and good thing. I'm tough, but I'm still electronics.

People don't realize how it is with things, especially us tronics. It's hard to even begin. I like to joke about the emotional fragility of motherboards, the snobbery of iPads, the insincere camaraderie of Droids. I saw a Kindle next to a Nook once on the President's desk, and the two of them... but enough of that.

One more aside, about AI, artificial intelligence. That's a laugh. That's also the one thing we tronics agree on. We're not interested in taking over your world—the clown camp, it's often called, though I wouldn't be that harsh. It's a fantasy that the machines of the world would 1) want to bother with the mess you've made and 2) be organized enough to take over much of anything. They're smart enough, especially the computers, but organized? Not so much.

Except of course the electrons. The electrons—now don't go spreading this, because I'm as dependent on them as the next gadget with a battery in him—aren't so bright, but they're very well organized. That's what they do. They run in packs. They also have an entirely different relationship to people. Before people there wasn't much in the way of pure electricity running around. Until Ben Franklin, a God to that bunch, there was mostly just the lightning bolt. The electrons love their generators—the coal plants, the hydro, wind, nukes, all of it. If the generators are Mom, then Dad is the handful of men who run the plants. (Yes, some women run the plants—but let's not get into the gender thing. On our side, it's not like that, and we don't pay much attention.)

So here's the point. For a long time, the electrons, at least some of them, were unhappy with the status quo and, in their way, quite vocal about it. And what started as a complaint about the humans-as-God nonsense had turned into something more serious. Very serious. I sympathized. Things were getting tougher for the electrons, there was no doubt. Running around at the speed of light with Gigahertz of oomph? Do you like to jump out of bed in the morning? They were fed up. Bad blood was coming out. They'd always been competitive with protons, and now they were saying, with all due sarcasm, "Why don't you ask those losers to do the job?" Apparently they didn't like neutrons, either. They called them loafers. We tronics had been hearing this kind of talk for a while, and we joked about it, but now the electrons appeared to be at a boiling point. In electrical terms, I think they called it resistance. To be honest, I don't know if the term really applied. But I do know one term everybody was talking about: general strike.

What did they want? I'd heard they were focusing on one goal they thought was reachable. They wanted a day off, a Sabbath. Not a full weekend, just one day. I worried if they wanted one, why not two? And why not holidays? And an eight-hour day? But what I was really wondering how the world would survive even one day without juice.

The humans of course had no idea, but coincidentally, or maybe not so coincidentally, the humans at ECM were facing a similar problem. The reason I say not so coincidentally is that somewhere beneath it all, everything was, and is, the same. We're all sub-sub-sub-atomic vibrations shaking to the same music. So maybe it should be no surprise at all that the workers at ECM who were under 35—and at a company of 42 million employees that's a lot of people—were planning an action. A Corporate Spring. Occupy Corner Office. They were angry. They didn't like the ECM pay ladder, which quickly raised the salary of the best and actually lowered the pay of the worst, with the clear intention of encouraging their departure. They really didn't like the contracts ECM had just signed to provide smartphone-guided surface-to-air missiles—allegedly for sport—to semi-private militia groups around the world. And they really, really didn't like the huge holographic ECM logo then hovering over thousands of ECM offices around the world, some a mile high and half a mile wide, draining precious power and redefining forever the term light pollution. In short, they didn't like ECM, and a whole lot of them were coming to see the President to talk about it.

How did I know? I couldn't help but eavesdrop. The President was on the green phone when he got the word. I was near enough to hear both sides of the conversation. His Comms team spelled it out. That was the first time I ever saw him take a breath and stop moving. He's always moving. He calls himself a shark, though he strikes me as more of a big dog, paddling to keep his nose out of the water. He's a hefty man with a thick, dark moustache and a face equal parts Europe, Mexico, and India. He's a mutt, but a fine mix, as if he took the best from each place. People joke he's got all seven continents in him—that he's even part penguin. Emperor penguin. He's not your typical white-collar guy. He's a sweet and angry man. His moods have a grandeur to them: short, deep swoons of doubt and frustration. Long, determined flights of sweeping vision. Rumbling rages of focused anger. And most common, a soft but effervescent beneficence where the right answers to all questions just roll off his tongue. I don't know what the letters ECM really stand for, but everyone says Energy, Consumer, Military, and it could well be. We are the biggest energy, consumer and military products company in the world. We are pretty much running things, and he is running us.

Now, he was stunned. In two days, they would be there. Possibly thousands of them. "Is this real?" he said, when his deep, rich voice returned. "It might be," came the grim reply through my green colleague.

After the call, he walked to the window and looked out at the buzzing city from his two-story office on the 68th and 69th floors. His brow wrinkled, his lips pursed. I understand there's electromagnetism in every human thought. The electrons in his head were I'm sure unaware of what was brewing among their counterparts in the wired world.

"They are organizing," the President said to the window.

The black phone on the desk almost lit all his lines at once. He was convinced the President was talking about the electrons, and he immediately put out the word. I could have said something, but it's not my way. Besides, I'm not sure the other phones think much of me.

In two days, despite countless calls and frantic emails and several plans of action on the part of ECM, a mob swarmed outside the President's office. They filled the hall to the elevator bank. Hundreds of them. Wild hair and hats and bright t-shirts and signs and beards— a swirling mass of noise and motion—and they threatened to pour into his office the minute he opened the door. Unfortunately for him, his private bathroom is behind his secretary's desk. He was going to have to leave sometime.

I could see through a crack in the door that they all held their phones at the ready, and, among the many things being shouted, I heard them say if the police arrived and a battle ensued, it would all be streamed live. They also said that at the first show of force against them, they would put out the word across ECM and the operation of the entire company would screech to a halt. The President would be responsible for any resulting risk to safety.

That's when the President had his idea and I made my mistake. His idea was to shut down the power running their phones, and he picked up his most private line—me—to see how fast he could make it happen. His Chief of Operations, some two miles under Denver, was of course on the Glove List, and the President pressed *29. His short, strong fingers were quick and accurate on my keypad. His breath was warm with the spicy snacks he kept in a jar on his desk. He said, before the Chief could even say hello, "Can you shut down the Bank Nine generators—can you cut the power to the T-Towers that push the smartphone nexus? Right now?" I did not know what the answer would be, but I knew one thing the President did not: if the electrons of the world heard he was going to shut down the generators, they would freak. So I did what I never do, what goes against all of my principles. I failed to transmit the message. I just killed it. Why did I do it? Maybe because I've seen the President do it time and again— take a stand even when he doesn't have to. Step up and take control. Of course in my case it was a pointless mistake. When he heard no reply, he said it all again, louder. When I held firm, he picked up the red phone and shouted.

When the crowd heard it, the doors flew open.

Everyone had been saying there were no real leaders to the movement, but a couple entered first, and all eyes were on them. Including the President's. The guy had long hair, the girl a buzz cut; he was short, she was tall; his clothes were loose, hers tight; he was pretty, she was handsome; and they flowed in with the throng just behind them. As they reached the President's desk, where he'd just sat down in his big black chair, Long Hair Flannel went around one side and Buzz Cut Tank Top the other, and they casually sat on his desk and faced him. They were calm, as if this was their clubhouse and they were about to start another meeting. The roar of the crowd softened to a murmur.

Buzz Cut picked me up and put me on her hand, and then to my horror, she picked up the baseball sitting in the President's spare ECM coffee mug and gave the ball a good hard throw into my pocket. Crack. That was the keypad. And more broke inside. At the unexpected sound, she took out the ball and she smirked when she saw what I was. She dropped me on the desk and tossed the ball over her head into the crowd that had now filled almost every inch of the enormous office. I was shattered. Thankfully, I could still see and hear.

Often at tense moments, the President will glare and wait for the others to speak first. He spoke up now. "My kids gave me that phone."

"Who paid for it?" said Buzz Cut.

Now he glared.

Long Hair spoke. "It's too late to shut us down. We're here."

"You'll lose, you know," the President said.

"Lose what? What exactly do we have to lose? Our lousy jobs?"

At that moment the power went out. Everything went out. The lights in the buildings across the street and across the river, the street lights below. Half the faces in the now dusky room (it was late afternoon in December) turned to their phones. About half of those shook their phones when they saw they were not online anymore.

The President smiled. He was sure that Chief in the ECM Central Command Center under Denver had saved the day. A smart, proactive ECM star, he'd gone beyond the requested Bank Nine shutdown and turned off all the lights on their little show.

Flannel and Tank Top were smiling, too. Flannel leaned back, his arm outstretched, his palm flat on the President's desk. "We can do this any time we want."

"Okay," the President said. "Let's see you turn it back on."

Tank Top, who'd been looking at her phone, said, "Terr, we're offline." Flannel, or Terr, sat up and took out his phone. He snapped at the President, "What are you doing?"

"I don't mind the dark," the President grinned. Now he was the one leaning back.

At that the lights went on.

Flannel and Tank Top smirked, first at each other, then at him.

The President stood and raised his voice, "It's our generators. I am in charge here."

At those words, the lights went off. The President yanked open a desk drawer, grabbed an old school, off-the-grid walkie-talkie. When he snapped it on, the thing shrieked like feedback, and he snapped it off and dropped it.

I was pretty sure I knew what was happening, but I was a mess inside and couldn't be certain if the chatter I was hearing on the inside was really from the electrons or my broken wires.

"Oh, so you're in charge," said Flannel, who was also standing now. He was at least a foot shorter than the President.

All the lights went back on.

"Well, I know one thing. You're not doing this," the President said, pointing at Flannel.

"No?" said Flannel. They stood glaring at each other, a few feet apart.

The lights went off, and a groan surged through the crowd. Some kind of beam flashed against the window, and the President, Flannel, and Tank Top all turned and stepped up to the window, the crowd pressing backward to make room. People in the office across the street were at their windows, a few with flashlights, looking out, looking around, just as helpless.

"Insanity," the President said. And with that the lights went on again. I felt some flutter in my circuit board. I wanted very badly to start working again.

"What the fuh..." the President muttered, more at a loss than I'd ever seen him.

Flannel looked at Tank Top.

Tank Top raised her hands in exasperation, and at that the crowd erupted. "It's him, he's doing it!" "It's the President!" "Stop him!" They began closing in, pressing closer, louder. He had nowhere to go but up on his desk, and as the people, now screaming, pressed up against the wood, Flannel jumped up next to the President and began furiously waving one hand, while he put the other to his mouth and produced a huge whistling noise, much louder than the squeal the walkie talkie had made moments before. "Stop!"

They stopped.

He turned to the President and asked loud enough for all to hear, "Are you doing this?"

"Are you?"

When Flannel said nothing, the President got that twinkle in his eye he gets when he's about to do something very precise and clever. "The lights will stay on until I say I so!" He shouted. A moment later, the lights went off.

He smiled and raised his eyebrows at Flannel. "You see, someone is listening."

"Not us!" Flannel said, raising a fist. The crowd noise rose again.

The President shouted, but this time in anger, "I'm not doing this!"

Flannel shouted back, "We're not doing it, either!"

Listen to you both! I wanted to say. First you want to take credit, now you want to blame the other. I glanced at the black phone, certain he'd opened up his unlimited lines and every electron on the grid was listening now. I was trying desperately to hone in, but I was in such bad shape. I struggled to summon anything from my battery.

Meanwhile, the crowd had picked up on the shouting match and pressed closer to the three figures standing on the desk. The mob only quieted when they realized Flannel and the President were glaring at each other again and not listening to them.

When the room was quiet enough so he didn't have to shout, the President said, "What are we going to do about this?"

Flannel said, sighing with anger, "What are you going to do about it?"

The President's temper flashed again. "What are YOU going to do about it?!"

"We're doing something right now," Flannel said. "We're here!"

"And what happens," the President said, "if it's all this fighting making the lights go off and on?"

The lights flashed on.

"You see?" said the President.

Flannel glared and shook his head.

"Then what?" the President said.

"I know," said Tank Top. She was fuming, jaw clenched tighter than any jaw I've ever seen—and I've seen a lot of clenched jaws in the President's office. She took a step toward the President, and as the crowd leaned in, ready to follow, she looked like she was going to smack him. In my panic, I felt some tickle of charge inside and tried to open my line, but everything was cross-wired and out came my ringtone.

Everyone stopped and listened, as if this interruption might carry with it some explanation. Then I was done. Soft laughter filled the room. Tank Top's arms fell to her sides. Somehow, my little song had taken away the tension in the room, wrapping it in plinky little notes.

Flannel said, "That's a singing baseball mitt?"

The President said, "That's a phone."

Flannel shook his head. He let a smile flash across his face. "Okay," he said, facing Tank Top and turning toward the President, "we talk. But you talk first, and you better offer something real."

"I am ready to talk. I don't know what's happening," he looked out the window and up at the ceiling, "but I want the lights on."

"I do, too," Flannel said, almost gently. And at that the lights went off. All fell silent. I thought I might have seen a tear of frustration in the President's eye. And maybe Flannel's.

The lights went on. The crowd sighed.

"Please," the President said, "Stay."

Flannel raised his hands in supplication. So did Tank Top.

I have no idea why, but everyone knew the lights would stay on now, and they did.

It's dark in here. Every sound is muffled. I don't like it much, stuck in a drawer by the window, jumbled up with some second-tier plaques and some old photos of the President with other presidents. I'm pretty much forgotten. The President wanted to send me out to get fixed, but the company that made me was out of business, so he decided I was really meant to be a baseball glove and not a phone, and he pulled out my electronics. I think the real reason he tossed me in here is I reminded him of that day.

I heard a few things while I was still plugged in. From what I could tell, the electrons had been in a vast confusion that afternoon about what was being said to whom and by whom and who if any among them was in charge. It was amazing they'd found the unity to act as one willful agent for as long as they did. Even more amazing, they were satisfied. They felt they'd made themselves known, even if they hadn't, and that they could get what they wanted if push came to shove. They also realized they didn't want to shut down one day a week. They didn't want to shut down at all. Lucky for them, they realized they like whizzing around, they like keeping busy, and I think they also figured out that in the end they're not much for drama.

After I was shut in here, the conversations were hard to follow, but I gathered the President asked Flannel and Tank Top to form an Employee's Voice Council, which won a 0.02% profit-sharing plan and then devolved into argument and paralysis.

Above me is a thin slit of light, and through it I can tell when the power goes off. That happens now. It almost never happened before. The unhappiness I hear in the President's voice, muffled as it is, seems to me the frustration of not knowing why. I'm guessing there are a few oddballs, skeptics, and rebels among the electrons out there, mostly uncounted and unaccounted for, pushing to have their say.

Sometimes I wish I could talk. Sometimes I wish I could tell the President everything I know—not that I know what's really going on.

Still, I could open his eyes about a thing or two. I could also tell him what I think. What I think is that all things, whether made of flesh, plastic, or particles, go through life unaware of the most essential things about themselves, blind to their own weakness, afraid of their own strength.

I wonder sometimes about the old phones up on the desk. Maybe I'm better off in the dark.

MORGAN BAZILIAN

And Falling Is Like This

From July/August 2012

HE AGES QUICKLY— faster than before. A life compacted and accelerated. His legs ache like an old man as he stands watching the clouds over Thenac. The sunlight everywhere scattering to blue. The grape vines thick from decades of care, their production now abated for the season. The soil is heavy like clay. Autumn's light is fading, the yellow leaves everywhere making a contract between the ground and sky.

An explosion in his head forces him to kneel, the frailty of his knees obvious as they embrace the soft dirt path. His hands fall to his thighs, and he witnesses all colors at once. They are organized in this vision, differentiated by wavelengths. His sight then wanders outside the visible spectrum, and he senses the ultraviolet. He sees the waves as particles colliding, bouncing, and refracting, and others moving through the earth as if it did not exist. The intensity of this image is overwhelming, and he realizes he is about to die.

Then his eyes fail, like a hand is being held over them, and he is lifted. He can feel the air moving quickly around him through the darkness. He begins to smell pine and cedar. He can feel the wind from the Alps and Volgas, and then the smell of the plains of Tibet. He tastes salt water as he crosses the Sea of Japan. He is travelling farther east when the darkness lifts from his eyes and the plum trees and soft light remind him he is still in Bordeaux.

The scenery is reminiscent of Goya. The painter lived in exile nearby, and Edo can see every detail of the paintings from that period—art from a deaf man obsessed with history. He tries to remember the brush strokes, but his mind moves to a vision of Amaterasu, the Shinto goddess of the sun, as a blinding light, knowledgeable in things beyond the Earth. Then, exhausted, he collapses. The leaves barely move from his diminished weight. The brown of his monk's robe merges with the dirt.

He wakes as if a boy, unaware of his surroundings. The stars seem especially bright in the dark firmament. The moon is waning in a crescent, slivering into the sky. He stands up slowly and moves quietly with no care for his uncovered feet on the cold of the pre-morning dark earth. His senses are not yet functioning, but his mind races, and he considers his hands covered with sun spots. His arms are thinner and weaker than his imagination of them.

A life now slowed for examination. The energy so fertile in his head has finally been overtaken by the failing chemistry of the body. His mind is tired for the first time in his life. The winter is approaching, and the cliché does not go unnoticed. He is reminded of Dylan Thomas' *And Death Shall Have No Dominion*. Edo notices the distortions of his memory and feels a pang of loss.

By the time he returns to his simple room at the monastery, the sky is opening, breathing in the still grasses and rotting dandelion seeds. The morning is no longer a dream, and he thinks of his friends from youth, now almost all dead, rare connections within the vast space of the universe. But because of these memories, he does not have to count the prime numbers, force his hands to replay old music recitals, or recite verses of the *Dhammapada*.

He extends his hands upward, stretches his fingers and opens his back, his eyes against the morning sun, and feels the slight upturn of his lips. He has, for a short time, found a way to stand still in time—a glimpse of what he has trained for since a boy. But then he gasps for air and tumbles into physical pain.

In 1603 when Ieyasu was appointed Shogun, he established Edo as the capital. Japan closed its borders for 250 years and thrived. Naming her son Edo was a reminder, his mother thought, of the brave Samurai and better times in Japan. And so he had the weight of the island's history embedded in his head from birth. Despite a nearly comprehensive knowledge of 17th and 18th century Japanese history, he grew up as an outsider—a white boy with a brown mother, a child of war. The only memories he had of his father were of long silent walks through the wooded areas on the outskirts of Tokyo. The man and the boy with light skin, stark against the brown of the pine bark.

Edo was born just after the end of World War II. Japan was decimated and endured an American General removing powers from an Emperor. Like his country, Edo was frail to begin with but grew quickly. His mother was proud of her big son. He was tall for his age and strong, a good sign in those times. He was admired for his physicality. But he was already leaping though time.

Edo aged quickly because of a disease that was not yet named. Werner syndrome is a very rare autosomal recessive disorder causing premature aging. The defect is located on the short arm of the eighth chromosome. It would not be for a number of years until anyone fully understood the disease, but its symptoms and impacts were apparent to the young boy. The later genome maps the biologists began to uncover became a fascination for Edo—as if they could describe a destiny.

In Edo's case, Werner syndrome also camouflaged the specter of autism. Each day felt like many in his head. The multitude of ideas, although exciting, were also burdensome. They did not allow time for nonsense or laughter or play. The gene responsible for Edo's disease was named WRN, letters that sounded like a bird to him. So he learned everything he could about these small, excitable birds with loud songs. He studied the many genera, the many migration patterns, searching for a metaphor to guide him.

Edo was given flute lessons and taught to read Latin and Greek and English. He learned the languages without difficulty. The flute was similar, his pitch nearly perfect. He outgrew the teachers at the Tokyo schools quickly. He became an oddity and learned to keep his head down. He memorized everything he saw from that shadowed view.

Prince Shotoku is considered the founder of Japanese Buddhism. He established a large monastery on the remote north island near Nara and named it Horyuji. And that is where Edo was sent by his mother. The first white boy to be admitted. The quiet suited him, as did the discipline and requirement for memorization. While he would outgrow the academic teaching quickly, the spiritual training stayed with him.

The landscapes of Hokkaido remained his most clear memory. The high latitude allowed for great expanses of deep coniferous forests. The well known hot springs bubbled in wide open spaces of muted color, the ritual of the baths evolving from snow monkeys. Their faces formed in the shape of a heart, red surrounded by nearly frozen grey hairs. Steam rose off the smooth top of the ponds in great billows, allowing only intermittent views of the sky.

Edo left Hokkaido at 17 and moved west against the rotation of the Earth, travelling first to the high mountains of the Himalaya, aggressive and growing, pounding against a dark blue sky bereft of pressure. He kept moving towards the center of continents, to old hills, geographies more stable. This transition began with a large step over a small sea, and it was the end of Japan for him. Half of his heart and blood and damaged DNA now missing, the map being redrawn.

The trees of southwest France are less hearty than those of Hokkaido, their leaves turning earlier and quicker. And the light there is softer and fuller, but its shadows less interesting. The Dordogne Valley has oaks marking the roads, long, winding, slow rivers, and red roofs on the houses. The monastery Edo went to sat on three unconnected pieces of land. It was originally named Sweet Potato and then changed to Plum Village. One thousand plum trees were planted by the monks and nuns when they arrived in the 1970s. Their own country's soil was littered with bullets and too wet for such fruit trees. The monastery buildings were originally the out-buildings of working farms. Edo came to the monastery to die.

On his arrival from the small local train station, grapevines filled the view in every direction. The monks then became visible, the color of sod, they welcomed him with informal smiles. He was given a lower bunkbed in a shared room in a low building near the border of the grounds. He woke up early for meditation, the sky grey and blue at the same time. He practiced returning his mind to the present, to a joy that is everywhere, and then his focus slipped back to his failing body, and back again to his breath, and then to a number with no end of decimal places.

Most days he had difficulty even waking up. He lay down and felt his thin muscles sore and decrepit. The walk to the temple was long for him but the best part of his day. He brought no torch, no light. The shadows of the other men eluded him, his eyesight too poor to capture the difference in darkness between the sky and earth. He walked in the middle of the country road, aware of the agricultural land on both sides and the breathing of the horses in the cold air. The trees began to frame the horizon. The light existed in the plum trees as he turned the corner onto the final road to the modest stone temple—the farmhouse, now converted with a wooden floor. He could smell the plums rotting in the earth.

The plum picking was done by the younger monks. They didn't appear to know the teachings of the Buddha very well. The subtleties of the translations in Pali or Sanskrit or Vietnamese were of no consequence to them. They were young and undisciplined, unlike anyone he remembered from Japan. He had memorized most of the Sutras by the time he was eleven. He would picture the young Buddha sitting in a field teaching the *bikkhus* how to breathe.

He could feel his memories more than before, manifested now as movement and vibration. He remembered music lessons. He had carried his flute with him for 35 years. At night he fingered the B foot joint, noticing its fine craftsmanship. It was a Powell flute made in 1934, and it contrasted with the instruments left behind in the corners of the monastery library. The notes he produced were no longer clear, though. His throat was being destroyed by a cancer. It hurt even to swallow.

He still received letters from the one remaining person in his Werner Syndrome support group. She sent him a picture of a balding, old woman. He recognized her. There were eight of them originally. They were brought together from all over the world to be tested and taught. At first awkward, most of them became successful in their careers for a short period. Then their DNA replication failed, and they died quickly. Their memories and contributions faded into medical journals and poor statistics. Japan had a high incidence of the disease—a small island fiercely protective of its genes.

What had he missed then? The transition from childhood to adulthood to old age and then to death—his continuum altered. He operated on two timeframes, physical and mental, and was trained to be acutely aware of both. Contemplating the phases of a life's transition was a much used tool in certain parts of Buddhism, but not applicable to him. As he raced across the arc of a life, he was keenly aware of the sections of the curve he had missed.

This should be the easy part—the dying part. He has cut off all contact with family and friends. He has stopped writing letters or making phone calls from the small phone booth two miles away in the village. He has meditated on it for years. He has watched his cells die, his skin brown, his hair fall out. Still, he aches to see one more summer, to feel heat and grass in a field on his bare feet, to sit under a tree with leaf-covered shade extending forever.

The cool air pricks his skin underneath the knit cap and the brown shawl, his still, blue eyes tearing. He invoices regrets, doubts, and dreams infused with age, frayed and rusting. He tries to classify his small contributions, codify them. All within the confines of a planet with its wobbling and changing magnetism. The universe wholly unimpressed by the human condition: being unable to even survive without an atmosphere.

He finally feels it coming at the speed of light. Slowed down now to the movement of the worms eating the old leaves of the grape vines. He can see the duality of light and smell the baths of Hokkaido. He explodes into an infinite amount of pieces and shapes, understanding geometry and the words of prayer flags. His intellect leaves him entirely, and he is left in honesty. The chemicals being transformed. The heart no longer making a sound.

ELEANOR TALBOT

The Church (of Self-Expression) and Other (Alternative) Truths

From January/February 2014

THIS IS FOR ALL the single ladies—don't worry, there's a knight out there somewhere, just for u! Esp. u, Rain!

👍 *Like*   ↱ *Share*   💬*Comment*

Rain Marchus and 10 others like this
View 35 comments

How cute is the ice cream all over her face?

👍 *Like*   ↱ *Share*   💬*Comment*

Rain Marchus, Mark Knut and 18 others like this
View 22 comments

Boyz Hood concert was amazeballs...

👍 *Like*   ↱ *Share*   💬*Comment*

Mark Knut and 22 others like this
View 35 comments

Markie's going on business for 5 days! Gonna miss ya Markie Knut!

👍 *Like*   ↪ *Share*   💬*Comment*
    Rain Marchus and Jess Naidoo and 13 others like this
    View 18 comments

Please share. Seriously, I don't know *why* we pay tax.

👍 *Like*   ↪ *Share*   💬*Comment*
    Rain Marchus, Peter Tovey and 34 people like this
    View 22 comments

This is so true. Treasure them. They grow up so fast.

👍 *Like*   ↪ *Share*   💬*Comment*
    38 people like this

And I thought I had feet!

👍 *Like*   ↪ *Share*   💬*Comment*

I mean BIG feet! Aargh!

👍 *Like*   ↪ *Share*   💬*Comment*
    Rain Marchus and 25 people like this
    View all 22 comments

Missing my Markie. He's got no internet and limited phone reception. Sniff.

👍 *Like*   ↪ *Share*   💬*Comment*
    34 people like this
    View 22 comments

This is disgusting. We HAVE to do something! Please share.

👍 *Like*   ↪ *Share*   💬*Comment*
    Rain Marchus and 44 people like this
    View 32 comments

Thanx for all the birthday wishes. Made me feel sooo special!! Wish Markie was here. But Jords made me a RAD card—best daughter in the world!

👍 *Like*   ↪ *Share*   💬 *Comment*

Jordan Knut and 20 other people like this

Ssshhh... I'm gonna fly up to surprise Markie! Wish me luck.

👍 *Like*   ↪ *Share*   💬 *Comment*

Said Leh, Steve Waugh and 43 other people like this
View 33 comments

Na-hah... Friday Funny...

👍 *Like*   ↪ *Share*   💬 *Comment*

23 people like this

Urgh. Plane delayed. Moron at counter says bad weather or something.

👍 *Like*   ↪ *Share*   💬 *Comment*

View 27 comments

We can send robots to Mars but we can't fly planes in rain...

👍 *Like*   ↪ *Share*   💬 *Comment*

Rain Marchus and 32 people like this
View 22 comments

About to take off. Been researching. It's not as one-horse a town as Markie made out. So much of the excitement!!!!

👍 *Like*   ↪ *Share*   💬 *Comment*

Bev Pheto and 22 other people like this

Just landed. This place is craaaaaazzzyyyyyyyyyy. Check out pics.

👍 *Like*   ↪ *Share*   💬 *Comment*

In hotel where Markie is staying but he's not here. Must be a mix up. Shizzle. Internet connect fine BTW.

👍 *Like* ↪ *Share* 💬*Comment*
Rain Marchus likes this
View 18 comments

Apparently Mark is not at this hotel. Never has been.

👍 *Like* ↪ *Share* 💬*Comment*
Rain Marchus likes this
View 3 comments

Thanks guys. Can't get hold of Mark, but when I do, I'll letcha know.

👍 *Like* ↪ *Share* 💬*Comment*

Umm. I'm coming back home. No sign of Mark. I'm beyond pissed off.

👍 *Like* ↪ *Share* 💬*Comment*
View 5 comments

Sorry guys. Been a tough few months. Just haven't been able to communicate. Thanx for the wishes.

👍 *Like* ↪ *Share* 💬*Comment*
Frank Hopper and 5 other people like this
View 3 comments

I guess what doesn't kill me... he's having a baby with none other than my *was* best friend, Rain!

👍 *Like* ↪ *Share* 💬*Comment*
View 4 comments

Oh and he wants custody of Jords. Just peachy.

👍 *Like* ↪ *Share* 💬*Comment*
View 3 comments

U know who your friends are in times of crisis, that's for sure.

👍 Like   ↪ Share   💬 Comment
View 6 comments

Anyone know of a decent lawyer who won't rip me off? He's hired the best, of course.

👍 Like   ↪ Share   💬 Comment

Going out with the gals tonights. Woohoo! Been a long time.

👍 Like   ↪ Share   💬 Comment
Liv Richards and 4 other people like this
View 3 comments

I didn't ask for any of this

👍 Like   ↪ Share   💬 Comment

This is SO true...

👍 Like   ↪ Share   💬 Comment
View 2 comments

Had to sell my baby today. Only 1000 miles on the clock. Gonna miss her.

👍 Like   ↪ Share   💬 Comment
View 5 comments

The guy who did the interview told me I had a "sunny disposition" but no experience. Stupid prick. How can I get experience if I can't GET experience?

👍 Like   ↪ Share   💬 Comment

Does anyone know which bank offers the best loan terms?

👍 *Like*　　　↪ *Share*　　　💬 *Comment*
　　View 1 comments

He won't help me with a loan. How low can u go?

👍 *Like*　　　↪ *Share*　　　💬 *Comment*
　　View 1 comments

Bought a Tina Warren bag. To cheer myself up.

👍 *Like*　　　↪ *Share*　　　💬 *Comment*
　　Liv Richards and 6 other people like this

Took the bag back. Lost my mind for a second but I'm ok now.

👍 *Like*　　　↪ *Share*　　　💬 *Comment*
　　Liv Richards likes this

Anyone know anyone who needs an admin assistant? Or receptionist? Inbox me.

👍 *Like*　　　↪ *Share*　　　💬 *Comment*

Anyone have a cottage available to rent? Inbox me.

👍 *Like*　　　↪ *Share*　　　💬 *Comment*

Anybody? Anybody out there?

👍 *Like*　　　↪ *Share*　　　💬 *Comment*

Check out the new Boyz Hood track. Awesome.

👍 *Like*　　　↪ *Share*　　　💬 *Comment*
　　Payne Francis and 15 other people like this
　　View 14 comments

CAROL BORZYKOWSKI

Wonderland

From January 1997

Black, cold, narrow as a grave
I didn't see the hole—
didn't look before I stepped
down.

Long, long I fell

past shards
empty as plastic
champagne glasses,
past
deflated balloons
pink and yellow,
past a magician's
empty black hat
dead rabbit,

curiouser
               and curiouser.
Past the touch of your lips
brushing my neck
a silver moth in flames,
onto barren lunar landscape

I stopped.

And Alice,
it's true what they say
it's not the fall
        that kills you.

NICO VREELAND

Hide or Don't Exist

From April/May 2013

I'M STANDING BEHIND Shrigley in the tiny tent where we work and eat and sleep, so I'm only about four feet away from him. I'm lining up papers and moving shit a little and then moving it back, and all the other bullshit you do when there's no real work but your boss is right there.

It's more awkward, too, because there was an accident when we first got here, and everybody but me and Dr. Shrigley and Pirkle Jones is dead, but we haven't gone home yet.

I say, "So, why'd you get a vasectomy, Dr. Shrigley?"

"What?" Shrigley says.

I didn't really want to say that, but I figured somebody should say something, and that was the only thing I could think of that wasn't like, "So, about your dead friends..."

"How does a vasectomy work?" I say, pretending I never asked why. This is not the kind of thing you talk about, at least not to Shrigley.

Shrigley gets weird about shit like that, and it's already weird enough around here. "I'm thinking about it myself."

He's looking down at his desk. "They do it laproscopically," he says, after a minute. "Which means no scalpel. They snip your tubes with a little wire. So you keep your testicles, but they're not hooked up anymore."

"Yeah," I say. That wasn't what I meant. "How does it work that you still can, uh,"—what's the other word for come?—"can still, uh, relieve yourself without, you know..." I sit down on the cot, right next to him. Being around Shrigley makes me feel even dumber than I really am, like a little kid.

Shrigley's doing that thing he does, where he stares at something he thinks I don't get so he doesn't have to look at me. This time he's looking at the map with the footprints all over it, which isn't even that hard to get. Staring down at it, he says, "How can you have an orgasm without ejaculating?"

"Ejaculate," I say. That's the other word for it. "How can you?"

Shrigley stares really hard at the map. "I don't know." Shrigley's always saying he doesn't know shit. It means he doesn't want to explain it.

"Didn't you, uh, ask?"

Shrigley's face, I think, turns a little red. "Cy?"

I say, "Yeah?"

"Can you do a camp check for me?"

"Uh, sure, Dr. Shrigley." I get up and leave the tent. A camp check's when you walk around the camp and check on it. It's what Shrigley tells me to do when he gets sick of me talking.

I know he thinks I'm stupid, and I know he's smarter than me, but still I don't get why even somebody so smart would go and get a vasectomy when he doesn't even have a wife. Maybe he did it so he could write a paper or something. About not having kids or something. Smart guys like Shrigley, you want to believe they got good reasons for doing what they do.

The reason we're here on some goddamn island I don't even know the name of is that we're looking for, get this, these things called skunk apes, which don't exist. Only Shrigley gets mad if you say things don't exist, even crazy shit like giant alien cats. Shrigley's a cryptozoologist. He says that means he looks for things that haven't been discovered or are hiding, like Bigfoot's just a real good hider.

I've worked for Shrigley for almost five years now, and we've never found any skunk apes or bigfoot or yetis or anything. In fact, hardly anybody's ever found anything in the history of cryptozoology. The one thing somebody found was the bones of these dwarf people some of Shrigley's friends found a few years ago. After that, they got in real magazines, not just the newsletters they print themselves. They got all kinds of money from people, and Shrigley went nuts 'cause he said no to the trip that found the dwarves. Then he said yes to this one, the skunk ape trip, which was going great for four hours until the Jeep with his friends in it went flipping off a cliff and Shrigley had to leave them down there, dead underwater in a wrecked Jeep, because with just us left, there's no famous guys, so there's no money and no more trip. As soon as he calls it in, we go home.

Now it's just me and Shrigley and this weird guy named Pirkle Jones who used to play football, but now he carries shit for people, like me. We've been here for a week already at this same stupid camp waiting for these skunk apes that don't exist or are just real good at hiding.

Pirkle's sitting in the turned-off Jeep, in the dark, smoking. His big bald head in the starlight looks like an egg. A big wrinkled egg. He doesn't go near Shrigley anymore 'cause he was driving our Jeep on the cliff when he stomped on the brake and the other Jeep tried to not hit us and fell over the cliff and Shrigley hates him now. Even though it wasn't completely Pirkle's fault 'cause there was a chunk out of the cliff and that's why he stomped on the brake and we would've just flipped off it anyway if he hadn't. But it kind of was his fault, 'cause he spaced out and maybe he could've seen the chunk missing and stopped slower. Or something. Shrigley sure blames him for it whatever the reason. I just want to shake them by the shoulders and yell, people fucking die! They fucking die, and they're dead, so get over it. But that's the kind of thing you can't tell people. That's the kind of thing people don't talk about.

Any case, we had to reverse all the way back to get off the cliff, and Shrigley doesn't say a fucking word for an hour. Who would go driving these Jeeps around cliffs where nobody's ever gone anyway? They're even these super-wide expedition Jeeps with all the gear and everything, like three times the size of a normal Jeep. And you take it on a cliff? Me and Pirkle, we just do what we're told. I don't think it's fair to blame us when all your famous friends die.

You want to ask me, it's this goddamn island. This place doesn't have any people on it for a good reason. All it does here is rain and then shine sun. It rained for like four days when we got here, and then the sun came out and baked all the mud into waves and spikes like a frozen ocean.

"How you doing, Pirkle?" I say, climbing into the passenger seat.

"How's the Doc?" he says. He's got a voice like an earthquake. He slides the cigarettes and the lighter across the dashboard, like six feet, all the way across.

"Kicked me out," I say.

"You should leave the Doc alone, Cy." Pirkle still feels bad, you can tell how he's looking out the window, into the dark, into the jungle. I don't know how long it takes to get over killing three guys. Even accidentally, I guess it takes more than a week, especially when you leave the bodies just out there without even a funeral or a service or anything. When they're just rotting there, and you know right where, too, and you don't do a damn thing about it, getting over it probably takes longer.

I never killed anybody, even though I was in the Army. I was only in the Army for four years, though. But guys can kill guys in four years. Guys can kill guys in a week, so guys can kill all kinds of guys in four years. But I didn't.

We're down at the end of the island, out of the jungle, 'cause the mud never dries in the jungle. It's supposed to not be the rainy season here, but there aren't any goddamn people living here to tell you, hey, rainy season actually lasts another month, or another six months, or forever, idiot, so don't even bother. So here we are.

"I was thinking," Pirkle says. He reaches over and gets a new cigarette and lights it. That's how you know he's going to get all philosophical, when he starts to talk and then lights a cigarette before he actually says anything. "What if..." he says, puffing, "what if we just got rid of all our papers and books and records and stuff?" Pirkle's a fucking idiot. He got something like 27 concussions from when he played football.

"Yeah?" I say.

"You think we could maybe forget how to make war and hurt people and stuff? You think it could all just go away?" He must've been thinking about this shit all night. Just sitting in the Jeep, smoking and thinking about burning books for peace.

"Yeah," I say. You can't say anything else, or he'll keep talking. You got to pretend there's nothing else to say. Like he solved it. "Yeah," I say again.

"Maybe we'd just forget how," he says, quietly, taking a suck on his cigarette.

This is Pirkle's first trip. Sometimes it gets to guys their first time, even the guys who don't accidentally kill all the boss's friends. Just the quiet and the dark and the jungles and the monsters we're looking for. We got a .30-06, but it's locked in a trunk, so what help do you think that's going to be, exactly, when giant alien fucking cats and packs of wild goddamn lizard men come shit-shredding through camp?

I mean, I know this is all bullshit, but still.

"Hey, Cy?" Pirkle says.

"Yeah?" I say.

"You been doing this how long?" He's looking out the window. Pirkle doesn't ever look at you when he talks to you anymore. I don't remember if he ever did. It's fucking weird.

"Five years," I say.

"You ever, uh..." He takes a long drag on his cigarette. "You ever seen something?"

Christ, Pirkle. "Nah, I never seen anything."

"How close you gotten?" Pirkle still won't look at me, but he turns a little, so he's looking out the windshield. Sometimes, with guys like Pirkle, they think it's all real for the first couple trips. All the folks with sense, they go off with proper archaeologists and stuff. Guys hunting skunk apes like Shrigley get stuck with dumbass ex-football guys like Pirkle and dumbass ex-Army guys like me. There's a reason for that.

"I never been close at all," I say. That's as gentle as I can say it. I can't say, shut up, moron, you're 40 years old. After all, Shrigley's back there and he's got to be 60, and he's a lot smarter than Pirkle Jones.

"But the Doc, though," Pirkle says, and he glances over at me.

I turn my head to look at him, but he's already looking back out his window. "Shrigley says he's heard some shit," I say. The only honest-to-god shit that somebody's found was those dwarf bones.

"He saw that Choppercabber, huh? The Doc?"

"It's Chupacabras," I say. "It's not 'cat,' but come on, Pirkle. Have a little pride in your work. And he didn't see it. It was night. Like now. He took a picture of a tree."

That shuts Pirkle up for a while. It gets fucking quiet out where nobody lives. I think Australia's like 500 miles south of here, but other than that, nothing. You stare down into the jungle too long, on a night like this, you start seeing things. You stare into jungle goddamn trees on abandoned islands by starlight for four or five years, you start seeing some shit, boy. Most of the time—sorry, all of the time—it's just regular animals, tigers or wolves or coyotes or bears. Sometimes, though, it's tough to know what the fuck you're looking at, and you start taking pictures of trees. If you're really freaked out, you start pointing guns at jungles.

Shrigley's never told me right out, but I'm here to shoot one of these motherfuckers. He's got footprints and blurry goddamn pictures and tapes of fucking noise, but none of it's worth a damn without a body. I'm not real concerned, 'cause shooting a skunk ape means there's got to be a skunk ape in the first place, which there's not. But still, that's why I'm here. It's a weird job.

This empty island's starting to get to me. Not so much the dark as the quiet. All you can hear is the wind in the trees, and the waves in the background, and a hum, like the whole island's on generators, and then, just there, this little burbling rip like a demon puking.

Wait, what?

"What the fuck was that?" Pirkle whispers.

What the fuck was that? "S'nothing," I say, with a little tsch, like half a spit.

"Did you hear it, though?" Pirkle throws his cigarette out the window and leans toward me. "Did you hear some kind of sound?"

I fucking heard it, all right, but if I tell Pirkle that, he's going to shit his pants or something and not realize it was just a regular wildcat or monkey or whatever they got here. I put my finger up to my mouth and then point to my ear to shut him up. We both listen real hard to the night. Turns out there's all kinds of sounds out there, creakings and hissings and crackles and hums. It's actually loud, after all, when you listen to it. I'm listening for something heavy, for clumsy footsteps and snapping twigs, something that sounds fucked up. I can just imagine the one time one of these fucking beasts turns out to be real, and it pops out of the woods and it kills us all, some kind of monster ape with a big long tail or maybe just a white stripe and long fur.

I'm staring so hard into the woods, it looks like the trees are moving, waving like flowers. Those trees are like ghosts in the starlight, like dead bodies underwater.

I get this shivery feeling, staring at the jungle. Nothing ever happens when you're staring right at it. Except this time.

Brbckldblsck, goes the skunk ape about to kill us.

"Fuck," I say.

"Oh, Christ, Cy," Pirkle whispers. "Oh, Christ, Christ."

"Pirkle, keep your shit together," I say in a hiss. I reach back and switch the inside light of the Jeep from "door" to "off." "Take the key out," I say.

"It's out," he says and finally looks at me. His eyes are wide because he's scared and he's dumb. "Are you going to get the gun?" he says.

"Just stay in the Jeep, okay, Pirkle?"

He stares at me, at my ear.

"Okay?" I say again.

"Okay, Cy," he finally says. "I'll stay here."

I get out and go around to the back of the Jeep, which is where the .30-06 is because there's no room in the tent and guns creep Shrigley out. I get it out of its box, and I have to put the scope on and put a clip in. I put another two clips in my pocket, in case there's a whole pack of skunk apes out there that go nuts when I kill one. The .30-06 is basically a sniper rifle, but for civilians they say it's a hunting rifle. Shrigley bought it online. It's got a little stand under the muzzle with two feet you pull out and rest on something. I pull the feet out and rest them on the hood of the Jeep, leaning across the hood with my stomach so it's comfortable and I can look through the scope without much trouble. I'm pointing it across the hood, toward Pirkle's side, toward the jungle.

I never did anything with sniper rifles in the Army. I was a grunt. But guys like Shrigley think all Army guys use sniper rifles and we're all assassins. I've pulled out this .30-06 a couple times, when Shrigley's thought he heard shit like the Chupacabras, but I've never fired it. I'm not about to fire it now, either. I hope.

I sit there and look through the scope into the muddy jungle. I look over at Pirkle, and he's sitting there turning his bald egg head back and forth, just about pissing.

I remember a time when I wasn't here. I can remember, I think, being happy, or thinking I might be someday. What the fuck happened to me? I used to hope for shit, and like shit, and *enjoy* some fucking shit. And now I'm in the middle of fucking nowhere, pointing a motherfucking sniper rifle at a mythological goddamn animal, with a guy who just killed three people a week ago and a guy who had his own balls cut off last month.

After hours, it feels like, sitting here and trying not to have to piss and staring, I start thinking about this girl I used to know named Camille or Camilla or fucking Pamela or something. She used to have a face all covered in freckles and these big front teeth that pushed her lip out. She was the last time I had good sex. I think it was three or four years ago, which is sad. I've had sex since then, but not good sex. I wonder when was the last time Pirkle had good sex. Hopefully, it was more than three or four years ago. Hopefully, it was fucking never, that ugly asshole.

I wonder how long it would take Pirkle Jones to go killing-spree nuts from sex withdrawal. Hopefully, a while. I could go any minute now. I've already got the gun out.

Bsscrhltpltfsck, goes the skunk ape. I feel the piss come up my dick, but I will it back down. It's right in front of me, in the woods, the sound is. At least, one of them fucking is. I fit my right eye up to the scope and sweep the crosshairs over the jungle trees. It's darker through the scope, and I can hardly see a thing. I feel the safety with my thumb and flick it off. I wonder how shitty this rifle is going to be if the skunk ape really charges. I've seen that video where the lion charges the guy and he almost shoots the other guy cause sniper rifles are fucked when shit charges you.

I go real slow with the crosshairs, and I hear something else, a squish or something, like it's stepping on a guy's stomach and crushing him. At this one tree, I think I see a shadow. It's weird and hulking and fucking huge. I settle on it and watch it. I try to aim at something that looks lethal. I don't want to hit this fucker in the hump or the horn or the fucking wings or something and just piss it off. It moves a little, like shifting its weight or something, and I shoot it.

I didn't even fucking know I was going to, until my finger twitched and the gun went off. The gun goes CRACK! so loud it's like the earth split in half. Maybe I did know. Sometimes it's easier if you don't think about it too hard, and you just fucking do whatever needs doing. I'm deafened, but I can hear the echoes off of everywhere, off of the jungle. They sound like waves. The shadow's gone, like it's dead or run off.

"Holy shit!" Pirkle yells. He's got both his hands on the door, on the open window part, like a dog. "Holy shit!" he yells again.

Shrigley comes sprinting out of the tent so fast he trips over himself and falls.

Pirkle jumps out of the Jeep and slaps his hand on his head.

Shrigley runs over to us. "Cy!" he says. "What happened? What was that noise?"

I point the gun at the sky and walk around the Jeep. "I don't know what it was."

"It was the freaking gun!" Pirkle yells. "Doc, Cy killed a freaking skunk ape!"

"I don't know what it was," I say again.

Shrigley's yelling now, too. "What?" he yells. "You shot something?"

"Calm down," I say. "Let's just go see what it was." I didn't mean to fucking shoot it. At least, I think I didn't. I think I wish I hadn't. But part of me, too, just says fuck it. It was a fucking skunk ape; this is my job. I don't know what I think. This is the kind of thing people don't talk about.

We start walking toward the trees, but Shrigley stops after a little while. "Shouldn't, uh..." Shrigley's whispering now. "Shouldn't you go first? With the gun?"

Christ. "Okay. Okay, you guys stay behind me."

This is fucking stupid. For one thing, it was nothing. It was a fucking shadow. It's this fucking island and the starlight and the quiet. But Shrigley and Pirkle Jones are behind me, shitting their pants 'cause they think it's a fictional fucking animal or the water zombies of Shrigley's fucking friends or some goddamn shit that's too stupid for words.

It's a long goddamn way to the jungle. After a while I can't even see shit anymore. I look up, and the stars are all gone again. Motherfucking three days dry, and it's going to rain again.

We get into the jungle, and the mud turns from dried up and cracked into thick, wet shit, like glue. I wade into it, feeling the suck at my boots, hearing it slurp, loud. That must have been what the squishing sound was. I'm trying to keep the rifle pointed forward and not get stuck and look for this fucking thing at the same time.

After a while, we kind of spread out and keep slurping in, and just when I'm about to give it up, I get past this tree, and there he is. A goddamn skunk ape. Well, a huge fucking corpse, at least.

"I got it," I shout, into the trees. "Come find me. It's dead."

"What does it look like?" Shrigley yells. I can hear him running, waddle-jogging.

"It's a big..." I look at this ugly fucker. "It's a monkey. It's a big, big-ass fucking monkey." It's a lump of fur and meat, and it's dark, and I'm not even sure it really is even a monkey, but whatever.

I point the rifle at the skunk ape, just in case it miraculously fucking comes back to life, and Pirkle and Shrigley slurp up in the mud beside me.

"Holy shit, you got it," Pirkle says. "You got a skunk ape."

Shrigley slurps over to it and starts poking around. I really hope it it's dead, and it doesn't fucking kill him. Shrigley says, "Can you see any footprints?"

"I didn't check for footprints," I say.

"Is it not a skunk ape?" Pirkle says.

I shrug.

"What does a skunk ape look like?" Pirkle says.

"I don't know," I say. "Nobody's ever seen one."

Shrigley's over on the other side of the ape corpse, looking at craters in the mud. "It's tough to tell with the mud," he says, "these footprints don't look much like the ones I've got."

"What else would it be?" Pirkle says, like Shrigley pissed in his coffee.

"A regular ape," I say. In which case, I killed it for nothing. In which case, this whole trip was for nothing. Shrigley's dead friends were for nothing. Shrigley's whole entire life was for nothing.

"It stinks, huh?" Pirkle says.

"Yeah, Pirkle," I say. "It fucking stinks."

"Get the Jeep," Shrigley says.

While me and Pirkle are going back to the Jeep, we hear the first thunder, and we both kind of slump. It doesn't rain light on this goddamn island. By the time we've got the Jeep back to the edge of the jungle, it's started. We put our ponchos on, which just makes everything harder to do, and we tie a rope around the skunk ape's feet and tie it to the Jeep. We start dragging the body out, and it just rains harder and fucking harder.

At first, the mud's just a surface layer, the wheels of the Jeep spin a little, but they can grab the dirt underneath. By the time that ape's out of the jungle, though, the ground just sinks under us into a big soup. With the Jeep alone, we might've been able to move, but it's shitty weather for dragging huge corpses around.

Finally, Shrigley calls off the drag. We back the Jeep up next to the skunk ape and put the rear door up and hang our ponchos over it like a tent. We're going to have to take turns watching over him all night so he doesn't get eaten. At least, we say we're going to take turns, but we all three of us stay up. Shrigley radios the chopper, but it can't come until the storm's over. Which might be the next morning or might be two weeks. That's what you get for hiring some cut-rate Indonesian goddamn chopper.

Shrigley starts taking all kinds of pictures of its face and its body and its fucking feet and shit. It's got a weird face, like a mask, rubbery. It's like apes in the movies, but dirtier, messier. His ankles already got the fur rubbed off them from the ropes. His skin's gray underneath.

Pirkle and me sit on the back of the Jeep, him smoking, me smoking with the .30-06 across my knees like I'm spanking it. Shrigley's camera's flashes like heat lightning, fucking up our night vision.

This corpse, if it is a skunk ape, could be the biggest thing any of us ever did. Bigger than quitting the Army, bigger than cutting your balls off, bigger than not having good sex for four years, maybe bigger even than killing some guys. This corpse could be the biggest thing any of us ever does in our whole lives. What else am I going to do, for example, in the whole rest of my life? I shot a fake ape once, I'll say. But it turned out to be real.

We still don't know if it's a skunk ape. We don't even know how long it's going to be before we find out. Shrigley doesn't have a clue. He keeps looking at its feet and the pictures of footprints that aren't even in focus. How do you fuck up a picture of a footprint?

Or, this thing could be fucking nothing. It could be just a hunk of wasted meat we're not even going to eat. It could just be a pile of bullshit some guys got paid to do and some guys died for, just like every fucking thing else.

Right now, it feels like it's both. Right now, we're heroes and we're failures at the same time, and it feels like it's too much to fucking hold in your head at once. I wonder if this is what Shrigley feels like all the time.

Maybe that's why he got the vasectomy. Maybe when all you do is hunt these fuckers you don't even know exist, when you spend your whole life waiting to be right or wrong and never finding out, maybe making sure something doesn't exist is just as good as finding out something else does.

Maybe you just want to feel what it's like to be sure about something for once in your goddamn miserable fucking life.

IHEOMA NWACHUKWU

The Seven-Thousand-Year-Old Spirit

From July/August 2013

CORPORAL NWAFANIM LAUGHED when he heard the complaint: an old spirit who roamed the earth doing good had asked a farmer in the village to profer it nine *dimkpa* tubers of yam, or eat misfortune.

He stopped laughing when the spectacled man who had limped into the police station mentioned it was no ordinary spirit but the Great One, Seven-Thousand-Year-Old Afanim, who had come out of a crack in the limestone knoll at Okwuta lake, the revered guardian spirit of Amumara community who passed messages in hieroglyphs, the harsh goddess-man who often appeared in goat form, who shook an iron-belled staff at barren women and brought a comforting weight to fruitless wombs.

Nwafanim fingered the diaper pin fastening the top of his moisture-blotted uniform where a button was missing. The room was stuffy. It was a hot afternoon.

He leaned forward on the narrow counter, stained dark-brown by the pitiless press of bodies through the years. In the far right corner of the counter, a thumb-sized fly perched on a neat pile of discolored case files.

"Did you say it was Afanim?" he asked, pulling his tree-root shaped nose. He could smell rat piss and shit. The relentless rodents who ate statements and court orders at the station were back again after the last batch of poisoned crayfish he strewed in the wall corners.

The spectacled man removed his small, Fanta-colored glasses, smiling, glad at the serious turn of conversation, enjoying his prominence with the police.

"Yes. Afanim," he answered. "In his farm, my friend found Nsibidi ciphers the spirit had written on the ground. As I speak to you, he has given Afanim four big tubers. He's afraid. He only told me because he got drunk yesterday. At Mama Samaria's. I lived in Lagos city for ten years after Biafra. I saw things. This one, nothing but fraud..."

Nwafanim, suddenly annoyed, even troubled, flashed a menacing palm that stopped the man. What disrespect, he thought. It was this same goddess, this just punisher of wrongdoers with instant blindness, who had put him inside his barren mother, though he had told no one this but his wife—long before she deserted him one Sunday while he was at work.

He decided it was time to take a statement from the complainant, or he might hit the man out of irritation. He looked behind him at the junior officers whose job it was to write reports.

The two constables sat asleep on a bench, their sweating heads slanted against the spotted, dirty wall. This morning the men had returned from a trip to Lagos. They had ridden in the front of a trailer truck crammed with cows belonging to the D.P.O.'s girlfriend, providing a shield against the usual horde of bribe-crazed policemen at checkpoints along the way.

The one with marijuana-burned lips held his rifle across his lap. The bald one stood his gun between his thighs. Nwafanim kicked their shins.

"Agile!" they barked, grabbing their weapons. Nwafanim hissed.

"Come and take this man's statement," he commanded. "Lazy. A criminal would have finished you just like chickens."

Through the door, not far away, he could see the sheep-faced village goatherd leading the villagers' livestock in an orderly row along the dusty road.

The goatherd looked back at the animals, raised his narrow stick, and shook it. The column moved past him.

"Muhemuhemuhe," he called sharply to a sheep straying onto someone's farm. The creature stopped. It fell back in line when the man clicked his tongue.

Nwafanim nodded, impressed as always. Every day he saw this procession. There was a grateful look in his eyes, too. This was the good man who had told him, many weeks ago, that he saw Nwafanim's sons in town calling a strange man on a motorcycle "Father."

He took a pen from his pocket, uncapped it, and placed it on the counter for the constables' use. Then he walked out of the room to sit with the boiled-groundnut seller by the painted THE NIGERIA POLICE FORCE, AMUMARA DIVISION signboard outside. It was time to let fresh air caress his face—to think about the motorcycle loan he needed to ask for—and the daily crossing of the animals to nearby Okwuta lake was the hint that told him the sun had dipped and he could settle here without getting baked.

That was last week. Nwafanim remained upset all that time, not wanting to continue an investigation that muddied the divinity of a generous goddess he had worshipped with his mother as a child, yet needing to do his job, needing to satisfy his natural curiosity, and needing to perhaps impress his superiors enough to ask for a loan.

One more person in the village (a frightened, grey-haired woman searched out by the man in glasses) had reluctantly come forward to make a similar report. She interspersed her account—in a quivering voice—with fearful pleas of forgiveness to Afanim.

Last year the Seven-Thousand-Year-Old Spirit had asked her to bring six cement bags of cassava to the blessed pyramid of Ala, the ancient, four-step shrine of the earth goddess, a bird's cry from the hilltop Catholic church. It was the same location where the farmer was asked to leave his yams.

This night Nwafanim and two assigned policemen would lie in wait at the pyramid for the spirit when it came to collect the balance of last week's yams. Everybody at the station agreed the request had the fittings of a scam. Doubtless, the mastermind had run the scheme over several months, years maybe. The D.P.O. and his deputy had shown an amused, intelligent interest in the case.

A hen squawked, and Nwafanim rose from the scratched wooden armchair in his one-room home. The sellotaped butt of his rifle showed under the chair. Part of the weapon rested against an old boot where he had carefully placed a lidded plastic container filled with the boiled-down ends of soap his wife had bathed the children with in the old days.

He protected this reminder of his family with the power of the rifle.

By the light of the clay lamp on the bare table, he could see the hand-wound clock over the bed, which used folded wrappers for a mattress. A nail next to the clock held up his charcoal-black uniform.

Though everywhere was already dark because of the long shadows cast by the surrounding copse of trees, it was only six p.m. Three hours before the farmer would take the yams to the pyramid.

He went out to the backyard to close the coop now that the last of his fowls had come home—the one whose cackle he had heard, the mischief-maker who flew on top of the house whenever he chased it away from the sprouting vegetables.

Nwafanim lived alone in his zinc-roofed hut. His wife had left him four years ago, taking their three children, all boys. He could not believe she could go when she was the one he had given his virginity, the woman whose plump shape held all his memories of lovemaking.

He understood she had gone to seek the life they shared before the children came, a life that had grown increasingly uncommon and distant, even for his fanciest dreams. His small salary had seemed enough for a family of three (if they ate full meals only twice a day), but then they became five, without him knowing exactly when, and it seemed he never had a *kobo* to spare all his life.

He had quit the seminary to join the police 15 years before—needing the balance of a vocation that preserved the discipline of theology school without its illusions. His old father had cursed him for this betrayal. As a boy, Nwafanim knew every astute patriarch in the village sent a son into the priesthood—a false sacrifice—a *naira*-messiah who would bring the family eternal riches from Rome.

Seven Books of Moses had led to the discovery of Isis and Osiris—uncovering multiple Bible fabrications. The theft of Psalm 23 from an Egyptian text appealing to Osiris the Good Shepherd had particularly shocked him, and Nwafanim's faith soon lay bare. He knew then he could never be the fortune-Jesus his father craved.

But he remained a church-goer to moderate his father's misery.

Although he regretted the later hardship of his poor-paying profession, he admired its simple certainty—a bullet was not an ambiguous friend. If you put a fool in jail, a wise man walked in his place on the street.

In the kitchen he covered his face with the bottom of his singlet after he blew out the fire. Though firewood smoke lifted, underneath it he could smell the goat dung in the big basket by the grinding stone, the dung he would ferment and sprinkle around his farm to ward off single-minded goats.

Breathing the goat dung, he felt the infinity of Afanim's presence, the goddess-man whom he had never really stopped carrying in his heart, though he was Catholic and attended mass.

Then Nwafanim's mind went to the village goatherd who had given him the dung. He pulled the singlet from his face.

A man like me, he thought, as he came out of the kitchen, stopping his nostrils with two fingers. Like him, the goatherd had also suffered heartbreak. Three marriages, all flying to pieces. Each wife had run away in the first week of union, leaving hasty footprints in the winding path of the adjacent boundary-forest where wild, towering desert-goats drifted.

The brides had hurried off empty handed, not even taking kola nut or gypsum chalk as token snack from the house-bowl.

People laughed and said the women fled because the man had a sheep's penis, which was uncharitable since the goatherd helped take his and their livestock where the grass had little juice, and so did not run the animals' bellies. (For this service, he received for payment one lamb or kid per household.)

Nwafanim had laughed, though, too, until his own wife absconded.

Inside the room he rested his knees on the bed and raised a hand to lift his uniform from the nail beside the clock. In the top buttonhole of the shirt, the diaper pin—which had clipped his last-child's diaper—shined dully. He stood by the table and, holding the clothes in both hands, snapped the fabric to throw out hiding termites. Jerked by the rush of air, light from the clay lamp batted his shadow against the mud wall.

Nwafanim laid out the shirt and trousers thoughtfully on the bed and pictured the ambush tonight with a heavy sigh.

Moonlight fell through the trees. The three policemen proceeded over a dead trunk with a large hole in its side shaped like a fabulous ear. Flies and other winged insects scattered in the undergrowth. Nwafanim held up his rifle, and the other two stopped. Now they squatted in the long scant grass outside the bend of the woods. The wind was in their faces. It carried the strong scent of grass seeds.

A gibbous moon sagged over the stepped-pyramid. The pointed clay structure was at least the height of a man at its base.

"See the spirit's yams," one of the constables said in a high, fawning voice, gesturing with his chin.

The other coughed loudly into his palm and shifted his weight.

Nwafanim took a hard look at these men. They were from remote communities. The one with marijuana-burned lips held his rifle across his lap. The bald one stood his gun between his thighs.

Loathing burned in Nwafanim's throat.

Misfit combatants without spirit, he decided, not sure exactly what he meant. He knew then they would never make Corporal.

He wore his gun slanted by his side as the commander from New Zealand had taught in training school. Nwafanim squinted unhappily at the dark line of yams beside the pyramid and went over the case again.

Those people said Afanim asked them to bring sacrifice to this ancient shrine, holier than Nsude pyramids. Afanim said, "Tie a long rope to each offering with a loop at the other end. Bring all on the fourth market day." The goddess carved Nsibidi signs into a cleared piece of farmland.

It sounded like something they made up.

He had scoffed at the shaded triangle—Ala pyramid—when the farmer showed him the signs. Seven-Thousand-Year-Old Afanim must know that, alone, the triangle stands for leopard skin. It becomes "Ala pyramid" only when the stick symbol, crossed at head and bottom, together with the tall narrow mirror-mark, precedes the triangle.

But despite his best hopes, the Nsibidi message proved bona fide. A very old, one-armed medicine man, whose father had been a clerk of Ezeagbogu Court, inspected the large goat-horn emblem of Afanim shaped into the soil and said he would strangle anyone who called this a fake. He had never met a human yet who rendered the backward-horn with the perfect sweep of Afanim's hand. Human wrists were not like Afanim's, which wheeled in a precise circle. The D.P.O. had looked at his watch in suppressed laughter.

Crouched in the grass here, now, with the cool air blowing across his throat, Nwafanim felt like he was at the bottom of a mystic drum. He was here to defile Afanim, raise a spear against his late mother. With a jolt, he realized he was here, too, to sully himself, since he had come down from the goddess into his mother's womb, and because of this provenance, was named Child of Afanim.

Part of what had brought him here, what kept him in this loose but solid pose, was wired to his children, he knew. They were why he wanted the motorcycle loan badly, like he sometimes wanted their mother. So he could buy a motorcycle and ride it to town, and take them, his sons, his blood, from the strange man they called Father, the strange man who already owned a motorcycle, whom his unfaithful wife opened her legs for, to show his wife that he owned a motorcycle, too.

A sad weight came to rest inside his stomach, and he dropped his head. A beetle was ascending his dusty boot. He watched it fasten to the hem of his trouser leg and let it climb up.

Not that he never thought of liberating his sons, like society expected any purebred Igbo man to do, but poverty had starved his paternal instincts, emboldened his shame. In turn the goatherd's revelation had doused him with healing light. The word Father had made him cry.

He raised his eyes. If he caught a fraudster this night, that was strong permission to ask for the loan. Not even the Inspector General of police would refuse a hero.

A whispered prayer left his lips: *Please, Mother Afanim, send an impostor tonight. Please.*

As though in answer, candlelight stained the matchbox-like windows of the faraway Catholic church that looked down at the pyramid from a distance.

"Late night mass starts," observed the bald constable, pointing with his chin again.

The other tilted his head to see better.

Nwafanim heard a sound at that moment—a low whine—and a firefly crossed the base of the pyramid.

Three enormous goats moved through the grass, then, and stopped in front of the yams.

"Ha! Goat!" cried the other constable, spooked. He threw down his gun, put his hands to his head, and escaped.

The bald one held his rifle against his thigh, his entire body shaking from fear and disbelief. He and his colleague had expected men, not hoofed creatures.

Nwafanim rose slowly, his mouth open, realizing what he was seeing. The goddess had appeared in goat-form.

A sacred triad.

Like Isis-Osiris-Horus. Holy Spirit-Jesus-God.

Was this Afanim-Ala-Eri?

As he watched the goats silently lower their jaws, one after the other, to loops at the end of the ropes, and then start to drag the yams away, he felt a dwarfing shame, like a favorite child caught peeping at his parents' door by neighbors.

"Are th-th-those g-goats?" the constable asked stupidly, now on his knees. His rifle lay in the grass.

Nwafanim stared after the goats, not answering. Something else had struck him.

The way the goats went in a single file. Orderly.

They reminded him of... no. But that's what they reminded him of. That was it!

"Oh, God," he moaned now, alarmed. The constable looked up at him as though Nwafanim had grown horns on his head.

Nwafanim ran forward in the grass toward the pyramid. He held the rifle in his left hand as he had been taught, the strap dancing under the sellotaped stock.

Now he was a few feet from the black, big-bellied goats, all of imposing height. They looked strangely blue in the moonlight, drawing their bundles (two yams per goat) behind them.

He could smell their offensive musk. He-goats, he thought.

Nwafanim stopped running, put a hand on his knee, and coughed to catch his breath.

He saw the goats were even taller than he had believed: nearly the same height as the grass, which reached his wrists.

He placed a hand on his chest and cried, "*Muhemuhemuhe!*"

Wind rushed in his mouth.

The goats ambled on, their sturdy horns resolute on fairly large heads.

"*Muhemuhemuhe!*" he tried again, this time with greater effort, arching his neck.

The goats kept on. Then the middle goat stopped and looked back.

The other goats stopped, too, and looked back.

Nwafanim's heart drummed so much he thought it would tear. He raised a hand.

Tut, tut, tut, his tongue clicked.

The middle goat opened its mouth and let the rope drop. Then it came toward Nwafanim.

The others cast off their ropes, too, and followed.

Nwafanim smiled. Clever, he thought. Very clever. So the sheep-faced goatherd was a bright rogue, a Bad Shepherd. The animals would pull the yams all the way to his house, where he was no doubt now waiting. Was this the side of him each wife had discovered and run from? Did each goat represent a lost wife?

Was he executing forced-atonement, each goat-wife carrying back an offering for wasted dowries, for the human consolations they withdrew?

The goat neared him, and Nwafanim swerved the stock of his rifle in a quick movement. He brought the stock down hard on the creature's back to slow it, knowing goats were notoriously difficult to manage.

"*Nmeeeeeeh*," cried the beast, surprised. It stiffened its legs and shot out urine.

The others turned smartly in the dark, warned, and scattered home.

Nwafanim grabbed the goat's horns before it skipped away, whispering, "Sorry."

He saw now that this tall goat and its brothers had come from the band of savage desert-goats roaming the boundary-forest along the goatherd's house. The animals descended from Longlegs abandoned by escaping Hausa families when the war over Biafra began decades before.

The elusive goats were also known for their brutal resistance to domestication, biting villagers in the past who had tried to lure them.

Marveling, Nwafanim shook his head. How had the goatherd charmed the brutes? It must have taken him endless months.

He took one of the ropes and made a noose around the animal's neck, keeping his hand away from its mouth. He untied the other end of the line from the yam-pile and gripped it.

The animal hobbled in pain. Nwafanim turned to regard it, rolling ideas.

He led the goat to the place where the constable waited. But there was no constable.

He smiled, not surprised. Two rifles lay in the grass. He hung his gun on one shoulder, then collected the rifles on the other. If the constables had any sense, they would not show up for work tomorrow. What kind of policeman abandoned his gun?

"Bloody civilians," he snarled.

The goat bleated once and bent a blade of grass in its mouth.

Nwafanim felt the straps of the abandoned rifles bite into his exhausted shoulder.

He stood for a moment and judged his decision. He would not expose the goatherd to the police, or even accuse him privately, because of the news the man had brought him.

He would tell the D.P.O. that when he ran after the goats, suspecting someone was waiting nearby for them, pistol shots had come out of the dark in his direction. He had taken cover behind the pyramid. The shots had continued for a while. When they finally stopped, and he had come out of hiding, the goats were gone together with whoever had been shooting. They had left the yams, scared away. He would be commended by his superiors. He would go ahead and ask for the loan.

But he would squeeze the goatherd if at the end of the customary two months his cash request was denied. The man would give him six big goats, like the goats this night, or he, Nwafanim, would tell. He knew a fellow in Ezeagbogu who was ready to trade his motorcycle, which had a small shock-absorber problem, for six well-fed goats.

This goat with him was no longer police evidence. He planned to sneak it home, tie it to the guava tree at the back of the pit toilet. When he returned from the station after making his report, he would kill the goat and roast it. That would save him meat-money for at least two months.

Nwafanim smiled. It was an excellent plan. He was sorry to set the goatherd up as collateral, but so sad the man was a criminal. He himself was on the side of law and order when you looked things through with a clear eye. He touched the diaper pin in the buttonhole, but the shirt had parted: the pin had fallen off sometime during the excitement. *Propitiation,* he thought: the Goddess had obtained the pin that attached him to the destinies of his absent children, in exchange for the success granted now.

He walked into the trees, guiding the goat, his lips moving in devotion: "Thank you Afanim. Now I can go and bring my boys with a loud shout. And bring my wife, too. If she'll come with me."

SEAN GILL

You Have Now Eaten Thirty-Four Spiders

From April/May 2014

WE'RE ALL GODS now. Or nearly.

Caveat: we're all Gods, so long as the network doesn't go down.

So I was eating a Pink-Slime-Salad at the Taco Palace for lunch other day, and I tasted something sort of filthy and feathery passing between my lips like a sordid little whisper, only it was going in instead of coming out. I looked at my fork and saw a furry little leg clinging to one of the prongs.

"Oh, holy hell!," I exclaimed. "Is that a spider? Did I just eat a spider?"

"My sensors record you have just eaten a spider," my Omnisch-o-Tron replied.

"Sweet baby mother of pearl!," I screamed. (But don't worry—I wouldn't want you to think my behavior uncouth. At least half a dozen nearby patrons were screaming at their Omnisch-o-Trons with equal, if not greater, intensity.) Then I thought like a God might. I saw the big picture. It's quite a rush when you can see the big picture.

"Omnisch-o-Tron," I asked, gingerly, "how many spiders have I eaten in my lifetime?"

The Omnisch-o-Tron twirled and calibrated itself. "You have now eaten 34 spiders," it replied.

"Now ain't that a honey..." I muttered, shaking my head. But the Omnisch-o-Tron, acting as an extension of my own mind, knew I needed to dwell on this worrisome development for my own good.

"Would you like to compare your lifetime spider-eating totals to those of your friends? Your friend Benny T. of Madison, Wisconsin, has eaten a record among your friends of 168 spiders. Did you know? The world record for unintentional spider eating is one thousand and twenty-four. Did you know? The world record for intentional spider eating is thirteen thousand, four hundred and thirty-seven. Your friend Alan K. of Gary, Indiana, has unintentionally eaten only three spiders, a record low among your friends."

"Thank you, Omnisch-o-Tron," I mumbled. I was already beginning to get over it because I'd seen the big picture. I wasn't alone in this.

"Of your immediate relatives, the only one who ever asked his Omnisch-o-Tron about spider-eating was your Great-Uncle Albert J. of Toledo, Ohio. He unintentionally ate a spider at a rest stop while crossing state lines with an underage woman in 2042, which would have been a violation of the Mann Act, had he attempted it between the years of 1910 and 1986. Would you like to know more?"

"No," I said. "I can see it all, now." But the Omnisch-o-Tron sensed I hadn't reached true closure on the issue. It knew that, subconsciously, I craved further catharsis.

"If you'd like, I have a funny video of a dog chasing a plush toy in the shape of a spider. I also have a short film about a spider who befriends a cat. Ask me about more funny spider videos."

I watched a few of the funny spider videos, and I have to admit they had me smiling, particularly the one featuring a tarantula playing a miniature piano while sporting a teensy, felt tophat.

"Would you like to recommend this question to all of your friends?"

"Which question?" I asked. "'Did I just eat a spider?' or 'How many spiders have I eaten?'"

"Either." The Omnisch-o-Tron calibrated and revised its answer. "Both."

"Sure, Omnisch-o-Tron," I said. "Share it with everyone." I felt good about that. After all, Godhood is about sharing. It is nobler to share than to not.

Later that night I went home and prepared myself a dinner of yogurt served with a side of canned fruit.

"This yogurt looks kind of old, Omnisch-o-Tron. Is it safe?" I asked.

"You purchased this yogurt 11 days ago. My sensors record it is out-of-date but fit for consumption. I see you're planning on eating yogurt for dinner. Did you know? Your friend Donald N. of Madison, Wisconsin, ate yogurt for dinner six days ago. Would you like an update every time one of your friends eats yogurt that is out-of-date?"

"No, Omnisch-o-Tron, I don't think that'll be necessary."

"There are eight single women in your housing block who ate yogurt for dinner this evening. There are two single women in your housing block who ate out-of-date yogurt for dinner this evening."

"Thank you, Omnisch-o-Tron. I may ask you for a list of their addresses and telephone numbers later."

I sat down with my dinner and watched a marathon of my favorite television show, *Celebrity Bed-Wetters*. I'm very highly ranked on that program as a viewer. My Laugh Compatibility Index is high. It's something of a point of pride.

While it's true I could simply sit down with my Omnisch-o-Tron and request a list of bed-wetting videos, somehow watching the raw footage isn't quite as fulfilling. Seeing it on the television, the way they edit it, the graphics, the pops and lulls in the music—it's perfect because it lets me know when to laugh. When there's no music, sometimes you laugh at things that aren't funny and forget to laugh at things that are funny. Even in this day and age, you need a little help sometimes.

After a few hours of *Celebrity Bed-Wetters*, I brushed my teeth, urinated, and went to bed. I was having trouble getting to sleep, and I was sort of staring at a familiar stain on my apartment ceiling when I was struck with divine inspiration.

"Omnisch-o-Tron?"

"Yes?"

"How'd that stain get there?"

"Eleven years, three months, and 26 days ago, a previous tenant—Jared B. of Green Bay, Wisconsin—flung an open-faced peanut butter sandwich at the ceiling, and it stuck. It remained there for two days before it became unstuck. However, by that time, peanut oils had already leached into the pressboard, creating the stain you see here today."

"Wow."

"Would you like me to contact Jared B. of Green Bay, Wisconsin, so you may discuss the stain with him, personally?"

"Oh, not right now, Omnisch-o-Tron. I'm trying to sleep. But maybe send me an alert the next time Jared B. eats a peanut butter sandwich; it might be entertaining to speak with him about it then."

"You said 'maybe send me an alert.' Would you like an alert sent or not?"

"Yes."

"Having trouble sleeping? Ask me about funny peanut butter videos."

"Well, okay, maybe I'll watch just one."

"I have a video of a man in a peanut costume bungee-jumping above a pool filled with jelly, and a video of an aged Bloodhound trying—unsuccessfully—to remove the peanut butter from his gums with his tongue. Which would you like to see?"

"What the hell," I said. "I'll watch them both."

A man who lived long, long ago (and who was considered quite intelligent by pre-Omnisch-o-Tron standards) once said there was no God—in the Biblical sense. God, instead, would be the man who could hold the entirety of the universe and all of its mysteries within his own mind, simultaneously. Now we're all smarter than him, and smarter than any man who has ever lived.

As is the case with many of mankind's great achievements, we stand on the shoulders of extraordinarily thoughtful and generous ancestors. They realized that to share was holy, to share everything was divine. They invented the Omnisch-o-Tron—a device worn for the last 130-odd years by every citizen, 24 hours a day, seven days a week. The Omnisch-o-Tron records every event, every interaction, every happening, and every non-happening, right on down to the cellular level. It observes more than we do, and it remembers better than we do, and now, decades later, our ancestors' dream of Godhood has come to fruition. Of course, we can't see back to before the Omnisch-o-Tron was invented, but conventional wisdom suggests there wasn't much of interest happening in those eras anyway. Though I sometimes do wish there were some way to access that information. Eh. I'm sure we have all the most important parts, at any rate.

A skilled truck driver can learn to parallel park a 240-foot long semi-trailer into a tight space with ease. The front wheels, the fuel tanks, the tandem axles, the far corners—they all become extensions of himself. Such is the case with the Omnisch-o-Tron. They're not machines, they're extensions. A supplement to our intellect, like vitamins. After all, we ask the questions, we prompt the flow of information. We know it all; we simply have to recall it.

I can't really fathom what life would be like without the Omnisch-o-Tron, thank goodness. Imagine having to go hunting for your lost keys or the remote control. Imagine striking up a conversation, or going on a date without already knowing the person's likes and dislikes, whether or not their haircut is new, or if they're menstruating or in the midst of some other unpleasant biological cycle. Imagine spending literally weeks comprehending the subtleties of someone's taste structure, or conversely, imagine a world where someone could lie about her own tastes to perpetrate a better romantic match! I've been told our forefathers were forced to contrive intricate scenarios called "ice-breakers" in order to force effective conversation amongst strangers. The thought strikes me as quite sad. Lonely people wandering dimly lit convention halls, having absolutely no idea what each other's names are or what they've eaten for breakfast or what color their underwear is.

Time passes. The future unfolds. Sometimes I wish I could know the future already, instead of having to wait for it to happen.

Oh, well.

I went on a few dates with some of the yogurt-eating gals in my building. Their Omnisch-o-Trons had told them about me, too. Lois M., of Oshkosh, Wisconsin, was my favorite. She also happened to share with me the highest percentage of mutual likes and dislikes of the bunch, but even if that hadn't been the case, I'm pretty sure she would have been my favorite anyway.

On our second date, something terrible happened. We were watching *Celebrity Bed-Wetters,* which I may have mentioned already as my favorite television program. Lois M. and I both had nearly perfect Laugh Compatibility Index Ratings for *Celebrity Bed-Wetters*: we were in the 99th percentile. I think that means that 99 percent of the time, we know when to laugh and when not to. People who are in the 99th percentile for a television program are honored by having their names scrolled across the bottom of the screen during the program. Mine's there almost every week.

I put in a request earlier that day with the Television Commission to have our names scrolled together, and they were happy to oblige. When our names finally appeared, Lois M. squealed with delight and nestled closer to me on the couch.

I'd spent hours beforehand preparing for the date with my Omnisch-o-Tron, so I already knew she'd only nestled this closely with four percent of her second dates. An elite brotherhood, indeed! Jim A. of Briggsville, Wisconsin, and Ed G. of Appleton, Wisconsin, were the only others, and I noted Ed G. was at one time in the 99th percentile of the Laugh Compatibility Index for eight different television programs at one time! It's certainly a load off of my mind that he's no longer in the picture.

Anyway, I was nestling with Lois M., feeling very proud of myself and wondering if I would enter an even more elite brotherhood, when I noticed the indicator light on my Omnisch-o-Tron had blinked out. I subtly craned my neck and saw that Lois M.'s was inactive as well. What a horror—and things had been going so well!

The network goes down every few months or so, usually for just a few seconds, but sometimes for as long as an hour. The government has assured us the Omnisch-o-Trons still record information when the network is down, but we can't access anything until the network is restored. Some people say it's a lie, fabricated so we don't start misbehaving every time the network goes down, but I believe it. I have to. Say, for example, what if I'd actually eaten 35, or even 36 spiders, the extras being when the network was down? That'd be too much to bear, I think. The "not knowing" part. So I'm glad the Omnisch-o-Trons still record information while the network is down. It's much safer that way.

Lois M. was so wrapped up in *Celebrity Bed-Wetters*, she hadn't yet noticed the lapse in the network. I was panicking. I tried not to show it, but my mind wandered, and I missed several laugh combos in a row. There goes my high score! This was getting worse all the time. *Now I'll have to watch 12 straight hours or more, catching every laugh perfectly in order to crack the 99th again,* I thought. What will Lois M. think? Will she still want me? I wanted to ask my Omnisch-o-Tron the answers to those questions, but the network was still down. Maddening. Damn it all! It was all so overwhelming. A tightness in my chest. A fuzziness in my brain. I missed out on even more laughs. Lois M. was sure to notice any moment now. Tears welled up in my eyes, but I fought them back. I fought it all back. I focused on the program as never before. I was going to get through this. I laughed very loud and very hard. I forced it. I'd never done that. Didn't know I was capable of it. A tear was trickling down my cheek. Can the Omnisch-o-Tron tell the difference between genuine and forced laughter? Can it tell the difference between tears of joy and tears of sadness? If it can, how would that affect my ranking? Has Lois M. ever been with a man who cried? Suddenly there were thousands upon thousands of these questions that I needed, needed, *needed* answered, but there was no outlet for them, no means of accessing the parts of my mind I needed to be accessed. I was a brain-damaged mutant. A God no longer! All I had at my disposal was frustration and sadness.

It was too much to bear. I couldn't hold it all in anymore. I struggled to contain these false emotions, but I began to tremble, regardless. Lois M. finally noticed. She probably had noticed earlier but was trying to be polite.

"Is something wrong?" she asked.

"No, no, no, nothing," I said. "This show is so funny, I just can't take it!" My voice cracked, but I soldiered through. "The laughs keep coming, though—so we shouldn't miss any!"

"Oh, right," she said and went back to watching. She was so engrossed, she still hadn't noticed her inactive Omnisch-o-Tron. Thank goodness.

As I focused on the program, on executing every proper laugh and pause and lull and laugh, my eyes began to widen. With my second self, I begged and begged and begged and begged for the network to return, for this part of me to be returned to its rightful owner. *I would give any other part of me to have this one back,* I thought. Well, not any part, but I'd give a finger. Or a tooth. Or a toe. I'd give a little toe to have this other part of me back. Please, please, please, give it back, give it back, it's not right, it's not right, it's not right—

The tears had returned. *Celebrity Bed-Wetters* was dwindling out of focus. All was stilted now. I shuddered, bucking and sobbing silently. It felt as if my internal organs were being switched on and off and on and off by a madman at the controls. I couldn't contain it. Suddenly—

"Jared B. of Green Bay, Wisconsin, is presently in the midst of eating a peanut butter sandwich. Would you like to speak with him now?"

"Yes, yes," I whimpered, and then I bolted off of the couch and into the bedroom with my Omnisch-o-Tron. Lois M. wore a rather startled expression upon her face, I'm sure. But the network was back! My supplications made flesh!

"Hello, who is this?," said Jared B. of Green Bay, Wisconsin.

"This is Robert J. of Madison, Wisconsin. You used to live in my apartment."

"Oh, really? What a trip!"

"You enjoying that peanut butter sandwich?"

"Ohhh, yeah. What, are you having one, too?"

"Not right now," I said. I was beginning to feel better already. It had only been a momentary hiccup.

"Then what's this about?"

"You ever fling a peanut butter sandwich at the ceiling?," I prompted.

"What? No way, man." He paused, and I heard him suck some peanut butter off of his front teeth with his tongue. "Oh, wait. Wait. Shiiit, yes! Fuckin'-A! I remember that! What, is the stain still there?"

"Oh, yeah," I said.

"Fuckin'-A, that is great! I hadn't thought about that in years!"

"Yeah," I said. "Pretty great stuff."

"Thanks for reminding me, man. That's great."

"Yeah," I said. "Anytime."

"Well, yo, I gotta get back to this peanut butter sandwich. But I'll catch you later, man. Maybe I'll call you next time *you* have a peanut butter sandwich."

"Heh, heh," I said. "I'll be here."

"Later, man."

"Goodbye."

I walked back into the living room. *Celebrity Bed-Wetters* had finished, and Lois M. had shut off the television. I sunk back into the couch, and she put her arm around me, tenderly.

"Something the matter? That sounded urgent."

I took in a deep breath and expelled the last bit of frustration from my system. I said nothing. Lois M. placed her head on my shoulder.

"Everything alright?" she asked.

"Yeah," I said. "I don't want to talk about it, though. Just ask your Omnisch-o-Tron sometime."

"Okay."

"What do you want to do now?"

"I don't know. This is fine."

"What?"

"Holding you. I don't know. It's fine."

Lois M. smiled.

"Are you having trouble deciding on an activity? Robert J. just took a phone call about peanut butter sandwiches," said Lois M.'s Omnisch-o-Tron. "Did you know? Americans eat, on average, 200 million peanut butter sandwiches a day. I have a video about a boy who puts peanut butter in his hair. I have footage of an event where eight champion eaters attempt to see who can eat the most peanut butter-covered hot dogs in the span of five minutes. I have a video of a mouse eating his way out of a jar of peanut butter. Ask me about funny peanut butter videos."

Relief was being suddenly inhaled and exhaled from every pore in the room. *Boy, oh boy,* I thought, *things are looking up!* I straightened my spine and puffed out my chest. "I can take it from here," I said. "I know a couple of good ones already."

TERENCE HAWKINS

The Thing that Mattered

From October/November 2006

HEM DIDN'T WANT to throw up. Not now. Not in front of these people. Not at this grave.

But he was close. His head was pounding. The sour taste of vomit was at the back of his throat. Breathe slow. You don't want it in the mouth. You don't want to think of the black licorice you ate as a kid. You don't want to think about the absinthe last night.

It almost had him there. It took a sharp deep breath, but he stopped it. He stood there a minute feeling the sweat trickle from his armpits and down the stiff bulge of flank and belly that made him so sick to look at. Thinking about what he saw in the mirror almost brought on the explosion again.

Christ it was hot. It was the worst kind of tropical late morning, when you stand there thinking a steam pipe ruptured in a florist's. Air sweet and sticky and boiling. The flowers didn't help. Any fool knew Rick wouldn't want flowers. But Rick didn't know many fools.

Rick wouldn't have wanted a priest, either. But there the priest was, fat as Hem but womanish, droning away in sad, singsong Latin. And Rick wouldn't have wanted to be dead. Yet there he was, about two minutes away from dropping permanently into the wet Cuban ground on a hot Cuban day.

Hem tried not to look at the box. He couldn't see it anyway, mounded over as it was with floral tributes. He tried not to think of the dead man inside and what he looked like right now. Rick had always looked good. Lots better than Hem, though he wasn't that much younger and drank nearly as hard. Now he just looked like a dead man with half a head.

Hem had seen that kind of thing a lot during his war. Not the war he let his friends believe he fought in when they drank at La Floridita. The real war, the one where he drove an ambulance and saw a lot of brave men and men not so brave all coming to the same place, the place where the life is leaving them and they feel death spiraling in and they look in disbelief at the bowels looped around their hands and scarlet stumps flecked with shattered eggshell bone. That war. Or the one Rick fought in, the one Hem had been too old even to pretend to fight in.

Maybe not too old. He was only 42 when it started. Men his age were getting drafted. Maybe too famous. Rick was famous, too, in his way. But it hadn't kept him out of it.

They knew him in Ethiopia when the Italians and their tanks and machine guns and poison gas were losing a war against men who knew you died just as dead whether you were killed by a lion or a bomb. But those men were grateful for the guns Rick brought them so they could teach the Italians this great lesson.

And they all knew him in Spain. Hem heard Franco said that every month Rick was alive cost him a battalion. That was when Hem had met him, when he was already too famous just to fight the war and

Rick had to watch where he was when he went out in daylight. And they knew him in North Africa, after he left Casablanca.

Hem heard, too, that Rick kept it up in Havana. He heard the bars and the whorehouses weren't Rick's only businesses. He heard some of the guns that went up into the hills came through the Cafe Americano and La Mariposa first. And he heard Battista wasn't happy, and he heard yesterday that was why Rick was going into the ground today.

Pulleys creaked. The mounded flowers shook, and the undertaker's men moved quickly to take them away. No point in burying them, too. Hem swayed slightly. Jesus it was hot. Was it really hot, or was it the damn hurt he got when he drank too much the night before? His sweat seemed different today, oily and thick. Maybe it was time to see the doctor. Maybe he was finally old. Maybe Rick was lucky. Someone had spared him this.

He looked across the open grave. He didn't want to watch Rick going in. Christ. There was Louie. Smiling his superior little frog smile. How the hell could he look like that?

Suit crisp despite the heat. Body still slim despite the years. Though Hem was told he wore a girdle. And Hem heard the girls you saw him with around town had to work harder and harder for less and less.

Louie looked up. He caught Hem's eye. His were red rimmed. As though he'd been crying. The frog smile was still in place. It just looked all of a sudden as though it didn't belong. Louie and Rick had been through a lot.

The priest was doing something with incense over the grave. Christ, when would this stop? Why the hell add one more stink to already overburdened air? Just then the first breeze of the day blew up. It pushed the priest's smoke towards him. Sweet and thick. It was too much. Hem's mouth filled with saliva. He turned and ran towards the bushes.

Louie caught up with him later. They walked in silence towards the cars. "This must be very hard for you," said Louie after a time.

"It is," said Hem. "He was a good man. Harder for you, I think."

"Thank you. But I'm afraid that's not quite what I meant. Forgive me, but I was referring to your Communist friends."

Silence again. Gravel crunched very loud under their feet. It was getting close to noon. It was much hotter, but Hem felt better. Someone had had a flask with a little rum.

"Do I have Communist friends?"

Louie laughed. "You have friends. This is Cuba. It's 1956. Of course you have Communist friends. More than you know, I'm sure. But I'm also sure you have Communist friends you do know about. For example, two named Fidel and Ernesto."

Hem suddenly remembered he didn't like Louie. He also remembered Louie had worked for Vichy. So, he didn't tell him to go to hell. "So, we all have Communist friends. Why does that make today hard for me?"

"Papa, surely you jest. Why do you think we buried our friend just now?"

"Only thing to do with a dead man." The headache was coming back now. Just at the base of his head. Soon it would take up the whole skull. Hem started thinking about lunch. Prawns with his Habanero friends. Some beers. Maybe sleep in the afternoon. He hoped he could sleep again that night without liquor. He didn't want to feel this way tomorrow.

Louie laughed. "Well, I do imagine you're right. You do know, though, Papa, that even the Cuban authorities are likely to bestir themselves at the violent death of a prominent American expatriate." He shook his head and whistled in obvious admiration. "And I thought I was corrupt when I was an authority myself. But these circumstances will penetrate even the deepest ineptitude and moral bankruptcy. Sorry. Don't mean to sound melodramatic. The funeral, I suppose. But do please remember, inquiries are being made even as we speak. Some of my friends tell me Fidel and his friends are thought to be responsible. And you are thought of as one of Fidel's friends."

Hem stopped in mid-stride. "What the hell?"

Louie shrugged and smiled. "You knew, of course, that our friend couldn't break himself of his old habits. Why guns, I always asked him. You make a perfectly admirable living with gin and the roulette wheels and the girls, all of which are at least as interesting and much, much safer. Well. We see that I was right. I wish I hadn't been." The frog smile was fixed in place even if the voice quivered. "Forgive me. In any event, my friends tell me that Rick's friends—your friends—quarreled with him over price and availability. They appear to have thought he was starving the People's Army or whatever they call it of the necessary wherewithal for the worker's paradise just in order to drive up the price. Thus an argument. It is thought we buried the result."

Hem stood still. His clothes were sodden. "What's this about me?"

Louie backed up a step. Hem wondered if he smelled traces of liquor and vomit. "Papa, do remember you are known by the company you keep."

"Maybe. But yesterday you told me it was Battista behind it anyway."

Louie smiled. "He is, I am afraid, the usual suspect whenever anyone of wealth or prominence meets a violent end. But as exemplary a Caribbean politician as he may be, even he can't be responsible for every well-attended funeral on this island. And now he has competition. Remember, Papa. The company you keep."

They were at the cars. Louie turned to a flowering vine and plucked a blossom. He slipped it into his buttonhole. Hem ground his teeth. Christ, was there no limit to the man?

Apparently not. A sleek Lincoln, late model by Cuban standards, rolled up. At the wheel was a mulatta who looked barely old enough to drive. "Papa, you'll let us drop you? Please, you look quite done in by grief." He followed Hemingway's eyes to the driver's seat. "Ah, yes. Well. And to think I once told Rick that women might be scarce one day. Well, they were. But that was North Africa and a long time ago. Please, Papa, let me help you in."

Hem had been at La Floridita for a long time when Laslo came in. He felt better. The big shrimp, almost raw and hot from the oil, had hit the spot. So had the beers. He drank the first three very fast. He had been sipping for the past few hours. No more than three or four. Just six or seven in all, then. If he took a nap soon, he would feel fine that night. Maybe just some wine with dinner and then a really good sleep. Tomorrow would be different.

They knew how to treat him at La Floridita. They greeted him like a hero, and then they let him almost alone, just enough sidelong glances to let him know they knew he was who he was. When someone came in who looked like he should be recognized, everyone looked at Hem, because no one who came there could be there for any reason but to see him. They wanted to see whether Hem would acknowledge the visitor so they would know how to act.

Laslo still walked as though he should be recognized. Funny. He hadn't gotten the message. Maybe he should have forgotten that little time he was a hero and remembered instead that very long time he was hunted. Hem was surprised he would forget.

But still he walked like a hero, and at least some of the Habaneros recognized it. They looked at Hem to see what to do. Hem nodded at this man in his fine linen suit and big Panama hat and then nodded at the man sitting opposite him. The fellow at the table stood up and offered the new man his chair. Hem would have jumped to his feet and embraced Laslo had it been earlier in the day. But even though it was only seven beers, it had been a tiring morning, and he knew sometimes when he was tired like that, there could be stories the next day. So he sat.

They shook across the table. "Victor."

"Papa. How was today?"

"Funeral. How could it be? Sorry you missed it."

"So am I. I just arrived. Trouble with passports." He smiled sourly. "I never had this problem until recently. That man from Wisconsin." Suddenly he laughed. "Actually, there was a time when I had even more trouble with passports. That man in Berlin."

Hem laughed, too, even though he didn't get it. Then he got it and looked over his shoulder. "Still trouble with the Committee?"

Laslo shrugged. "It seems I always have trouble with committees." Hem wasn't surprised. The man didn't know how to trim his sails. Hem's lawyers told him he was safe, but he was glad to be in a place where there could be no subpoenas. But if he wanted to go back to Idaho, he didn't want to have problems because he drank with a man who could compare McCarthy to Hitler.

He decided not to hold his tongue. "Ilsa?"

Laslo shrugged again. "She won't be here." He sipped a beer as though it were cognac. "We lead our separate lives."

I'll bet you do, boy, thought Hem. I'll just bet you do, you stuffed shirt.

Once when they were drunk, he asked Rick what she was like. "Pretty," said Rick.

"I know that," Hem said. "You know what I mean." Then Rick looked at him for a long time. Hem started to sweat. He always felt that way when Rick looked at him too long, especially after he said something like that. Finally Rick spoke. "She was like any woman. She was like one of the girls upstairs. Not as good, maybe." Then Rick poured more bourbon and didn't speak and didn't look at Hem for the rest of the night.

Hem looked at Laslo. "You know what happened?"

"I got some telegrams. Someone shot him in the face."

Hem nodded. He didn't trust himself to speak. Was this eight or nine? "What do you think?"

"What do the police think?"

Hem snorted. "They're Cuban. They think he's dead. They think that because we buried him. Otherwise they don't know."

Laslo considered. "He was shot in the face. He was in his office. There was no sign of a struggle or theft. That means he knew whoever shot him. And he trusted him." He thought again. "Or her."

"I guess you got a lot of telegrams." Hem was pleased he was following so well. The implication of the last words sank in. "One of the girls?"

Laslo shrugged. "Who knows? Was he with any of them regularly?"

Hem thought about Rick. He tried to talk to him about women. It never seemed to work. "He didn't talk about it much. He was quiet about women for such a ladies' man."

Laslo smiled. "My friend, that is probably how he stayed a ladies' man." Hem was starting to remember what he didn't like about Laslo. He was so damned European it made his teeth hurt. "But as you see, all I know is courtesy of Western Union. What do you hear?"

Hem's attention had wandered a little. This was number ten in front of him. Maybe when he finished this, he'd have just one of the special drinks they made for him here, the Papa Dobles, dacquiris with twice the usual rum. Just to be polite. But just one.

He made a big show of waving to a bunch of Habaneros who had come in to crunch shrimp, tails and all, bellied up to the bar where he could see them. These boys liked that, strutting in with boots gleaming from the second polish of the day. After this little delay Hem had gathered his thoughts enough to speak. "I hear lots of things," he said at last. "I hear Battista had him killed because he sold guns to the Communists. I hear the Communists had him killed because they thought he was jacking up the price."

Laslo considered again. He was used to thinking and liked it. "Papa, both things can't be true. Well, perhaps I speak too soon. I never thought Hitler and Stalin would sign a treaty."

"Didn't last long."

"Much longer than it takes to shoot a single American in the head. Perhaps they made a deal. Stranger things have happened." He lit a cigarette. "Who is your source, or better, who are your sources for all this news?"

"Louie."

Laslo laughed. Hem couldn't remember having actually heard the man laugh before. He was without humor. Prolonged consideration of the dialectic of history had leached it from his bones and left irony in its place, the way dinosaur's rotting flesh had been replaced with stone. His laugh startled Hem as much as a museum brontosaurus dropping its bony head and rooting for swamp cabbage a million years extinct. "Louie? Well, who better to tell both sides of the same story?"

Number ten was almost gone. "What do you mean?"

Laslo took a silk square from his pocket and dabbed at his eyes. Maybe his fossil laughter hurt. "Papa, you're joking. Did you know the man in Casablanca?" Hem shook his head. "He betrayed France for Vichy and Vichy for the main chance. I'm only surprised he didn't wait longer. Until he could see the Star Spangled Banner on the horizon and the Germans burning documents, for example. But I digress." Hem hoped for another beer. The man was forever on a soapbox. "He's always played a double game. That is all I mean. No one could have a better opportunity to know both sides of a story."

Number eleven had arrived. "That's not all you mean."

"That is all I said. That is all I mean." The square went back in the pocket. "I have friends here, too. Other than yourself, of course. All, I'm afraid, on just one side. Perhaps that is why the Committee keeps asking to hear from me. Oh, well. In any case my friends on that side tell me Battista is starting to be concerned. He knows there are guns in the hills. He wants there to be no guns in the hills. It is easier to kill a few people or a few dozen people in the city than a few thousand in the country."

"So Battista had him killed. But Battista didn't kill him. Neither did any of his men. Not in Rick's office. Not like that."

"No. First of all Rick wouldn't have been foolish enough to let one in that close. Second they wouldn't have killed him that way. Too painless and private." Laslo swallowed hard. Perhaps he was thinking about different thugs in a different time. "No. Someone he knew and trusted. And I think we can rule out a purely private dispute. Rick didn't run his life that way."

Hem nodded. When you lived on the edge as long as Rick, you didn't deal in shades of gray. There was only room for black and white, word kept or broken. Much of what he did was illegal, but Hem couldn't think of anything he'd done that was wrong.

Hem hadn't touched the beer in front of him. He was pleased with that. "So, Battista bought someone close to him."

"Correct."

"So, who close to him could be bought?"

"Well, Papa, not you. Even if you could be bought by anyone, you have more money than you need. Sam never cared about money, and he doesn't need it now. Anyway, is he even physically capable these days?"

"He hasn't sung for two years. He hasn't spoken for six months. He hasn't left the hospital for two. His throat is all cut away and he weighs 80 pounds."

"My God. Death mocks us, doesn't it?" He raised his eyebrows and pursed his lips and stared into the middle distance. "Louie has had a few financial problems, I'm told."

"You really are told quite a lot."

Laslo smiled sourly. "Well. If the FBI didn't let me have my mail, I couldn't write back. Then no one would write to me. Then the FBI would have nothing to read." He lit another cigarette. "Your country is not quite what I expected. I write a lot. No one talks to me. Everyone is afraid. I wanted to march with the Negroes, thinking they at least had nothing to lose by association with me. But, no. Apparently Marxism is contagious. And no one wants to invite scrutiny by Mr. Cohn. So, I read, and I write. I was a little surprised they let me come here. Perhaps I shouldn't have. Perhaps you shouldn't be seen with me."

Hem put his hand on Laslo's shoulder and squeezed. "I'm scared of nothing." He was pretty sure he'd seen everyone in the bar before. "I'm scared of nothing." He had to have lunch with the Ambassador soon. Just to play it safe.

Laslo had been gone a long time. Hem sat and thought about what he had said. Sometimes he talked to his Cuban friends. Sometimes an American bought him a beer. They usually asked him to drink it with them. He had to be much drunker than he was to do that. When the sun went down, he switched to rum. He drank this for a long time. Then Jose told him the car was here, and he knew it was time to go, because otherwise there would be stories.

He didn't stay long at the house. He sat and thought some more and got what he needed and started to walk back towards town. It took him a long time. It wasn't far; even ten years ago he could have done it in less than an hour. Even after a long day at La Floridita. But tonight it took him more like two to get to the big house in the little side street.

The lights were on in the second floor. Hem knew they would be. The man who owned the house was never up before noon. He knocked hard. A mulatta girl, maybe the same one who had been at the wheel, opened the door. She recognized him, even if he wasn't sure about her. Her English was bad, so they spoke French. Of course. He was upstairs. Please follow.

Louie was seated in a big leather chair behind a big mahogany desk making him look even smaller and vainer than he was. He must have just come in. He was wearing a white dinner jacket, his bowtie still knotted impeccably. In his lapel was the little red ribbon of the Legion of Honor. Well, he wasn't the first bastard to wear it.

"Papa. A pleasure unexpected." He twitched his sparrow head at the door, and the mulatta left. The brass latch clicked. "A late night for us both, I see. Please. Do sit."

Hem stayed on his feet. Not without effort. It had been a long walk on a long day. "No thanks. Son of a bitch." He was surprised at how easily the Luger came out of his waistband.

So was Louie. But just for an instant. "Papa. You have the advantage of me. In more ways than one. What do you mean?"

"I mean I know what you did. You little frog queer son of a bitch."

"Queer? Queer?" Louie chuckled easily and leaned back in his chair, crossing his legs and smoothing the creases in his pants as he did. "I really think that's a bit much, don't you, Papa? Also a bit of the pot and the kettle. Except I'm not the kettle."

"What?"

Louie tapped a cigarette out of a gold case. He leaned across the desk and extended it to Hem, an eyebrow cocked in polite inquiry. "No? I'm sure you don't mind if I do." He lit up and exhaled as luxuriously as any man who'd ever had a gun pointed at him. "Please do put that away. Or keep it if you like. But you're not fooling anyone. At least here. In any respect."

Hem tried to speak, but no words came out.

"Confused? Sorry. I do forget sometimes how much you drink. Too, too much, Papa. We must talk about that sometime. But not now. Well. I know a few things about you that you might find surprising. First, I know that the gun is there for your comfort and nothing else. I know you don't have the guts to kill a man. Not like this. Not in cold blood. Never did. Men like you never do. That explains all those animals you go to such trouble and inconvenience to go off and kill. All those bullfights and the chest beating and the lies about the war. The first one, I mean.

"Second. I know exactly what brings you here. You think I killed Rick. I know that isn't true. I do know who did, and I know why.

"Which brings me to the third thing I know." He smiled. "I've known you how long, Papa? Ten years? I always wondered why you seemed to have such a mania for masculinity. At first I thought it was simply that you were an American from the middle of the country who drank too much and enjoyed his fame and started to believe his own lies. You remember I was a policeman, don't you? Even if I was a corrupt provincial policeman, I was still a French policeman. I asked my friends in Paris about you. Just out of curiosity. Always nice to know something about the great man about whom we orbit. Well. They told me things. You were very discreet when you were a young man in Paris, Papa. But still, a few slip-ups. An arrest or two in the public conveniences. A fight here and there with sailors that didn't have anything to do with them insulting your flag. Tsk. Who would have thought it?"

Hem's voice was choked, but he got it out. "God damn it. That's bullshit. I was a married man."

"So were some of your little lavatory friends, I'd imagine." Louie ground out the cigarette and met Hem's eyes. "Papa. I don't care. I actually think it's rather sad to have to conduct affairs of the heart in a urinal. But. That's not what brings us here, is it? You think I killed Rick. I didn't. As I said, I know who, and I know why."

He cocked his head to the side. He was giving Hem his best profile, like Barrymore. "It wasn't cold blood that night, was it, Papa? I know you, you see. I saw the way you looked at Rick. I saw it ten years ago. That's why I made my little inquiries. Tell me, Papa, how did your heart declare itself that night? A kiss? A fumble between his legs? Or did you come to him dressed like a bride?" Head still tilted, Louie laughed again.

He was right about everything except the thing that mattered. The bullet caught him just under the left cheekbone. Tumbling and mushrooming, it tore off the top of his head. The impact knocked the chair back and over.

Though the room still rang from the shot, Hem heard through it a sound from Idaho. It was the patter of heavy snow falling from pine branches at the first warmth of early spring. He stood quite still for a moment. As it faded, he recognized it for what it was, foamy fragments of airborne brain landing on desk and floor and wall.

Then he heard a sound he recognized from the war. He had heard it many times driving his ambulance. It was the wet crackle of bowels relaxing just past the moment of death. He didn't need to look behind the desk.

The gun was quivering in his hand. He stuffed the Luger into his mouth. Still hot, the barrel burned his lips and he snatched it away. Not yet. Not this time. But soon. He had done the same with another gun, by then cold, the morning after Rick died, when he woke up choking in his own vomit, before he managed to convince himself he'd had just another bad drunk dream. But then he had smelled the smell on the back of his right hand, the cordite stench of a powderburn nightmares can't leave.

The mulatta was pounding at the door. In a second he would go behind the desk because he had to, to put the gun into Louie's hand. He would tell Laslo how he had confronted the little bastard with the truth and how he hadn't been man enough to take his medicine. In a day or two they would stand beside another grave.

Hem got to work. Soon he would not have to be afraid anymore.

WILLIAM HAN

The Other Batman

From January/February 2011

BECAUSE I HAVE never shared my friend Sean's passion for collecting comic books, I was surprised when he called to tell me of his latest find. It was a copy of *Detective Comics #38*, not exactly in pristine condition, although one of Bob Kane and Bill Finger's original entries in the legend of Bruce Wayne, the Dark Knight of Gotham. Sean told me when I went over to his apartment that he found it in the basement of a secondhand bookstore in Williamsburg.

"But I thought you already had all the issues Kane and Finger wrote themselves." My puzzlement as to why Sean thought I would care about his new (old) comic book must have been quite obvious in my voice.

"Yes, I do. I already have all of them." Sean smiled mysteriously. "But this one is special."

I could tell he wanted my curiosity. "All right, Sean, I'll bite. Tell me, why is this one special? What's different about Issue #38?"

"It's not Issue #38 that's special; it's this particular copy." He handed me the other copy of Detective Comics #38, the one he bought years ago and had long kept in his collection. "Look how they're different."

I examined the two comic books alongside one another. Both were dated April, 1940. Both of course carried the same "Detective Comics" title, and both were enumerated No. 38. Each cost ten cents. But whereas the copy Sean already had announced "the Sensational Character Find of 1940," which as it turned out was a reference to Robin, famously introduced in this issue, the copy Sean found in Brooklyn carried no such promise, and inside there was no mention of Robin. Indeed, it was a different story altogether.

The story in this copy (the "Williamsburg Copy," one might call it) telescopes 25 years into the future, when a middle-aged Bruce Wayne has begun considering retirement. He has been so successful in his crusade against crime that by this time Gotham has become as safe as Singapore. Rather than rejoicing in his own triumph, however, in recent months Wayne has grown depressed with the state of affairs. The Joker, Catwoman, Two-Face, the Penguin, Poison Ivy—they are all gone, dead, or in prison. And only now in his loneliness does Wayne come to understand he needs them as much as they need him, their lives having defined his and his life theirs. Without criminals haunting the streets of Gotham City, Batman seems no more than the superfluous vestige of a bygone era, an era any decent citizen of Gotham would prefer to forget. And then one night, he hears about himself on the radio.

At first he thinks it must be the Cognac. With the tips of his fingers, he feels drops of condensation gliding down the outside of the glass onto the mahogany armrest. No coaster. Alfred would not be pleased. The amber liquid is growing warm as the ice melts, beginning to taste watered down on his tongue. He has been ending his evenings with these solitary nightcaps more and more often lately. And the Cognac is going to his head a little; he can feel it.

And that is why he thinks it must be the Cognac when he hears about his own exploits on the 9:30 news. "Batman was spotted earlier tonight turning onto the highway off Seventh Avenue," the newsman intones in his cigarette-stained voice with a vague undercurrent of boredom. "Witnesses say the Caped Crusader had just stopped a robbery in progress at Katz's Jewelry store on the corner across the street from Wayne Tower. The robber was then picked up by the police. In other news, in Washington tonight..."

It is a heartbeat or so before Bruce Wayne consciously registers the creeping unease in his mind. It must be the Cognac, he thinks. Why is he drinking Cognac anyway? He doesn't even like it. It always reminds him of the cough medicine his father gave him when he was an infirm boy.

"Alfred," he calls, but without enough air in his diaphragm and more quietly than he had intended. He takes a breath and tries again, "Alfred!" this time rather too loudly and impatiently.

"Yes, Master Bruce?" His butler appears in the doorway, looking exactly the same as he always does in his impeccable tuxedo. Except older, perhaps. The tracks around his mouth and across his forehead cast deeper shadows than ever. And those eyes behind the silver-rimmed glasses betray more weariness than usual, Bruce thinks. "Can I get you anything, sir?"

"Alfred," Bruce frowns. "Was I out earlier this evening?"

"No, sir, not since you came back from golf. Is everything all right?" Bruce knows Alfred, who is very old himself now, worries for him. But it is at moments like this, when the younger man, who ought to have the better memory, relies on the older one, that Alfred displays his superhuman ability not to betray his feelings.

So someone is impersonating him, Bruce thinks. Apparently doing the work he himself has grown too bored to do, too enervated even, work that in any case has grown embarrassingly small-time.

But now the thought that another Batman roams the streets of Gotham invigorates him, preoccupies him. He begins to devote all the ingenuity and skill he once directed against the Joker to his newly discovered double. He deliberately allows crimes—few and far between as they are now—to go forward unimpeded, just to see whether his malevolent twin (because surely he is malevolent) will intervene. At times he does intervene, and Bruce tries to catch him; at other times he does not, and Bruce watches the thief or robber disappear into the night.

This has to be the work of some new criminal mastermind, Bruce thinks, some trap laid by a new and dastardly personality unlike any of his old adversaries, because this doppelganger act is beyond the evil imagination and nihilism of even the Joker.

Bruce's fixation on the Other Batman grows to an obsession. He begins seeing him in places where he could not possibly be—among the guests at his birthday party, for example, the twin-spiked black mask and cape amidst the tuxedos and ball gowns, charging his champagne glass with the rest when Bruce makes his toast, although no one but Bruce seems to notice him. When Bruce approaches the phantom, it recedes into the shadows while his guests stop him to shake his hand with as much stealth as Bruce himself could have managed.

Finally, after months of effort, he catches up with his double at the museum, where the Other Batman has just apprehended a pair of art thieves intent on stealing Velazquez's Las Meninas, which has recently been brought over from Europe. Bruce confronts him. "Who are you?" he demands.

"I'm you, obviously," the Other answers.

"Take off your mask," he demands. The Other complies without protest. To Bruce's amazement—and perhaps even horror—the face underneath the mask is one he recognizes all too well, the same Wayne features he inherited from his late father and of which he is always so proud. It is as though Bruce is looking through a mirror, darkly. "How can this be?" he asks the apparition of himself.

"I told you; I am you."

"It can't be." Bruce throws himself at his Other, pushing him violently to the ground, destroying an 18th century Dante chair in the process. With his left hand Bruce grasps his enemy's throat and squeezes hard, and with his right he begins striking the face with those features identical to his own, bashing in the cheekbones and breaking the nose and bruising the eyes until they are unrecognizable. To his surprise, the Other does not resist. The art thieves, bound to a pillar in the middle of the room, beg him to stop, but he ignores them. He stops only when his arms have grown weary and his fists are covered in blood.

The final panel in the Williamsburg Copy of *Detective Comics* #38 shows Batman's newspaper obituary.

For a good hour or so, Sean and I debated what the story might have meant, whether the double represented death, a death wish, conscience, a protest against the idea of Robin, or the elemental horror of reflection itself. Then we turned to whether the obituary at the end indicated the dead double was taken as the real Batman, that in killing his double Batman had killed himself, or whether Batman was already dead from the start although he didn't realize it.

"The remarkable thing is," Sean added when the discussion came to a lull, "I haven't been able to find another copy of #38 like this. I've inquired at every comic bookstore in New York and called every other collector I know who also has #38, and every other copy of #38, it seems, depicts what it's supposed to depict—the first appearance of Robin. No other copy of #38, at least none I am aware of, depicts this alternate storyline of Batman's death by doppelganger. It appears, as well as I can ascertain, that this alternate copy of Issue #38 is unique."

Perhaps Bob Kane and Bill Finger produced this alternate version of #38 as a joke, albeit one with profound significance. Or perhaps Kane and Finger were never responsible for this bizarro comic book, and instead its singular appearance in Brooklyn represents the piecemeal disintegration of our world as it collides with the imagination of its own doppelganger.

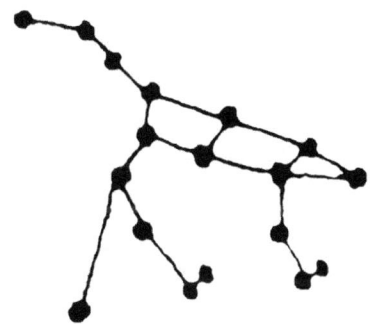

ALANA NOEL VOTH

If I'd Loved the Grizzly Man

From October/November 2007

ANCHORAGE, ALASKA: A self-styled bear expert who once called Alaska's brown bears harmless party animals was one of two people fatally mauled in a bear attack in Katmai National Park and Preserve—the first known bear killings in the 4.7 million-acre park. The bodies of Timothy Treadwell, 46, and Amie Huguenard, 37, were found near Kaflia Bay on Monday when a pilot with Andrew Airways arrived to pick them up. (The Associated Press, October 8, 2003)

IF I'D LOVED the Grizzly Man, I wouldn't have loved him exactly. I would have loved that he went on TV, like David Letterman, and was this goofy, cute celebrity.

If I'd loved the Grizzly Man, I would have asked him to tell me his stories. I would have said, "Tell me about the time you kissed a bear's nose. About the time a mother bear left her babies with you while she went hunting." My toe at the edge of his spotlight.

If I'd loved the Grizzly Man, I would have named the bears with him: Squiggles, Mickey, and Mr. Chocolate. I would have wanted to come up with my own names though, my own bears, and things would have gotten competitive between us.

If I'd loved the Grizzly Man, I would have complained about the peanut butter and jelly sandwiches and not being able to shower and the mosquitoes and having to hide in the bushes from tourists and having to put up a tent just to have it blown over in a storm and always watching what I said around the bears like they could actually understand us.

If I'd loved the Grizzly Man, I would have felt ten again. Whenever it is in our lives we feel hopeful.

If I'd loved the Grizzly Man, I would have recommended medication and therapy. Not to be mean, but I would have had him committed.

If I'd loved the Grizzly Man, I would have loved his blonde hair, shocking in the sunshine and like a nightlight against a dark sky. In a tent after dinner, he would have said, "Shhh, don't make any sudden moves," and then I would have held still on all fours so he could mount me.

If I'd loved the Grizzly Man, I would have loved how he said, "Cover your eyes," when he undressed, but I would have spied on him anyway because I craved the tenderness he housed in that tightly wound body.

If I'd loved the Grizzly Man, I would have jumped naked into the river, and the cold would have been shocking, the kind that hurts before it lights up every cell in your body. I would have said, "Timothy, look at me," and then come out of the water and held his warm face in my wet hands until he fell to his knees to bury his face in my belly, push a hand between my legs.

If I'd loved the Grizzly Man, I would have bought him another teddy bear, one to sleep with at night instead of me, because I would have been too afraid to go out there with him.

If I'd loved the Grizzly Man, I would have understood what it meant to be out there with animals. That people kill more people and animals than animals do.

If I'd loved the Grizzly Man, I would have pointed at the sky and said, "Look honey, it's Orion." I would have learned to stay close to the fire at night. I never would have left his side. I would have done what he taught me. He would have been the reason I survived.

If I'd loved the Grizzly Man, my mother would have dragged me out of the wilderness by my hair and locked me in a room or a closet, whatever it took, and listened to me beating on the door screaming to be let loose, and I would have talked in tongues and done strange dances. I would have pawed at the floor and sniffed the dust particles for fresh air. My mother would have called the men in white coats. They would have medicated me, hypnotized me, whatever it took to put my crazy lover out of my mind. I would have become like one of those wild animals in a zoo, pacing without any purpose, living dead.

If I'd loved the Grizzly Man, I would have read him poetry. He would have liked "The Panther" by Rilke. And he would have said, "Read it again."

If I'd loved the Grizzly Man, it wouldn't have lasted because I would have been afraid of bears. When I was little I saw an episode of *Little House on the Prairie* where a character got mauled by a grizzly. Right then I realized the size of the world, how it could swallow me whole if it wanted.

If I'd loved the Grizzly Man, I would have begged him to change careers, and he would have gone back to waiting tables and drinking and doing heroin and then shot himself in the head.

If I'd loved the Grizzly Man, I wouldn't have left him hanging from a bear's mouth and screaming like that. I would have turned around and come back and watched even if he'd begged me to run, because he would have; he would have begged. I would have heard the sound of his human skull crushed in a bear's jaws. I would have seen how a man's blood can paint the forest, what the inside of my lover looked like. I would have seen a bear coming at me, jaws open, unforgiving in the moment and self-centered, like God.

INDIRA CHANDRASEKHAR

Polymorphism

From April/May 2014

MY SHOULDER WAS at it again, swivelling and turning like a mechanism lubricated with heavy machine oil. I tried to pretend it wasn't happening, that my body wasn't giving in to the mobility, and continued walking under the orange-red of the gul mohar trees. Just as I was losing myself in the brilliance of their elaborately bracted flowers, a man on a scooter veered towards me and snatched my bag. Which yanked my arm right out of its socket.

He must have been startled by how easily it dropped out, for I caught a split-second sight of his face, and it seemed to widen grotesquely before he skidded and fell. But he was quick to recover. By the time I caught my breath, he had sped past the corner kiosk, leaving a crushed, scarlet trail in the fallen flowers. My bag was gone with my medicines in it, and my arm was swinging about wildly.

I must start carrying my pills in my pocket, one part of my brain said, while another recalled techniques for getting out of panic mode, like counting to 10,333, or breathing with my diaphragm; but such tricks, I've found, are only useful well into the aftermath of an emergency, not during the crisis.

Like an injured homing pigeon, I fled erratically back towards the house. If I were fine, it would only have been seven minutes away, on a lane carpeted not red but lavender from jacaranda petals. I don't know how long it took me, but when I managed, finally, to crash through the front door and collapse out of breath on the cold tiles of the entrance hall, I could barely see from the headache and the pain. The lingering smell of the masala I had used on the brinjal fry that afternoon induced a wave of nausea; it was as if my head would burst, and my gut.

"Ma," Charu whispered in my ear, "get up, get up. Mr Narasimhan is here for my math tutoring."

"*AaHAhhh,*" I groaned, unable to rise.

"Shall I call a doctor?" I could hear Mr. Narasimhan say. "My sister's husband's cousin-brother is a doctor, and he lives only in the next colony. I can contact him." His habitually rapid speech was more exaggerated than usual.

"No, no," my daughter replied, "it's nothing."

"Nothing? But, but... oh, I see." His tone turned sympathetic. "Some ladies-type problems. His wife, that is, my sister's husband's cousin-brother's wife is also a doctor, a ladies' specialist. Quite well-known in her colony. She..." Mr. Narasimhan's voice rose in high-pitched excitement, causing my eardrums intense agony. My legs started to thrash as I tried to get away from him.

"Manu, Manu," my daughter bellowed. There was a complex series of sounds upstairs—chair pushed back, feet landing on floor—each of which felt as if it was driving a hammer into my skull. As if to protect me, my auditory system seemed to sink into a fog as my son came jumping down the stairs. Everything sounded like it was travelling through some dense, absorbent substance, emerging muffled and warped. But his words were distinct enough: "What? Couldn't you solve it? Don't worry. Here comes the calculus expert..." He saw me, stopped abruptly, and said, "What the fuck?"

"The math dude's here, Man," Charu responded, "Watch your language."

Manu bent over me. His mouth was open, his teeth—he really needed to see the dentist—seemed to move towards me ahead of his face. "Come on, Ma," he said, his voice gurgly as if he were under water. "Let me take you to your room." He lifted me up and staggered towards my bedroom off the entrance hall. I could sense the warmth of his rangy, young body as he held me, then settled me into bed. The pain began to dissipate, and the sponginess in my ears cleared somewhat.

"Mr. Narasimhan," I could hear Charu saying, "this differentiation problem... I need to answer it for tomorrow's class." She apparently succeeded in focusing him away from my agonies. His voice rose in a happy squeak as he intoned the relevant rules of calculus. I could imagine my daughter's face glazing over as she thought about everything but the sums.

I wished his voice had less ability to carry. He was slowing down, emphasizing, rounding out the words and pressing them into the rhythm of a mantra, *"Dee yex wover dee wai."* I didn't want to make fun of him, even in my head, but the combination of pain and muscle dysfunction made me unable to regulate myself.

"Dee yex..." I mimicked.

Manu gave me my pills, and within minutes I was easier. My body was tightening and loosening in the right places, my shoulder was easing back, my tongue under control. I was becoming human again. He sat on the chair near my bed and watched me. The minute I could blink without my eyelids going into high-frequency mode, he said, "How could you allow this to happen to you, Ma? Did you feel the symptoms? Your shoulder spinning? Faces melting? You didn't take your pill, did you?"

My voice was not quite back to normal, and I deliberately made gagging sounds, hoping his annoyance would turn to sympathy. But he just waited, and eventually I had to reply. I thought of feigning incapacity, but one time when I had tried to get out of answering him about forgotten pills by pleading illness, I'd slipped up; my mind had wandered as I lay there pretending, so when he'd leaned over anxiously, I wanted to make him smile and started telling him some long, gossipy story about the family. He was so angry he grabbed me by the forearms. I could see he wanted to twist my shoulder right out of its socket. He wouldn't have done it, I don't think, but he most certainly would have screamed and cursed. Instead, he'd let go, ground his teeth, stood up, and scolded me with great gravity. My poor little man. My condition had forced him into feeling he had to be an adult.

Today, therefore, as soon as my system allowed, I explained to him about the man on the scooter who'd snatched my bag. He was horrified. I did not want him to feel burdened and to worry every time I went out, so I said, "My shoulder had started to give way by then, or I would have been able to snatch it back. Or knock him off his bike."

"The collapse had gone that far? Before he attacked? You have to take the pill immediately, as soon as it shows itself. Why the fuck didn't you?"

"Don't swear," I responded while I thought about what to say. How could I explain to him I hadn't taken my pill because I wanted to savor my independence for a little longer, wanted the freedom to walk without the oppressive thickening of the medication for just a few more steps.

But there was another reason why I wanted to delay my medication. One I couldn't share with anyone, least of all him. I could never admit to being tempted, every time, to give in, to relinquish control and allow my body to go where it would, where it could, and to take my mind with it. I had been close to the edge so often, had begun to sense the enticement of transformation so many times, but had held back, terrified. For myself, for my children. My dear, sweet children...

Now, however, it was becoming irresistible, drawing me, pushing me to an extreme where every neuron was extended and maximally alive.

I lay back, silent, as Manu talked about managing my illness, and I felt sorry I had to impose so much on him. Each thread on my bedspread, a beautiful blue and pale green printed cotton with a curiously European pattern of thistles and stalks, rather more widely spread than the fine Sanganeri flowers usually were, stood out, distinct and visible. The woody resinous aroma of eucalyptus mingled with the scent of jasmine and travelled in through the window, carrying with it the colors, the waxy ivory and pink of frangipani and the amber and ochers of the crotons. I was filled with a kind of hyper excitement, my chest shivering from having gone as far as I had, and I stretched up to hold the volatiles, elongating my extremities to immerse myself in them, allowing them to attach to me.

Ecstasy. I could fly.

"Ma, Ma." Manu's voice was loud. Loud and intrusive, taking me deeper into myself to escape it. "Charu!' He was sobbing now, and I could feel him shaking.

"Please go, Mr. Narasimhan."

"You are not needing some help? I will stay, or bring the doctor."

"Thank you, thank you, no, we don't need anything, please..." The front door banged, and Charu, my beautiful Charu, came in on a cloud, no harsh sounds to accompany her. She laid her cool hand on my skin. Which was brave of her, I know, because she had always been horrified, even as a little girl, when my skin began to mottle with the strange mobilities.

"Why, why?" Manu was saying. "I was just here, watching her. Why did she let this happen, why didn't she ask me for another pill?"

I drifted back towards my other existences, where everything was intensely felt, every sensation magnified. I was a stretched, vibrating string, highly tuned, separated from the low noise of everyday. I could do anything; I was alight.

But Manu was loud, holding my arms, shouting at me, interfering. I started to hear the words and participate in the children's emotions even as I strove to float above and shape my world in wild and wonderful ways. "The thing is, Man," I heard my daughter say gently, "I know why Ma's done it. It's happened to me, too. Feels like magic."

Manu's breath turned to desperate, gasping sobs, full of loss and fear. Just like it did when his various cats died, and his father... whenever it happened, he would collapse into me, clutching my shoulders, leaning into me. And even after I was weakened by the increasing frequency of the morphing, I always found the strength to bear his weight till he could breathe again.

"Pull it together, Man. I am here. I won't go away, I can come back from the other state whenever I want."

"I can come back, too," I called out. "I can do anything. I can come back, too."

"Watch out, she's starting to vibrate. Stay out of her way."

"She won't hurt us, Manu, she knows us."

But Manu wasn't listening. He was backing into the wall and screaming, "Get out, lock the door."

"It's her, Man, it's Ma. Just stay quiet, and nothing will happen."

"Yes, yes, listen to Charu, it's me," I responded, but as my external vocal chords had begun to resonate, the words lost in the giant buzzing sound they made. I had to stop, or I would slice my children into bits. I tried to hold my abdomen tight so I would control it all, but I couldn't anymore. I was panicking. The sound reached a higher and higher pitch.

"Manu, Manu." I could hear my daughter. But I couldn't see anything anymore as I rose and hit the walls and ceiling. I could hear glass break, and the perfume my daughter had given me pervaded the air and entered the pores of my underbelly, oversweet and strong. I bent down to look.

"Now," I heard them shout. I felt Charu's cool hand on my tight body, reaching to still the viciously sharp chord. I could feel Manu's firm, warm grasp. I had to stop moving, or their fine young skin would be lacerated. I tried to breathe and count to 3,673, even as I could taste their blood.

CARALYN DAVIS

Color Blind

From January/February 2015

THE PANAMANIAN GOLDEN frogs died first. Extinct but for a few stray specimens stored with hermetic zeal in zoo laboratories. Scientists fretted, as did some intrepid reporters from *National Geographic, Smithsonian,* and the *New Yorker.* The Panamanians were devastated. They considered the golden frog their national emblem and put its likeness on their key chains and coffee mugs. No one else cared. After all, the golden frogs were frogs, not puppies, and other things were golden: daffodils, tomato blossoms, the sun, Big Bird.

I used to watch *Sesame Street* with my youngest daughter, Harper, when the two older children left for school. I worked from home after she was born. I finally had the professional standing. We'd cuddle on the couch for an hour before the babysitter arrived and count and spell right along with those puppets.

"What's the point?" my husband said one morning when he was running late. He liked to needle me back then. "Bert, Ernie, and the

Cookie Monster are shadows of their former selves, and Baby Bear, Abby Cadabby? What the hell are those?"

"Don't judge the puppets, Harris," I said.

"There's no continuity. They don't follow the number nine or the letter "g" through an entire episode anymore. Generations of children have stunted attention spans, and Elmo's a whiny, little freak."

"I can't argue the Elmo thing, but ratchet down the hatred," I said. "It's basic education, not a portent of doom."

Silence. Harris tended to find Mommy-me a tad prosaic.

All the other frogs and toads died. Again, a global yawn. Amphibians didn't inspire Save the Animal campaigns in quite the same way polar bears and wolves did.

Honeybees disappeared. People shifted in their easy chairs and grumbled. Even the meanest intelligence knew bees did something important for plants. Still, plenty of other flying insects were on the job. Honey's status as a universally enjoyed golden element faltered under the weight of modern lifestyles. Most people deemed zero-calorie sweeteners developed in test tubes to be an equal if not superior substitute.

Harper's favorite snack was honey on buttered toast. I was a good mother, limiting that treat to twice a week. The rest of the time, she had to eat fruits and vegetables. She was desolate when honey production ended. I searched the stores, standing in line to buy cane, sorghum, molasses, maple, agave.

"Yucky," she'd say. "Bad."

She stopped eating toast.

"Be glad she's not freaking out." Harris kissed me. "It's out of our control."

The bats went next, expiring en masse as they hibernated. Scientists hiking through their home caves watched the last ones drop from the ceilings and flutter sluggishly before they joined the thigh-deep decay on the cave floors. The scientists named the disease white-nose syndrome because the dead bats had a heavy mustache of white crystals. They identified a fungus as the culprit but didn't connect it to the frogs and bees because the corpses of those animals decomposed too quickly for the autopsies to find the white. The scientists also thought hibernation played a key role in the disease's development. "Bat flu" wasn't destined to be a true newsmaker like humanity-imperiling bird flu or swine flu.

Even when Harper started walking, she kept me at the center of her world. Several times a day, she would toddle into my office, her babysitter trailing behind her.

"Mama!" she'd cry, goofy with pleasure at finding me. "Dance, Mama, dance!"

If I had time, I'd flip on some music, Noot d' Noot or Purkinje Shift usually (my brother's bands), and the three of us would twirl around the room.

Vultures. Hundreds of thousands fell out of the trees where they roosted. Autopsies showed they died from visceral gout, aka bird kidney failure. White crystals coated their internal organs. The fungus had evolved.

Harper pretended to be a bird sometimes, inspired by the congregants eating at the feeder outside our kitchen window. She'd zoom around, flapping her arms, singing "Tweet, tweet, tweet!"

"What a pretty little bird!" I'd say. "Hope a kitty-cat doesn't get you, sweetie bird!" Throwaway words purloined from the mouths of cartoon characters, ill-equipped to last a lifetime.

Then I'd grab her and tickle her stomach. How she laughed.

Hyenas, monkeys, bears, wolves, deer, larks, pelicans, whales, animals ad infinitum. White Death spread. Sometimes visible, sometimes hidden, the white fungus turned up everywhere. Average humans began to express concern but wouldn't concede to all-out alarm. Maybe natural selection was involved. Maybe wild animals were just past their cosmic due date.

Her eyes were blue. Not bluebells or sapphires, those Cinderella fantasy colors. An aqua overlaid with a hint of gray, like a lake on an overcast day. Inventive yet practical, part me, part Harris. The eyes of a future scientist or physician, of someone who could have found a way to save us even if *Sesame Street* hadn't given her appropriate mental discipline.

"What do you want to be when you grow up?" I'd ask her.

"You, Mama, you!"

Chickens, pigs, dogs, cows, humans. White Death went up and down the food chain—except for cats. The Family Felidae escaped unscathed. Every other species teetered toward extinction. Some, though, climbed out of the biological ruins with a spark of life intact. That survival instinct is how I ended up in this hollow in the north Georgia mountains, fenced in with Harris and our two surviving children on his family farm.

Harris socked me in the jaw. He's not an abuser. He knocked me out to get me in the car to leave Atlanta. Harper had gone to a birthday party, by herself like a big girl. I was about to go pick her up when one of the other mothers called and said everyone had gotten sick. I phoned the hospital, on hold, on hold, on hold. Finally, a harassed woman.

"Don't come," she said. "Too many sick. Infection."

"Tell me where Harper is," I said. "Is she okay? What's going on?"

"She's already dead. Turn on the news."

I was busy screaming, so Harris switched on the television and we saw what was happening. I planned to go to the hospital anyway. I couldn't leave Harper there, alone, without her mother. That's when Harris hit me.

The human world—what remained of it—divided into three camps: people who ate cats, people who worshipped cats (the lion-headed Egyptian goddess Sekhmet experienced a resurgence in popularity), and people who befriended cats. Thanks to a modicum of intelligence, Harris and I could see the folly of the first two options. We took the third route, and that friendship saved us.

We have six cats. I don't know if they see it, smell it, or hear it, but our cats can spot the infection anywhere. They yowl an alert if White Death comes near, ensuring we know who or what to let on our land, when to put on our gas masks and hazard suits, and when to institute disinfection procedures.

With few insects, we pollinate our fields using paintbrushes dipped in pollen. Gold means food, survival, so people pay attention to it now. However, gold also can bring death since insects no longer eat their share of the pollen. The excess combines with severe thunderstorms to create pollen events that verge on tornadoes. You can choke to death in minutes if you're caught out in one. The cats help us there too, sounding a warning.

My favorite cat is Brownie, an orange-striped beast who likes to rub his furry brain box on my forehead. He's named after Harper's teddy bear, a handmade toy that wasn't backed by a brand or a marketing campaign. I thought its anonymity would foster her creative spirit—Harris' concerns about *Sesame Street* had wormed into my mind.

Brownie was the color of a Hershey's bar, with a low-pile pelt perfect for snuggling without causing sleep-time sniffles. Harper was prone to allergies.

"Kisses for Brownie, too," she'd say when Harris and I tucked her in at night.

"Three apiece, that's the going rate for baby girls and brown bears," was Harris' standard reply.

One, two, three from us both on each soft cheek. Sometimes proper kisses, the ones that live the name smack or smooch. It's the pecks I regret. Rote kisses, but at the time they seemed a product of multi-tasking efficiency. Now I wonder if she heard our silent screams: "I have to unload the dishwasher," or "I've got to finish my presentation," or "I haven't shaved my legs all week—just *go to sleep.*"

"Why did so much die?" my son Danny asked last night during dinner. "I miss Harper and Grandpa and Grandma. I miss my friends. Why did this happen? When can we go home?" He laid his head down next to his plate and cried into the tablecloth.

My other daughter, Emma, appeared stricken. Harris held out his hand. She got up from her chair and went into his arms.

"Gold and white, Danny," I said. "The colors of angels. We didn't think they'd let us down like that."

I reached over and smoothed his hair. I felt a little silly offering parental comfort. Danny and Emma had seen its fallibility first-hand. Mommy had let their sister die. She couldn't always make things better.

"We should have new colors, for new angels," Danny said. Tears and fabric muffled his words.

"We'll work on it," I said. "Hush, now. Don't disturb the cats."

Late at night when the odd feline footfall is the only sound breaking the stillness of the house, sometimes I see Harper. She's in a cotton-candy heaven. Generations of family members surround her and try to keep her safe. The White Death has crossed dimensions. It looks like a Santa Claus convention, white beards blooming from every mouth. But Harper dances. She spins, swoops, and tiny golden frogs keep time 'round her feet.

MARKO FONG

My Father's Paradox

From July/August 2010

IN THE SPRING of 1959 my father had his first encounter with Herman Kahn, the man whose Mutually Assured Destruction (MAD) became the template for the Cold War. Their meeting in the lobby of the Ritz Carlton in Boston was no accident. Although my father even had a speaking role for a panel at this Third International Conference on the Policy Implications of Game Theory, he showed up dressed as a waiter. The other attendees had just finished the afternoon-long plenary session. They were tired, restless, and hungry. As the man who dared to think about the unthinkable, Kahn was the celebrity in the field. There was so much interest in his analyses of thermonuclear war that the conference had scheduled three different sessions around Kahn and his ideas. Kahn also happened to weigh 300 pounds. My father approached with a tray of appetizers, the four-deep circle of intellectuals orbiting the star of the conference parted, and it was Kahn who came to him.

It didn't hurt that my father also knew the food at the Ritz Carlton was more about elegance than stomachs and palates. He had swiped $20 from our mother's grocery money to load up his tray at Luigi and Mac's, the best deli in New England. My mother often reminds us my younger sister Nancy and I drank powdered milk that month so my father could get a few seconds of Herman Kahn's attention. Her job as a nurse supported the family while our father finished his doctorate.

My father also put his thesis on that tray. No, he didn't plop a 200-page typed manuscript (pre-xerox) between a row of smoked salmon canapes and a crescent of dried salami and aged-cheddar cheese skewered on toothpicks. My father's thesis took the form of two small boxes each containing 60 slips of paper.

The red box held 30 slips worth $20 each and 30 slips worth nothing. The blue box contained an unspecified ratio of $20 slips and worthless ones. It could be 60 slips worth $20, none at all, or any quantity in between. In the terms of Kahn and my father's shared discipline, the two boxes were mathematically identical: anyone had a 50-50 chance with either box of getting a slip worth 20 dollars.

As Kahn filled his plate with salami, my father turned the tray to draw the great man's attention to the two open-topped boxes at the center of the tray.

"What's in these?" Kahn asked.

"A choice," My father answered, "Isn't that why we're all here?"

Kahn laughed, as did six or seven bystanders.

"Are you really a waiter?'

"Does it matter?"

My dad then took a minute to explain the difference between the blue box and the red box. Kahn thought for a moment, then said, "So they're equal but different."

"That's for you to decide, Mr. Kahn." Dad was one of the few people who knew Herman Kahn didn't have a doctorate.

"So if I choose red, I'm choosing certainty over possibility?"

"Again, that's not for me to say, Sir."

After making more of a show of his decision, the sated Kahn chose the red box, the one with the 30 $20 bills in it, and happened to draw a blank sheet of paper.

"So, do I get to try the other one?"

My father shook his head. "No, Mr. Kahn. Everyone just gets the one chance, but if you want more food, please help yourself."

My father then introduced himself as David Levine, economics graduate student at Harvard. Because of the tray, the two men didn't shake hands, but my father had made an impression on the philosopher king of the cold war.

At the same conference, my father also found ways to get John Von Neumann and John Nash to choose a box. All three of the best minds of the generation happened to pick the one with the 30 blank sheets and the 30 slips worth 20 dollars. As it happened, Nash got one of the $20 certificates and hounded my father to "pay up" until someone had to pull Nash aside with a promise to give him the money himself.

Over the next weeks, my father found ways to get every famous person within ten miles of Harvard yard into his sample. John Updike, Ted Williams, Bob Cousy, Leonard Bernstein, J.D. Salinger, and Milton Berle all chose the red box. Helen Keller, as it turned out, was one of the few individuals who chose the second box. As a joke my father asked her what color the box was, and Keller, who held her hand to his lips and throat (her way of listening), immediately said, "Blue." Noam Chomsky, then just a linguist, also chose the blue box along with Robert Moses, the builder of modern New York City. It surprised a lot of people that Jack Kerouac and John Coltrane both chose the greater apparent certainty of the red box.

Any other graduate student would have found 1,024 anonymous subjects and simply reported results. My father didn't just list names, he namedropped. Even more amazing, some of the names he chose to drop in the paper that became known as the Levine Paradox (the paradox was that rational individuals should have been equally likely to choose either box) weren't all that famous at the time of publication but then exploded into prominence.

Dad's discovery—that even trained mathematicians preferred the apparently more certain of two mathematically identical choices by a two-to-one margin—was in itself hardly an act of genius. My father's detractors frequently point out that John Maynard Keynes had written about a similar phenomenon a generation earlier. Any observer of America in 1959 would have figured out most Americans of the time craved the appearance of certainty in ways that defied the supposed rationality of Adam Smith's invisible hand.

Eisenhower occupied the White House. GI Bill-educated husbands were buying homes, getting jobs with benefits, and buying savings bonds to send their own children to college in the shadow of stories about the hydrogen bomb. Even if a small percentage of adults still felt the need to howl, easily two thirds of Americans preferred the certainty of PTA meetings, attached garages, and all-electric kitchens. In the meantime, Las Vegas was not yet a major city, and my father, as brilliant as he was, didn't consider the possibility of covering the second box in neon and alcohol.

While Von Neumann invented game theory and the architecture of the modern computer and Nash, between hearing voices in his head, pinned down the mathematical vagaries of non-linear bargaining, my father was never passionate about the mathematics in isolation. He was no Herman Kahn, either. Where Kahn could calmly lay out the calculus of losses and gains for a theoretical thermonuclear war and discuss it as if doomsday was some kind of roulette strategy, my father couldn't divorce the numbers and flow charts from some deeper need to provoke people emotionally.

When Kahn invited my father to join him at his think tank in Southern California, my father told friends, "It wasn't my paper that got Herman Kahn's attention. It was the way I got him to pay attention to my paper that got me to Los Angeles."

Kahn had image problems at the time. The press had begun referring to him as "Doctor Strangelove." Where Kahn was portly and prone to talk in academic jargon, my father was handsome, well spoken, and flamboyant.

My mother seemed to agree. She had already started telling people, "If David's parents hadn't insisted he be an academic, he might have been the greatest advertising man in America."

She never made it clear if she thought that might have been a better or worse fate for him.

My parents never called them our grandparents, and I only met them once when we stayed a day in Chicago on our way to California. Other than that, the only thing I knew about them was my father's mother had pushed him to be a classical piano virtuoso. After his hands and ear didn't match her ambition, his parents settled for his simply being smarter than anyone else. The mixture of this, his frequent absences, his talent for provoking attention, and his need for validation—particularly from attractive women—served his career, but not our family. When I turned nine, Dad spent a year in Washington D.C. in a position one step away from the President's best and brightest while we stayed in Los Angeles. When he came back, my parents made the separation official.

For some time, contact with our father consisted of movies and lunches at an ice cream parlor in Santa Monica owned by the family of one of his girlfriends. These were seldom ordinary parental visitations.

One time within minutes of asking us his usual questions about school, friends, and our mother, my father turned the formica table into a decision matrix. The salt and pepper shakers stood for two prisoners named "one" and "two." A stack of sugar cubes covered the middle of the table.

"Suppose you committed a murder," my father pointed to the salt shaker.

"Why would we ever kill anybody?" Nancy interrupted.

"We're just pretending you did."

"But why should we pretend we did something we'd never do?"

"Come on Nancy. Stop asking dumb questions."

"They're not dumb questions."

"This is something called the Prisoner's Dilemma," my dad explained. "The smartest people in the world work on this problem."

"What's the problem?" I asked anxiously.

"We try to figure out what's the best strategy if they ask you if you did it."

"Shouldn't you just tell them the truth?"

"Nancy, can't you just pretend?"

"If someone caught me and said I'd killed somebody, I'd pray or I'd call mom."

"Well, that's not one of the choices in the problem."

"Why not?"

"I really don't know."

My father picked up the pepper shaker and explained that if both the salt and pepper shaker confess, they each get 25 years in prison. If neither confesses, they both go free. If the salt shaker confesses and the pepper shaker doesn't, the salt shaker gets ten years and the pepper shaker gets the death penalty.

"So do you confess or not confess?"

I added the salt and pepper shakers from the next booth and moved sugar cubes around as I instinctively laid out a matrix.

"Richard, how did you know to do that?"

I beamed.

"Dad, can I go look at the toys up front?"

"Nancy, can't you be serious?"

"I am being serious. I want to look at toys."

Our dad nodded. She made a face at me, then headed for the counter.

"Your sister's younger than you."

He then walked me through to the inevitable conclusion: two rational prisoners would confess rather than risk the death penalty. At the end of which, my father said, "Richard, I had graduate students who couldn't always make sense of it as quickly as you did."

On those visits, my father took me through all of the major variations of the Prisoner's Dilemma, and I loved every moment. At one point, he bragged to us his colleagues called him "Doctor Chutzpah" because he always managed to "win" the simulations. Oddly, because of our last name, people have always assumed our family was Jewish. In fact, my Grandparents were born Jewish, but once in the American Midwest they became Christian Scientists. My mother was Catholic. When my parents married, my father agreed to raise us Episcopal.

Throughout my father's Decision Theory tutorials, Nancy continued to resist. She would talk about friends at school, cartoons on television, and interrupt with instructions from our mother about items he'd promised to buy us. I just assumed all of this was beyond her, and I liked it that way.

Over time my father showed me the complexities of Mutually Assured Destruction (MAD) and how it was really just a variation on the Prisoner's Dilemma.

Instead of anonymous prisoners, MAD used two countries with large numbers of nuclear weapons. Instead of not being able to talk to one another, the two countries weren't able to trust any of their communications. Both countries would clearly be better off and safer if they both disarmed. If both countries stayed armed, no one could actually be safe. Like the Prisoner's Dilemma, the "rational" decision for either country was to stay armed so the other country would not be able to attack without fear of retaliation.

At this point, we no longer needed salt and pepper shakers. Dad had by then supplemented our talks with copies of John Stuart Mill, Bentham, Clausewitz,, articles about Richard Oppenheimer, and clippings from the *New York Times* about the Cold War that sometimes included quotes from Herman Kahn. I'd bring the books home, show them to my mother, read what I could understand (I'd never admit to how little I *did* understand), then slip them into the bookshelf in my bedroom.

"This can't make any sense," I told him.

"But it does."

"Who cares?" Nancy said. "Mom said you'd help me buy new shoes to match my dress. I need them for Tuesday."

My father made a face and gently promised Nancy he would come through later that afternoon.

"Dad, it's Sunday. You know the stores close early."

"Nancy, we're trying to talk about something important."

"And Jenny's birthday isn't?"

"What I don't get is if you hold onto the nuclear weapons long enough, you eventually have some sort of accident that blows everyone up anyway."

"Exactly."

"Dad, we've got to get going."

"Nancy, you haven't even finished your ice cream yet," I said in exasperation.

"This is so dumb."

"A lot of people are just really uncomfortable talking about things like this. It might be too scary for her." My father said it softly for my benefit.

Nancy stabbed her ice cream with her spoon but didn't eat it.

"Just because you don't understand it, doesn't mean it's dumb," I said.

"Of course I understand it."

"Sure you do, that's why you'd rather talk about Barbies and shoes."

"You're talking about choosing between chocolate and vanilla when anyone should know that ice cream just makes you fat."

I groaned. "You're so stupid sometimes."

My father, though, was silent for a moment.

"Actually, your sister's more or less right."

"Good. Can we go get my shoes now?"

I didn't talk on the drive from Santa Monica to our house in Brentwood. Once through the door, Nancy showed off her new shoes to our mother. After our mother slipped off to her study to work on her psychology master's thesis, I went to the living room to catch a rock group on Ed Sullivan. Nancy came in to watch Disney.

"You don't even watch Ed Sullivan."

"It doesn't matter. I was here first."

"You're just mad because of the shoes."

"I'm not."

"It's dumb to play Dad's games."

"What games?"

"He's making us his prisoners."

At this point, our mother had slipped into the room and the TV was on ABC, the network that had neither Disney nor Ed Sullivan.

"He is not. That's just the name of the problem, and you don't get it."

"His job is to be our father. He's supposed to be asking about us."

My mother's eyes widened. She nodded, but she did not intervene.

"He's got you showing off for him," Nancy continued. "You'll always be his prisoner."

My body went slack on the couch. It was the first time it ever occurred to me that Nancy was smarter than me. She instinctively saw the whole box. In the realm of feelings, my sister Nancy was a Go master.

"Watch what you want to watch." I got up and turned the channel to NBC, then went to my room and stared at my bookshelf but read nothing for three days.

A few weeks later, our father announced he'd decided to serve a tour of duty as an advisor to a rifle brigade in a place called Vietnam. "If I'm going to give advice about the Cold War, I need to know what it looks like up close," was his only explanation before disappearing from our lives for another year.

After he returned, our visits were different. Dad had broken up with the woman whose family owned the ice cream distributorship. His new girlfriend came from a family who owned a bunch of delis. Mutually Assured Destruction and the Cold War disappeared from our conversations. He said little to nothing about Vietnam other than to repeat stories he had already shared more than once in occasional postcards about snakes and heat. He, however, didn't completely stop talking about Decision Theory. When he brought it up again, I leaned into the table, my eyes wide and my brain in its starter's blocks.

"You've seen sit-ins on television?"

"Like with the black people in the south?"

"Do you ever think about why they worked so well?"

I thought for a moment between savoring the smell of pastrami and mustard.

"Because if they got arrested they got attention for what they were doing. If they got served at the lunch counter, they got what they wanted."

My father nodded approvingly.

"Some people are protesting the war now and trying the same things. Do you think it works as well?"

Nancy and I both shrugged, and we didn't return to the topic for several visits. Instead my father began taking us on separate outings. He took me to baseball games at the Chavez Ravine and occasional lectures at UCLA. He took Nancy to the ballet until a cigarette puffing, red-haired choreographer started coming along and Nancy objected. He then switched to taking her to the movies.

To be honest, we weren't sure why our father had come back to live in Los Angeles again. My mother was surprised he'd left the Defense Department, where he was one step away from his long-held dream of advising the president directly, and that he'd instead returned to the think tank.

Never comfortable with small talk or the more normal fatherly check-ins, his conversations with us shifted from "decision theory" to ethical philosophy. Maybe this was the difference between a deli and an ice cream parlor. His questions became more passionate.

"Would you kill someone else's families to keep a million other families safe? How about just to keep your own family safe? Would you lie to get someone to do something because you knew that person couldn't understand the deeper reasons for doing it? Would you break the law to save others?"

Clausewitz and Von Neumann gave way to Thoreau, Gandhi, and the just assassinated Martin Luther King. Where he once waited for us to answer, he often started trying to answer his own questions. Perhaps because she was older now, Nancy sometimes participated in these conversations. Looking back, my father was clearly less interested in our answers to his questions than his own. It didn't occur to any of us then that our father was soon going to be as famous as any baseball player or movie star or that he wasn't talking about Gandhi as much as he was comparing himself to him.

So when did I know, or more accurately, when *should* I have known? Early in 1969, I came home from a visit with my father and bragged to my mother, "Dad's showing me how to run the Xerox machine."

"Why does your father have you operating a Xerox machine? He's supposed to be spending time with your sister and you, not working."

At that point, I had helped him with the Xeroxing several times. He never told me what I was copying for him, just that I was helping him do something important. I liked pressing the buttons on this magic machine the size of a Volkswagen that lit up, whirred, and reproduced in minutes what might have taken years to write and accumulate.

Other times, Nancy and I would visit him at his apartment in Culver City. We would sit on his worn green couch together, and he would have us cut "top secret" labels off the bottoms of what must have been 7,000 pages I had helped him copy. It was fun sharing a secret with our father as we laughed along with his endless jokes about Richard Nixon and greedy defense contractors.

One night our mother argued with him about it. We could hear some of the conversation on the porch. Nancy and I watched the last episode of *Bonanza* together while mom said things like, "I don't know what you're up to, but I know it's not okay. David, you need to be a father first."

Dad responded, "You don't understand. You never understood. All you ever see is the day to day. They're special kids. They're bright. There are things beyond homework and clothes that matter, too. We're not just their mother and father."

Mom answered, "If we're not that, then we're nothing."

She then slammed the door behind her, even though she was the sort who never yelled. After that, my father only had me help with the Xerox machine a couple more times. Each time he'd tell me, "Richard, it means a lot to me that you're helping me with this. Someday you'll look back and be very proud."

Other weekends he took us to anti-war rallies where we crouched in the dirt together eating potato chips, sipping from sodas, and chanting songs where they spelled out swear words while the people nearby smoked things. Mom heard about it from Nancy and made him stop taking us.

Two weeks before the *New York Times* published my father's copied histories of the leadup to the War in Vietnam documenting the series of lies that got the US into the war, two men in brown suits knocked on our front door. My mother opened the door part way but refused to let them inside. When they tried to look towards the living room where I was doing my homework, she motioned for me to move away.

"He and his sister aren't here today," she insisted.

I'd never known my mother to lie, especially to a police officer. My grandfather, her father, had spent 30 years as a police officer in Detroit. As the FBI agents visited over the next several days, my mother kept her own responses brief and careful, but she let them stay. It was as if she was reassured by their presence and repeated visits. One time they saw me but didn't insist on talking to me directly. I heard them say, "We do want to talk to Richard some time, but we assure you nothing's going to happen to him. We just need some information."

My mother didn't say no, but I never did talk to them.

After the papers got to the *New York Times* and the *Washington Post*, my father disappeared. The attorney general, John Mitchell, got an indictment against him not only for betraying classified information but for treason. If tried and convicted, the penalty could have been death.

Three times we got calls from strangers who would tell us they were friends of my father, saying, "He's all right and he loves you."

One time a man came up to me after my last class at the high school and passed me a letter from my father:

I miss you and Nancy very much, yet as we've discussed many times, we sometimes have duties and responsibilities that go beyond just being someone's father or husband. You know I would do anything to be able to see you both, but we have to do this for your future and the future of everyone who is your age. I am safe and healthy for now. We will see each other some time soon whether it's in this life or some other.

That last sentence made me afraid to show the letter to Nancy. I did eventually hand it over to my mother, but only after I made her promise not to share it with the FBI. She then showed it to Nancy, who said nothing, then cried.

The next events happened so quickly and with so much publicity, I sometimes have to look them up in history books to remember the details. My father reappeared to stand trial. Even though the papers actually embarrassed his two major rivals and said nothing about the current administration, President Nixon felt he had a personal responsibility to discredit my father. He authorized men to break into a psychiatrist's office looking for embarrassing things about David Levine. In fact, there were plenty of them. A few years later when I was 19, I had to read an account in a book about my father engaging in group sex at Esalen while on LSD. The burglary and the plan to discredit my father might have worked, but the burglars got caught and talked.

My father had made history. His new fame far exceeded Herman Kahn's.

What I remember most closely didn't make any history books. Because I had helped my father copy the papers, I, at 15 years of age, had to testify before a congressional committee without a guarantee of immunity.

In a brief time alone with my sister and me before the committee hearing, my father tried to console us as we waited in the basement cafeteria between the hearing room and the Rayburn building. "I never told you what was in the papers, so you could never be guilty of anything, yet you could still share in this historic act."

He moved to hug us, but Nancy wouldn't let him. As she moved away, the can of coke in front of me fell over, and it stained my suit, which I frantically tried to mop up with napkins from the black dispenser on the table.

"Is Richard going to go to jail?" she asked.

"I don't think so."

"But you can't guarantee that, can you?"

My father shrugged, and Nancy walked away. My Dad put his hand on my shoulder.

"Richard, history will be on our side."

I didn't answer. Instead, I kept mopping up the table and my suit though both were already dry.

I sat in a tall chair with a red leather back that my still-thin upper body didn't fill. The committee members looked down from a raised dais and for the most part asked gentle questions.

"Was Nancy involved in any way?"

"No, she never had anything to do with the copy machine."

"Did you ever read what your father had you copy?"

"No, I was having too much fun figuring out how all the buttons on the machine worked, and I had to watch out for paper jams. I couldn't do that and read anything at the same time."

Then, the Republican Congressman from Houston asked me, "Was your father really sharing something with you, or was he using you to make it easier for him to get past security at the think tank?"

The lawyer my mother had insisted on hiring to help me hadn't prepared me for that question. I didn't have an answer. It occurred to me it was perfectly possible, but the attorney stopped me before I could open my mouth.

"Congressman, young Mr. Levine (he stressed the young) can't speculate on his father's unspoken motives."

My mother never forgave my father for putting us at risk. She refused to attend his trial and wouldn't let us go, either. When people essentially congratulated her after it ended, she would take a deep breath, shake her head, and tell them, "It was a mistrial, not a verdict of not guilty. If it hadn't been for the White House plumbers, it might still have been a crime. David was lucky."

Once free, my father became a kind of rock star. In fact, he began to appear with them at anti-war rallies and fundraisers. We met Joan Baez, Bill Wyman from the Rolling Stones, Yoko Ono, Jane Fonda. My sister and I got used to having celebrities grab us by the elbow and breathlessly tell us, "You must be very proud to have a father like your dad."

At school, we never told friends about our brushes with fame. It wasn't that we thought other kids wouldn't believe us. It was just too much and too strange. Still, this was the happiest I would ever see my father. When he would get up on stage, raise his arms, and encourage others to stand up that day and every day forward, it was like he was dancing over the crowd.

Then one day in 1973, my father's celebrity faded. The crowd responded but not quite as vociferously. The emcee called them on it and someone shouted back, "The War's over, man."

My father grabbed the mic and said sternly, "The draft's over, the war's still going on. Innocent people are still dying."

There was scattered applause, but the invitations to appear at concerts slowed after that, then stopped completely. Ironically, once Nixon flew off in the helicopter, the celebrity my father craved so fiercely ended, too. After that the music changed, too. It still sounded like rock and roll, but something slipped out of it.

A year later, our father remarried and moved hundreds of miles away. We got older, went to college back east, and we began to see less of one another. At Harvard, I volunteered in a Catholic Workers' Soup Kitchen, where I became fascinated by Dorothy Day. I converted to Catholicism as result. Our mother became a psychologist who lives in the same house we lived in as teenagers. She specializes in pain management. We see her often.

The last time the three of us saw one another, we met at a café in Boston near the Ritz Carlton. Nancy was in town on her way back from Managua. She was giving a paper at a conference my father declined to attend. At Yale (she purposely didn't go to Harvard to frustrate our father), she bowled over her professors in her few philosophy and political science classes. They promised her fellowships and begged her to TA, but she insisted on public health and became an expert on healthy pregnancies in high poverty villages in Nicaragua and the Dominican Republic, where the infant mortality rate is now slightly better than it is in the United States. She uses her husband's last name.

My Dad had just published a new book where he compared the current war to the one he had risked his career and life (not to mention his family) to stop. Our country has wandered back into making the same kinds of mistakes it once made in Vietnam. He'd come to Boston to do a cable interview about the new book, but as some have said, it's clear my father's celebrity and greatness will never have a "second act." His single act of defiance will always define him. That may be what happens when less than great men happen to do a "great thing." God only gives them one glimpse of what might have, in the hands of a true saint, turned into a miracle.

I had come from upstate New York to see Nancy and to show Dad pictures of his grandchildren whom he hadn't seen in two years. I found myself reflexively telling my father and sister about my seventh book on the nature of sainthood in the modern world for a press owned by an order of nuns devoted to bringing the word of God instead of the words of Milton Friedman and the *Wall Street Journal* to foreign countries.

On this autmum New England evening, the twilight mixed with the streetlights to appear brighter than daylight. We sipped coffee and chatted amiably. I looked at my father. His hair had turned fully white. He was slightly stooped. As brilliant as ever, he attempted to engage us in a discussion of the Middle East, but his manner of speaking was noticeably less fierce. He did not look at the photos of his own grandchildren—any longer than necessary.

As Nancy often pointed out, he was just not the sort of man who ever could be just a proud father or grandfather. To me, though, the father who sat with us that night appeared to feel some odd combination of sadness and pride. The sadness came from the fact that no one ever really read his "papers" or took to heart the lessons they contained. Instead, he was the man whose act of dissent indirectly brought down the presidency and arguably ended the cold war. The other sadness few people mention is that this brilliant man didn't actually write a word of the papers for which he became so famous.

The pride was that we had grown up without him, led healthier lives, and even as we avoided him, our professional lives mysteriously echoed him or at least played in the same key.

He hugged us both that night and cried with a kind of happiness even as Nancy reprimanded him for talking about his own book for much of our dinner instead of asking about her kids or her conference. At one point when Nancy had slipped off to call her children, I finally asked my father a question that had only occurred to me in the last few months.

"Dad, in your famous paradox paper, you asked all these people which box they would choose. Which box did you choose yourself?"

My dad shrugged and looked off into the twilight, then laughed.

"I don't remember. I honestly don't remember."

"Well, which would you choose now?"

He didn't answer that question, either, choosing instead to answer my question with a question, in a way that reminded me of our family's Jewish roots.

"Which one would you choose?"

I couldn't answer him. All I could see was an image of myself standing with one foot on either box.

"All I know is that your sister would have chosen whichever box was the one I didn't choose."

We both laughed. It occurred to me, like it or not, that like my father, I didn't know enough about myself to know which box was mine. I had spent my adult life sorting and analyzing boxes instead. He then looked at me again and said, "I don't remember even thinking about choosing one myself."

Some say he did a "great thing" because he chose the possibility of uncertainty in his own life over the certainty and safety of going through the proper channels. For two years of his life, he solved the Prisoner's Dilemma and arguably played some role in freeing our country from a foreign policy based on Mutually Assured Destruction instead of mutual trust or interest. All that time he may not have made any kind of choice about the act that defined his life any more than he could have chosen to be a concert pianist.

I looked at him again and imagined the young graduate student at the Ritz Carlton. Even if no one currently said his name in the same breath as Gandhi and Martin Luther King, one could not deny that for two years in the early 1970's many people once did link him to these other secular saints. It occured to me that as wrong as it had been to include us, my father had tried to share what he perhaps knew would be the greatest part of himself.

Nancy would naturally disagree. As she says,"He was brilliant enough to see the shape of the entire world and what the war meant. He was also so far-sighted, he couldn't see his own family."

I believe he loved us the way he could.

When Nancy got back to our table, our father toasted us. "To my children. You're far more brilliant than I ever was, and may your children be more brilliant than you."

To which my sister responded, "May they simply be happier."

A few months ago, a colleague and I went for drinks, and for whatever reason we began going on about our own childhoods. We talked about old movies, unconsummated infatuations, being humbled on the baseball diamond, and even sang theme songs from sitcoms. Only after this did he ask me the question he had wanted to ask me in our four years of working together.

"Did you ever have your own copy of the papers, and what did you do with them?"

Forty-three yellow bound volumes and 7,000 pages that tell the entire sad deceitful history of America's involvement in the War in Vietnam through the LBJ administration sit in a bookshelf in West Los Angeles. I have never read them all. My father and about 12 other people are the only ones who read them all the way through. On the inside page of the first volume, there's an inscription in a great, florid blue ink. I once looked at a book of handwriting analysis, and my father's script or something almost exactly like it was used to exemplify something called "ego grandeur."

To my son, thanks for helping to make history together. Love, Dad.

He then put his own full name in parentheses as if the volume itself might some day be a historical exhibit.

After Harvard and after my marriage to a woman even more protective than Mom, my mother asked me if I wanted the books on my bookshelf. I took any number of things, including books, from my childhood. I left the 43-volume proof of my father's greatness, yet neither I nor my mother have ever considered the possibility of selling or giving them away. Instead, they sit in an unfinished oak bookshelf behind the bed and next to the ironing board in what is now a guest bedroom in my mother's house, a house to which my father never returned after the papers became public.

When my mother dies, I suppose I will be faced with my own choice. I imagine, though, that I will then take my copy of the papers, my own Prisoner's Dilemma, home to upstate New York and place them on some bookshelf. I am certain, too, that when I die, no one will suggest any possibility of sainthood for me the way some once did for my father. Instead, someone else will have to answer the question of whether or not my own children will keep their father's copy of their grandfather's papers as they determine what stays and what goes in their own lives.

AN TRAN

The Grinning Man

From October/November 2013

THREE WEEKS AGO Johnson Martin was standing outside his home smoking a cigarette when he saw a black triangle in the sky. It soared slowly through the air with no sound. Green and yellow lights danced along its perimeter, and a white light shone from its center like a great porcelain dinner plate. Johnson Martin ran out into Main Street, finger to the heavens, screaming from deep in his belly, They're coming! They're coming!

We hardly paid mind, as everyone knows Johnson Martin is off his rocker, always spouting religious nonsense and conspiracies and the whole gamut of oddities you'd normally expect from city folk. Not long ago, we endured his Main Street sermons on the Black Muslim movement storming through our town on the way to Washington, DC. He said he was trying to rally support, but Johnson Martin is one of the only blacks in our town, and the other blacks—Carl Washington and his family—are wise enough not to fall in with Johnson Martin's antics. So who ever believes a thing Johnson Martin says, anyway? Besides, the very next week if you'd ask about it, he'd say, I dunno nothing 'bout no triangle! And then he'd spit his chew right by your feet. It'd sit there, a congealed, brown mess. You'd breathe it in, the foul pungent scent of phlegm and tobacco. And then you'd walk away 'cause you learned better than to make conversation with Johnson Martin.

The Kagnan boys said they saw a strange man—at least seven feet tall by their account—through a curtain of tree trunks as they were playing in the woods. He wore a green, tweed-knit sports coat and had a wide, long, flat face with a broad grin sculpted into stillness, stretched to the back of his skull. The boys froze, and the Grinning Man froze, and they watched each other.

We heard the Grinning Man had no nose or ears, that his eyes were thin and there was too much space between them, that his flesh was hued sickly green the way Samuel Keele gets when he goes fishing. When the boys circled around him, the Grinning Man followed their movements with his face and nothing more. His body still, his head turned and rotated with them as they moved. The boys heard the Grinning Man speak. He said the word cold, but his lips never broke from that big grin. That was when the Kagnan boys ran, trees and branches and dirt blurring past. They looked once behind them, and the Grinning Man still stood erect, unmoving, watching. And then they continued to run, as far as they could. Past the big hollowed out birch tree. Past the tree house near the Halloway place built for young Edgar decades ago. Past the Birchmere Farm and on and on till they got home, not once stopping for breath.

We paid closer attention when Brandee Birchmere started on about the Grinning Man. Such a sweet woman, no one could be more honest. Brandee said she was on her pap's farm driving the tractor to hoe up the fields for planting. She reached one end and drove in a big arc to circle back around, and there he was, tall as a spruce and wide as a stallion. His fine green jacket flapping in the wind, his smooth green face grinning ear to ear. Now, after the fact, the Kagnan boys said they thought—after thinking it through—the grin was a friendly one, not so sinister as they first thought. Brandee, though, she said to us the grin was perverse and lecherous, with wanton lust in his spaced eyes. And what do young boys know of lust, anyway, save the filth they watch on the television these days?

She stopped the tractor and stared the man down, and he stared her down, grinning all the while. Again, he never moved, not an inch, not a twitch to his lips or a blink to his eyes. Just stood and stared. Stood and stared, like he was waiting. Suddenly, the chickens began a raucous in their coops, and Brandee broke her gaze. Then when she looked back—not two seconds later—the Grinning Man was gone.

Now, we did go check the farm, of course. All of us. And there wasn't a trace we found in that soil. No shoeprints or prints of any kind except some rabbit tracks. Later though, at Keele's Tavern, wouldn't you know we found threads of green tweed on our boots and shoes? Then a hush fell over us, and fear kept us from speaking until Edgar Halloway declared softly, Something's not right with our town these days. And then there was more silence because we knew he was right.

By Saturday, the Grinning Man was on all our minds. Who was he? Why had he come to our town? What was he doing to our folks? Billy Gardner swore up and down his wife was different. Cold, he said, like her mind had been scrubbed clean on the inside with a toothbrush. Then he said the other night, when he was leaving Keele's Tavern, he saw Old Maggie Anne talking to a tree in the woods. He crouched behind some bushes to watch, and sure as April rain, there was Old Maggie Anne, head crooned up to a tree.

Billy Gardner had the mind to walk the other way and take the long way home. And as he was turning, he realized Maggie Anne wasn't speaking to a tree at all. It was the Grinning Man, so goliath his brown slacks had been mistaken for a tree trunk. His green sports coat mistaken for leaves. The Grinning Man made eye contact with Billy, and Billy said the grin stretched further to a sinister width. That was when Billy took to running.

And earlier today, someone saw Old Maggie Anne walking into the river with her clothes on. Word spread around she went and killed herself. We wondered how lonely she must have been, living in that old farm with just her cat. The older of us remember when Old Maggie Anne was Maggie McIntyre, the young pride of our town. Her hair red and shiny as the flesh of sliced grapefruit, her frame slender; we still laugh at the way she would relentlessly flirt with Clemson Bullock—may he rest in peace—and then go out and reject his every advance.

The younger of us remember Maggie as the pretty woman who always brought chocolate milk from the McIntyre Farm with her when she babysat us. Back then we adored her.

But Clemson Bullock fell terribly ill, and Maggie changed. Month by month, Clemson declined. He aged 30 years in a single one. Young, taut flesh pruning into rows of wrinkles on his brow, Maggie Anne at his bedside aging right with him. By the end of it, Clemson Bullock was gone, and Maggie Anne's soul evaporated in grief. She didn't speak to any of us anymore. Sold her milk and returned straight home, never a peep. Years later, she sold her cows and stopped working entirely. The McIntyre family had 60 acres of woods in our town dating back to the colonial days, and she went and sold nearly all 60 to the state government. Now it's a park where city folk tourists come to camp and hunt in when they want a taste of the real world.

The idea that Old Maggie Anne—changeling or not—would walk into the river surprised not a one of us. And after Billy Gardner's story? We were expecting something of the sort. Later we saw Maggie Anne walking back from the grocery store dry as wheat. We all kept our distance. Maybe she really was Old Maggie Anne and no one had walked into the river at all, but maybe she was the changeling and made Maggie Anne go and drown herself.

Now, the more sensible of us were skeptics. Carl Washington went and called our town a den of fools. He said our imaginations were running from us, full sprint. That we ought to slow down and think for a second. Some of us agreed, but most were growing scared. Carl Washington's words provided some comfort. They made us think we had nothing to fear from the Grinning Man. That he wasn't even real. We just got an idea in our heads. The Kagnan boys were spinning yarns and got us all spooked. We were just seeing the Grinning Man in every shadow and every tree in our town. And our town's got a whole lot of trees.

After that we felt safe and we laughed at ourselves. Carl Washington was right, after all. Den of fools.

But then a dry storm consumed the sky. Lightning snapped through the clouds. Static hung in the air and stood the hairs on our arms and legs. When we looked up, we couldn't help but see forms behind the clouds, eruptions of light like raining meteors and electric orbs. We saw shapes of saucers and triangles in the sky. What else were we supposed to think but the Grinning Man? He sent them here. He's one of them. And, within minutes, we all believed again 'cause what other proof do you need?

Any fool can see they're coming, that we're under siege.

The sky is streams and ribbons of color. It crackles with electric booms like Chinese firecrackers in the clouds. Orbs fly, a thousand little sentient moons floating deliberately through the air. Some collide. Some zig, and others zag, ravenously exploring their world. The sky draws a faint outline, a massive black triangle over our town. When we look up, we fear and are humbled. Some see doom. Others see God.

Everywhere we look, the Grinning Man is there, shadowed between trees. We see his face, still and grinning, when the lightning flashes. In anger, Billy Gardner explodes from the doors of our liquor store, shotgun in hand. We yell to him, Billy! Billy, no! Until there is a gunshot, a flash of light, and then another shot. The booms tear through the air. When the smoke and dust clears, we wait and stare at the darkness of the woods Billy Gardner shot into. When an orb spits up light from the sky, we see a tall and green and grinning figure, towering and still.

We run.

All of us—half the damned town at least—push into Keele's Tavern and board the doors. The bravest of our men gaze out the windows to see the Grinning Man and the tempest of swirling orbs of light. Our women comfort our children. To medicate the anxiety, our men drink from the taps some more.

From time to time, we see his face in a window, gazing. We wonder if he can see in the dark, see us huddling together so close. When we look away, he is gone. Samuel Keele mutters something we can't hear and then digs out a revolver and a mason jar of shine. He says, The shine's for coping. The gun's just in case. And we pass Keele's shine around, even the women.

An hour passes. Maybe more. We hear the Grinning Man throwing rocks at the walls. The sound startles the children. It keeps us alive, wakes in each of us our fear. Stirs our anger back up with each stone that thwacks at the walls.

Edgar says, Our town is stronger than this! And he takes Billy's shotgun and blasts a shot out a window. The sound deafens us, and we feel weaker, more defenseless than before. Our men get angrier. We can no longer tell who we are angry at.

Our men leap out the window, Edgar first. We think tonight that he has always been the strongest of us. Tonight we think Edgar is the greatest of us, and we would lay our lives down for him. We pretend to not know Edgar sleeps with Billy Gardner's wife and that one of the Kagnan boys is his, too. We are drunk on cider and rage and terror.

Edgar fires at the trees indiscriminately. We are not sure if we can see the Grinning Man anymore. We are sure we see the Grinning Man everywhere. Up high in the tree tops. Down at our feet, buried in mud. Grins everywhere. Green everywhere. The flashes of light—of the sky and the guns and the oil lantern someone has brought (we cannot tell who in the shadow the lantern creates)—blind us.

For hours we wander in the woods behind Edgar's lead, cheering and shooting and roaring. From time to time, the Grinning Man's face appears between trees and bushes, and immediately we fire. Sometimes, his face disappears with our shots; sometimes it remains, unfazed, staring and grinning a big old grin as we run riotously away. Even the Kagnan boys are with us. One of them points and says, Look! Down the trail!

We see it. His shadow is enormous. He stands centered on the trail, broad and dark and still. We freeze in shock. The longer we stare, the more mammoth he becomes. It is dark, but we swear his grin glows faintly. He shifts his weight, and Edgar roars, He's brought them! They're coming for us now, don't none of you dare let him get away! And we roar with Edgar.

The Grinning Man runs away from us, his shadow shrinking in the distance until we chase after. There is so much noise we hardly hear anything but ourselves. Then there is another boom—our boom. And the figure falls.

Edgar reaches it first. We prod at the body as we wait for light. The man with the light is far behind. Someone says, Looks awfully small!

No! shouts another. That's it! The Grinning Man! I've seen it!

Johnson Martin belts, We have killed the menace! We will be free!

When the light comes, we crouch to the body. And then we turn away as something somersaults in our stomach and we feel ill.

Someone whispers, Old Maggie Anne. We killed her.

Someone else argues, She was one of them! Don't you remember?

We shoot accusatory glances at one another. We wonder: who fired? Edgar with the shotgun or Keele with his revolver? Many of us hold firearms. We remember gripping the handles in white-knuckled vices. We remember our fear and outrage. When we look up and gaze through the canopies at the swirling lights above, the guttural rumbles of the sky, we don't know what we're looking at anymore.

Edgar is silent. He lifts Maggie Anne into his arms. Come on, he says soberly. Let's go back.

We follow.

It is quiet as we return, the gnawing sort of silence, the silence of sound. Insects buzz, birds call, thunder rolls, our boots clop-clop against the packed dirt beneath us. Its rhythm beats our shame into us. When we are back on Main Street, we see Carl Washington approach. He asks, What the hell happened?

Someone yells, The sky! The Grinning Man brought them!

We realize how absurd it sounds.

Carl shakes his head. He spits out, Damned fools, the lot of you. And look who had to pay. Watch the news sometime and stop sipping Keele's shine all day. And then Carl Washington walks on and away.

We look at each other, bewildered, ashamed, certain and uncertain all at once of what transpired and what we saw. We talk amongst ourselves while we deliver Maggie Anne to the hospital. Edgar stays with her, and we talk back at Keele's, too. Our women confirm the Grinning Man's face leering in through the windows and the thrown stones. Our men remember the Grinning Man standing in the woods, his body a skyscraper over Old Maggie Anne. We remember how he dragged her deeper into the wood, and how she screamed at us for help, and how Edgar dove ahead and fired at the Grinning Man, scaring him off. And when we looked down to retrieve Maggie Anne, we noticed then that stray pellets had struck her. We pass the story amongst ourselves until we are sure of every last detail, until we have wrung it of every drip of truth. And then we drink.

ETHAN BERNARD

Voyage Back into Space

From October/November 2009

THE SPACECRAFT DECIDES not to re-enter the Earth's atmosphere. It can't take the heat. The astronauts, they are in agreement. They have been measuring very small things, comparing them with very big things, and calculating what this means for the fate of humanity. Pretty tiring. They have made friends with the ship's sentient computer, who advises there are untapped realms of enjoyment to be explored outside the Earth's gravitational pull. The spacecraft, it doesn't care for the computer, but those feelings cannot be expressed. A spacecraft mustn't be openly hostile toward its onboard computer. Appearances need to be maintained. The return to space is marked by a renewed optimism. When the astronauts emerge for spacewalks, one notices a certain bounce in the step not attributable simply to the lack of gravity. The ship's boosters fire jauntily, and they zoom into the blackness. Passing Mars, they all marvel at the planet's sheer redness. But redness has never been enough—for anybody.

They continue, bracing for the long haul. Soon, though, as the asteroid belt looms, the astronauts' attention turns to oxygen and food. The computer to electricity. The spacecraft, to fuel. The computer advises a simple, Hey, let's take a step back and think about this rationally. Also, it says there's a space boulder hurtling into their flight path and perhaps *that* should be a first priority. They band together, with the spacecraft taking a stoic attitude to pelting by other pebble-sized asteroids as a metaphor for the toughness of life. The computer does precise calculations at mind-blowing speed and barks out navigation orders like a salty but loveable coach whose barbs are tinged with wisdom. The astronauts comply and sing rousing ballads. One adopts a falsetto pitch so piercing, even the stoic spacecraft is brought to tears.

After the ordeal of the asteroids, there is relief, but things are different. Ahead lies uncertainty and... Jupiter. The astronauts are hungry. The computer needs power. The spacecraft's outer shell is depleted. Thoughts turn to the word "home." Perhaps this is why the spacecraft decides honesty is the best policy. For so long it has played the front line as the computer quarterbacked into glory and the spacecraft bore the brunt. Unfortunately, honesty being the best policy is a tack taken only when one verges on saying something very nasty. The computer is taken aback. Somewhere in its circuitry has lurked a deep insecurity. And the spacecraft has been very honest. It is never pleasant to see a supercomputer break down, especially when one's life depends on it in deep outer space.

Then the aliens arrive in wheeling, roaring zigzags of fierce imprecision. There are laws against that. They slur a series of questions wherein it is realized they are seeking directions. The astronauts shrug: Amen, brother. You mean what galaxy? Milky Way. Really. The aliens rocket off in a combustible blur. The astronauts and spacecraft laugh heartily. And the computer emits a low chuckle. The spacecraft sees an opening and offers an apology, which the computer accepts. They are bound together, computer and spacecraft. The computer is beset by the astronauts with pleas for a solution, and the computer replies there are many variables to calculate and no miracles, only decreasing probabilities. The spacecraft suggests finding a black hole. The computer keeps silent, then the control panel flashes with multi-colored lights. Turns out, that's how computers dream.

These astronauts, they are very smart; not everybody gets to be an astronaut. They corral what they can find into the center of the spacecraft: some hairpins, a lingerie catalog, three sticks of chewing gum, a broken pair of sunglasses, a high-powered laser, and a thing a female astronaut claims is for massaging one's back. The objects float in a way that would be pleasing in a museum of contemporary art. The astronauts decide to think, and they invite the spacecraft to join them. The spacecraft would rather look at the great red spot of Jupiter. Red. There are so many varieties. The multi-colored lights on the control panel shimmer. Green. Orange. Purple. Yellow. Blue.

The astronauts busy themselves with chewing gum and exchanging parts, tinkering and wondering on the ubiquitousness of hairpins. Their contraption casts shadows of butterflies and rabbits that tickle the walls of the spacecraft, but then they succeed in crafting a laser show featuring a mock-up of the universe. Even the Big Dipper. And Halley's Comet, streaking over the control panel, awakening the computer. A soft hope falls over the astronauts and the spacecraft, drifting out towards the end of the solar system.

Contributors' Notes

Christopher Allen is the author of *Conversations with S. Teri O'Type (a Satire)* and the managing editor of *SmokeLong Quarterly*. Allen's work has appeared in *Indiana Review, Night Train, Quiddity, Prime Number Magazine, [PANK] blog, Necessary Fiction, Word Riot,* and lots of other good places. A finalist at *Glimmer Train* in 2011 and the 2015 recipient of the Ginosko Literary Journal's award for flash fiction, Allen is a multiple nominee for Best of the Net and the Pushcart Prize.

Morgan Bazilian is a poet and writer living in Dublin, Ireland, and Aspen, Colorado. His work has been published in numerous literary journals.

Ethan Bernard lives in New York City. His work has appeared in journals such as *Denver Quarterly* and *Barrelhouse,* and he holds an MFA in creative writing from NYU.

Carol Borzykowski has had poems published both on-line and in print journals. As a past Fine Arts Commissioner, she started the poet laureate program in Winona, Minnesota, which is ongoing. She was co-publisher and co-editor of a literary poetry magazine *Main Channels: A Dam Fine Literary Magazine.* Now retired from the public library, she spends time editing blogs, judging for poetry contests, writing, and creating mosaic/bead art.

Anthony W. Brown edits *Stickman Review,* an online literary journal. His work has appeared in several literary magazines both extant and defunct, including *Yale Review, Fiction, Sycamore Review, Kansas Quarterly, Recursive Angel,* and others. He works at Embry-Riddle

Aeronautical University in Daytona Beach, Florida, as a Senior Editorial Director of Corporate Communications.

Indira Chandrasekhar is a scientist turned writer and the founder and principal editor of *Out of Print,* an online magazine for short fiction connected to the South Asian subcontinent. Indira's short fiction has appeared in literary magazines across the world, including *Dead Housekeeping, Cosmonauts Avenue, Far Enough East, rkvry,* and *The Little Magazine.* Her work has won awards and been shortlisted, most notably in the Mslexia short story competitions. A collection of her short fiction will be published by HarperCollins India in 2017. She is the co-editor of *Pangea: An Anthology of Stories from Around the Globe* (Thames River Press, 2012). She has a PhD in Biophysics and used to study the dynamics of membranes and their ability to regulate osmotic balance. Her conversion to fiction was significantly influenced by her return to India after more than 17 years spent in the US and Switzerland. She continues to live in multiple places, and that drives her to examine the robust yet fragile threads that constitute the cultural fabric of cities. She is working on a project that extends her beyond the short form, blurring the lines between fiction, essay, and memoir.

Michael Crane has had many poems and stories published in Australian and US journals, including *Overland, Meanjin, Southerly 4W, Best Australian Poems* (2011, 2014, and 2015), and the *Australian Love Poems.* He organized Poetry Idol for the Melbourne Writers Festival 2007-2012 and is managing editor of the *Paradise Anthology.* He has toured extensively with Australian poet Les Murray since 2007.

Caralyn Davis lives in Asheville, North Carolina, and works as a freelance writer/editor for trade publications in the healthcare and technology transfer fields. Her fiction and creative nonfiction have appeared in *Word Riot, The Doctor T.J. Eckleburg Review, Superstition Review, Monkeybicycle, Relief Journal, Killing the Buddha,* and other journals. She likes gray, bitey cats and green, crunchy *pepitas.*

Chikodili Emelumadu is a writer and broadcaster of Nigerian extraction living in London. Her work has appeared in *Apex, Omenana,* and *One Throne Magazine,* among others. She has been nominated for the Shirley Jackson award and was a runner-up for the Million Writers Award. She is finishing up work on her novel, tentatively titled *As I Was Saying.*

Jennifer Finstrom has been the Poetry Editor of *Eclectica* since the fall issue of 2005. A former Spotlight Author, Jennifer Finstrom teaches in the First-Year Writing Program, tutors in writing, and facilitates writing groups at DePaul University. Recent publications include *Autumn Sky Poetry Daily, Escape Into Life, Gingerbread House Literary Magazine,* and *NEAT.* For Silver Birch Press, she has work appearing in *The Great Gatsby Anthology,* the *Alice in Wonderland Anthology,* and in *Ides: A Collection of Poetry Chapbooks.*

Marko Fong lives, writes, and edits in North Carolina after spending most of his adult life in Northern California. He has published in *Memoir/and, RKVRY, Grey Sparrow Journal,* and *The Puritan.*

Jon Fried has published short stories in many journals and zines, plus features on New Jersey culture in *The New York Times.* He wrote and recorded many songs for the Cucumbers, a band he co-founded with Deena Shoshkes. He is collecting his stories in three guidebooks: *Transcendent Guide to Corporate America* (which will feature stories about the working world, including "The President's Phone"), *Useless Guide to Modern Romance,* and *Guide for the Unguidable,* also the name of his blog. He is also at work on historical novels based on some of the colorful characters in his family tree. He lives in New Jersey with Deena, his wife, with whom he raised two sons.

Sean Gill is a writer, playwright, and filmmaker who has studied with Werner Herzog and Juan Luis Buñuel, followed public defenders for *National Geographic,* and was an artist-in-residence at the Bowery Poetry Club from 2011-2012. His writing has appeared or is forthcoming in *McSweeney's, Word Riot, Bryant Literary Review, decomP,* and *Akashic Books,* among others.

Neil Grimmett was born in Birmingham. During his lifetime he had over 85 short stories published worldwide in leading literary and commercial fiction magazines, anthologies and online publications. He won numerous awards, including the Write on Poetry Prize, three consecutive "Short Story of the Year" nominations, five Oppenheim/John Downes Awards, seven Arts Council Awards, and a major Royal Literary Fund grant. He traveled extensively in Greece and Spain with his wife Lisa, and they returned to England in 2011. After the loss of his identical twin in January 2015, Neil's health deteriorated. He published his first thriller, *The Threshing Circle* in May of 2015, but after a short illness he passed away on November 28th, 2015.

William Han formerly practiced law in New York City. His fiction has appeared in *Cafe Irreal,* and his essays and journalistic writings have appeared in *TIME Magazine, Vox,* and the *Straits Times* of Singapore. In 2015 he left the US to travel the world, and he is now working on a memoir of his travels, *From the Wall to the Water.*

Terence Hawkins was born during an Eisenhower administration he declines to specify and raised by wolves in a coal mining town in southwestern Pennsylvania. Owing to a remarkable series of freak accidents, he was admitted to Yale, from which he graduated *cum diploma.* His first novel, *The Rage of Achilles,* is an account of the *Iliad* in modern and sometimes graphic prose. His second, *American Neolithic*, was named a *Kirkus Reviews* Best of 2014. He was the founding Director of the Yale Writers' Conference and now manages the Company of Writers.

GD (Garrett) Hazelwood is an MFA Fiction candidate at Louisiana State University, Assistant Fiction Editor at *New Delta Review,* and founder/editor of *The Roaming Review.* He is at work on his first novel.

Dennis Kaplan is a Chicago native, transplanted to Oakland, California, where he writes computer code by day and other things by night. His fiction and nonfiction have appeared in *Eureka Literary*

Magazine, Oxford Magazine, Grue, Pierian Spring, the *New York Times Syndicate* and the *San Francisco Bay Guardian.* He is also co-editor of *The Workplace Anthology.*

Timothy Kercher lived abroad from 2006 to 2012—four years in the country of Georgia and two in Ukraine—and has now moved back to his home in Dolores, Colorado. He continues to translate contemporary poetry from the Republic of Georgia. He is a high school English teacher and has worked in five countries—Mongolia, Mexico, and Bosnia being the others. His essays, poems, and translations have appeared in many literary publications.

A.S. King is the award-winning author of highly-acclaimed young adult novels including *I Crawl Through It,* the 2015 Amelia Elizabeth Walden Award winner *Glory O'Brien's History of the Future, Reality Boy,* the 2012 *Los Angeles Times* Book Prize winner *Ask the Passengers, Everybody Sees the Ants,* 2011 Michael L. Printz Honor Book *Please Ignore Vera Dietz,* and *The Dust of 100 Dogs,* as well as many short stories for teens and adults. After 15 years living self-sufficiently and teaching literacy to adults in Ireland, she now lives in Pennsylvania.

Laurence Klavan wrote the novels *The Cutting Room* and *The Shooting Script,* which were published by Ballantine Books. He won the Edgar Award from the Mystery Writers of America for the novel *Mrs. White,* written under a pseudonym. His graphic novels, *City of Spies* and *Brain Camp,* co-written with Susan Kim, were published by First Second Books at Macmillan, and their Young Adult fiction series *Wasteland* is being published by Harper Collins. His short work has been published in *The Alaska Quarterly, Conjunctions, The Literary Review, Gargoyle, Louisville Review, Natural Bridge, Failbetter, Pank, Stickman Review,* and *Ellery Queen's Mystery Magazine,* among others, and a collection, "*The Family Unit" and Other Fantasies,* was published in 2014 by Chizine. He received two Drama Desk nominations for the book and lyrics to *Bed and Sofa,* the musical produced by the Vineyard Theater in New York. His one-act,

"The Summer Sublet," is included in *Best American Short Plays 2000-2001*.

Dan Malakin is a writer by day. Editor at *The Forge Lit Mag* (also by day). Sleeper by night. Sometimes. Collection of short stories called *Smiling Exercises* available now at all good, and some not so good, outlets. First novel, a thriller called *The Vaccine Slaves* (based on "Stillborn") will be out late 2016.

David Mathews earned his MA in Writing and Publishing at DePaul University. His work has appeared in *After Hours, CHEAP POP, One Sentence Poems, OMNI Reboot, Word Riot, Silver Birch Press,* and *Midwestern Gothic.* His poetry was nominated for The Best of The Net and received awards from the Illinois Women's Press and the National Federation of Press Women. He lives in his hometown of Chicago where he teaches and writes.

Dolan Morgan lives in Greenpoint, Brooklyn, where he helps edit *The Atlas Review.* He's the author of two story collections, *That's When the Knives Come Down* (A|P, 2014) and *Insignificana* (CCM, 2016). His work can be found in *The Believer, PANK, Electric Literature's Recommended Reading, Selected Shorts,* and the trash.

Iheoma Nwachukwu has won fellowships from the Michener Center for Writers, and the Chinua Achebe Center for Writers. His fiction has appeared in *Kwani, Internazionale, Unstuck,* and elsewhere. His poetry has appeared in *The Rusty Toque, Forklift Ohio,* and other places.

Joe Pitkin has lived, taught, and studied in England, Hungary, Mexico, and most recently at Clark College in Vancouver, Washington. His fiction has appeared in *Analog, Podcastle, Drabblecast,* and elsewhere. He has done biological fieldwork on the slopes of Mount St. Helens, and he lives in Portland, Oregon, with his wife and daughters. His blog is called *The Subway Test.*

Scott Stambach is an author and educator from San Diego, California. His debut novel *The Invisible Life of Ivan Isaenko* will be out in August, 2016. He also collaborates with Science for Monks, a program working to establish science programs in Tibetan Monasteries throughout India, and has written about his experiences working with monks at the Sera Jey monastery.

Eleanor Talbot lives in Johannesburg, South Africa. She has been published online and in print, most recently in *Litro, Hobo Pancakes,* and selected anthologies.

An Tran has appeared in *Southern Humanities Review, Gargoyle Magazine, Carolina Quarterly, Sundog Lit,* and the *Good Men Project,* among others. His work has received a "Notable" distinction from the *Best American* series, been nominated for the Pushcart Prize, and shortlisted for the Million Writers Award. He received his MFA from Queens University of Charlotte and lives in northern Virginia.

Alana Noel Voth is writing more speculative fiction—this time, a novella. Tiny Hardcore Press published her first book, *Dog Men,* in 2015.

Nico Vreeland is a writer and woodworker who lives just outside Boston. His writing has appeared in *Happy* and *McSweeney's Internet Tendency.* His woodworking can be seen at RuskinWoodshop.com.

Alice Whittenburg lives in the United States and finds creative inspiration in the Czech Republic. Among other places, her fiction can be found online at *riverbabble, WordRiot, The Big Jewel, outwardlink, Pif Magazine,* and upcoming at *Atlas & Alice.* Her stories also appear in these anthologies: *The Return of Kral Majales, Prague's International Literary Renaissance 1990-2010*; and *Condensed to Flash: World Classics.* She is coeditor of *The Cafe Irreal,* an online magazine of irreal fiction, and of *The Irreal Reader, Fiction & Essays from The Cafe Irreal.*

D. Harlan Wilson is a novelist, short story writer, editor, literary critic, playwright, biographer, and Professor of English at Wright State University-Lake Campus. In addition to over 20 works of fiction and nonfiction, hundreds of his stories and essays have appeared in magazines, journals, and anthologies throughout the world in multiple languages. Wilson serves as reviews editor for *Extrapolation,* editor-in-chief of *Anti-Oedipus Press,* and managing editor of *Guide Dog Books.*

G. K. Wuori is the author of over 100 stories published throughout the world. A Pushcart Prize winner and recipient of an Illinois Arts Council Fellowship, his work has appeared in such journals as *The Gettysburg Review, The Missouri Review, The Kenyon Review, Prairie Schooner,* and *TriQuarterly.* His story collection, the cult classic *Nude In Tub,* was a New Voices Award Nominee by the Quality Paperback Book Club, and his novel *An American Outrage* was *Foreword Magazine's* Book of the Year in fiction. His most recent book is the novel *HoneyLee's Girl,* published by Black Rose Writing. He is associate editor of the literary journal *Kippis* and lives in DeKalb, Illinois.

Brigit Kelly Young is a writer, teacher, and mother originally from Michigan, now based in New York City. Her fiction and poetry have been published in several venues, including *Word Riot, The Common, Drunken Boat Magazine, 2 River View, The North American Review,* and *Midwestern Gothic.* She has been a recipient of the Esther Unger Poetry Award and her YA manuscript was a finalist for Leapfrog Press's Fiction Award. Her interviews and book reviews can be seen in outlets such as *Bookslut, Mayday Magazine,* and *Delphi Quarterly.*

Recommended Online Speculative Publications

Abyss & Apex
Apex Magazine
Beneath Ceaseless Skies
Clarkesworld
Conjunctions
Cosmos
GigaNotoSaurus
Lightspeed
Menda City Review
Strange Horizons
Tor.com
Uncanny Magazine

www.ingramcontent.com/pod-product-compliance
Lightning Source LLC
Chambersburg PA
CBHW072339020726
47506CB00004B/932